A SPOT TO STAND

Living My Truth

Annie Davison

CONTENTS

PART ONE: THE WILDERNESS

Chapter One 1

Chapter Two 17

Chapter Three 27

Chapter Four 39

Chapter Five 54

Chapter Six 67

Chapter Seven 76

PART TWO: GENEVA

Chapter Eight 90

Chapter Nine 104

Chapter Ten 114

Chapter Eleven 128

PART THREE: PROVENCE

Chapter Twelve 145

Chapter Thirteen 160

Chapter Fourteen 176

Chapter Fifteen...189

PART FOUR: BACK HOME

Chapter Sixteen 205

Chapter Seventeen 217

Epilogue..230

'Give me but one firm spot on which to stand, and I will move the earth'

*A*rchimedes: 287-212BC

PART ONE

THE WILDERNESS

CHAPTER ONE

Rick and I married on 5 September 1970 at the Parish Church of St Mary the Virgin. I never thought of that church again until more recently, after a funeral, William and I walked past the church and of course I had to go in. Thirty years on.

I remember Marjorie Bidmead came to the wedding. Marjorie was fifty-five, permanently and proudly smart, as she was even into her mid eighties. I had met her when I was twenty, when I temped for the boss of the *Radio and Television Retailers' Association* in Fitzroy Square. I had just returned from three months in Paris, doing my first secretarial job abroad. I only worked for the RTRA for a total of two weeks, but thanks to Marjorie it changed my life. It was through her I became a journalist.

It was Richard Bentley, however, who originally gave me the idea. I had met Richard a year or so before I went to Paris, during my A level exams. At that time I was working full time in an office and studying at a local college in the evenings. I took Economics after one year at an outside venue – I forget where – and sat two more the following year, which is when I met Richard.

Richard lived in the cloisters of Windsor Castle, his father a Canon at Windsor. He was good looking - and attractive, simply by virtue of his romantic background. Meeting the Canon and Mrs Bentley was quite daunting, so although I liked Richard a lot, I'm relieved we stayed just friends. It was his determination to be a journalist that influenced me most. If he could do it, why couldn't I?

Marjorie was conference organiser at the RTRA. When, for the second week of my temporary employment, she invited me to go to Brighton as the Press Officer for their conference, I went, with no idea whatsoever what being a press officer entailed.

Mostly it meant typing in a room full of national radio and television reporters. I realised, too, it meant knowing what was going on in the conference and providing information,

1

neither of which I was able to do. But somehow I managed. I was amused to see that only one or two journalists would attend a particular presentation and then share the story with all the others. What they always attended in numbers, however, was the endless availability of free drinks. I remember a few years later a colleague telling me I would never make a journalist because I didn't drink enough!

One of the reporters at the conference, Mark somebody, was very willing to tell me I would make a journalist. 'If you really want to write, come to my room'! He was extremely unpleasant and offensive, which upset me. But in the end it was Brian Dean of the Daily Mail, who told me he had rung the wife of his colleague, crime reporter Owen Summers, on my behalf. She was editor of a national teenage magazine, *Fabulous* (later *Fab-208*), and if I wanted to apply for the job of editor's secretary, it was a start.

Indeed it was. Unity Hall Summers was one of the most influential women in my life. She terrified me! Which is strange considering she once told me that when I arrived for my interview – with my hair still 'up' in the glamorous curls the hairdresser at Brighton had created for the end of Conference ball, she said I had terrified her! The first thing she said was that I should call her Unity. She was thirty-eight, I was twenty, and in those days it still felt wrong to use a Christian name for someone older.

Unity was one of the last old-school tough newspaper women, in the Jean Rook mould, who had had to fight hard for their place in the profession. Considering her training, it seemed odd to me that she now chose to work on a teenage weekly magazine. Although I didn't know it then, she ran it more like a newspaper.

On my twenty-first birthday, Unity and deputy editor Betty Hale took me out to lunch and bought me champagne. I felt hugely grown up. I remember asking whether wanting to be a journalist very badly was enough, and they both said that this was half the battle. Within eighteen months I was moved to the Features Department and I learned my trade from one of the best. I have kept all these years the handwritten overview she did for me of how to write a feature....'establish where you are and why. Introduce him to the reader and your reaction...'

Writing was never easy for me, but what I lacked in natural talent I know I made up for with perseverance. I can remember the days and days I would pore over Donald Zec's personality interviews in the *Daily Mirror* and copy the rhythm of his words – de dum, de dum, de dum – line by line, into my own features. Even now I rewrite a lot, and have the profoundest admiration for daily newspaper journalists who prepare and write stories at the shortest notice.

Unity trained staff by the 'pulling through a hedge backwards' method. I shall never forget the time I had flu very badly – the first of only three times in my life. I was staying overnight at Rick's home on one occasion – years before we married – and the following morning I literally fell over with flu. Rick's mother called the doctor who said I couldn't be moved for seven days.

I was seriously unwell, and Mrs Gannon couldn't believe it when Betty Hale phoned with a message from Unity to say that if I were a 'proper journalist' I would complete a feature I was writing. To this day I don't know how I managed to do it, but despite Rick's mum's protestations, I did. When I read the article later I could feel it was written in a state of delirium. I was surprised Unity let it through, but perhaps she didn't have the heart not to.

On another occasion, towards the end of my time at *Fabulous*, although not a pop star enthusiast – and therefore wrote mostly about actors – it was decided I should do an interview with Paul McCartney. To all intents and purposes this was impossible, because by 1969 the Beatles were far too big. Once again Unity insisted that if I were a real journalist I would get the interview, whatever it took. Betty even suggested as a creative beginning to my research, I might hire a dog and camp out on the common until I bumped into Paul!

Fortunately I heard that a reception for Mary Hopkin was being held at the new Post Office Tower near Warren

3

Street. Paul was promoting her first single *Those Were the Days my Friend*, on the Apple label, and he had to be there.

Throughout my childhood I had been incredibly shy. My family were very silent and even though I made school friends easily, by the age of seventeen, I still couldn't speak to new people, particularly men, without feeling insecure. I felt I had no opinions of my own and therefore had no idea how to make interesting conversation.

It was at that stage I simply decided to change my life. I sat down on the floor and made a list of five things I was going to achieve. I determined to learn to drive, to take three A levels at evening classes, to read serious newspapers and find out what was going on in the world, and to make myself read difficult books.

I embarked on my programme systematically. I forced myself to read such nihilistic authors as Jean Paul Sartre, Franz Kafka and Simone de Beauvoir, 'acting as if' I understood them, until I found I actually did. I regularly read the broadsheet newspapers and periodicals like *New Society* and *The New Statesman*. After two gruelling years of evening study alongside full-time work, I took my A levels.

When the idea of becoming a journalist began to form, thanks to Richard Bentley, this too became a 'tool' in my education. I reasoned that as an interviewer I would be forced to talk to people, and yet I could hide behind the format of asking questions. Questions became my modus operandi for many years, driving friends and acquaintances mad with my inquisitiveness, until eventually I was confident enough to speak from experience and add my own life to conversations.

And so it was that my hugely improved will-powered self made a beeline for Paul McCartney at the Post Office Tower. I went straight for my quarry and cornered him. It was slightly disconcerting that he was moving one way on the turning floor of the tower restaurant and I was moving the other, but before we separated completely I managed to tell him my life depended on him giving me an interview that evening. To my relief he agreed to find me later.

I relaxed for a couple of hours but as the time went on and he didn't come back, I was sure he had forgotten and gone. There was nothing for it but to walk round the restaurant to see if I could find him, at which point I don't know who I was more afraid of, Paul or Unity. With Unity failure was somehow never an option.

I found Paul sitting with Linda. They had not yet married and the romance was still a rumour. I apologised and asked him if he might soon be available for the interview he had promised. Graciously he stood up immediately and we walked away from the crowd to talk.

I took shorthand notes standing up and although for me twenty minutes is far too short for a feature length article and I knew I would need a lot of extra information from the cuttings, my gratitude was huge. He apologised that he must get back to Linda because she wouldn't like him being away so long, and I like to think I knew the truth about their relationship a few weeks before most people realised how serious it was.

By 1970 when Rick and I married, I had left *Fabulous* to become the feature writer on a highly successful young people's magazine called *Petticoat*. The new editor, Terry Hornett, was the whizz-kid of the era; a young man who by extraordinary and implausible talent managed to hit the zeitgeist with women's magazines. He began as a tea boy at IPC and went on to form his own company and originate some of the most successful titles.

Terry took over *Petticoat* from Audrey Slaughter and my predecessor was Janet Street Porter. Lynne Franks was a fashion PR at the time, not the public relations guru she later became. But a new editor like a new broom always sweeps clean and eventually most of the editorial team were Terry imports.

It was a glamorous time to be in magazines, and apart from the monthly glossies, perhaps, there was nowhere better to be. I was just twenty-five and the three years from the date of my wedding were the happiest in my life. I remember walking along Piccadilly one morning, thinking I was the luckiest person alive.

I had never been sure about marrying Rick. We were introduced by a former boyfriend at a tennis club frequented by a group of 'smart young things', collectively confident in themselves in the safety of their fathers' wealth. While his own father was anything but wealthy, Rick could certainly play tennis. His father's estranged sister was a Mottram of Davis Cup legend, and he earned his spurs amongst this Crowd. The Crowd included Tim Bell who later became part of Saatchi and Saatchi and later the Conservative Party guru Sir Tim Bell.

Before we married, Rick and I had been going out and going nowhere in particular for three years. But when my father died of a heart attack aged fifty-nine in May 1970, I decided to stop prevaricating and agreed to marry Rick – as much for my mother's happiness as mine. I kept my maiden name, Wilson, because as journalists we did that then.

My family adored him. He was kind, gregarious, easy-going, and loved his mum. He had a fun, homespun musical talent on guitar and piano – particularly good at Fats Waller numbers – and an unfulfilled ambition to write and record a successful song. Above all, he was funny. I remember Unity saying the same about her husband Owen, that the most important attribute of all was humour.

When I look back I realise that Rick gave me the best gift any husband can give – my freedom. It was the dawn of the women's movement and I was in one of those few professions where already women were treated equally with men. But my desperate will to succeed, to escape the limited expectations I saw placed on me, was only made possible because I could take it for granted that Rick loved me.

He simply accepted me the way I was. With his easy, accepting nature he gave me the security and freedom, and thus the permission I needed to follow the path I was unknowingly treading. He let me be who I was, unconditionally. As my closest friend, companion and ally, who despite the disappointments we must both have felt, he was prepared to be loyal. I never questioned that he was right for me. We had married for life.

It was still early days in the sexual revolution and magazines like *Cosmopolitan* were just beginning to suggest that women couldn't be truly liberated unless they experienced multiple orgasms.

Working on *Petticoat* was fun. Before Carol Sarler came to join me as a second feature writer, I often wrote as many as six thousand words a week, which is a huge amount. I still wrote personality pieces - on such favourites as David Essex, Dennis Waterman, Sacha Distel. My only real disaster was interviewing Robert Wagner - who came to London with his then wife Natalie Wood - and fazed me into embarrassed silence. From time to time I went on film location or on a television set, and since I also wrote a film column I often went to preview screenings during the day or straight after work.

More importantly I wrote what I then called 'pseudo psychological' features, about every aspect of a young girl's life and experience that I could possibly think of. To my mind it was my way of offering service.

At one point on *Fabulous*, I had recognised that through my hard-fought attempts to haul myself out of my own painful emotional history, I had learned a useful skill. To begin with I described this skill as 'empathy', and employed it to reach a depth of friendship that I still find meaningful. But it also helped to draw out that 'added extra' from people I was interviewing. When in my capacity as Beauty Editor I interviewed French chanteuse Francoise Hardy I was proud that during our conversation this stunning ice-maiden melted in a way that no other reporter had achieved. She was in her own words 'hypertensive' and protective of herself, but to me she was delightful.

By the time I reached *Petticoat* I had changed my word to 'perceptive'. It was as though the momentum of life, once I had embarked on this more intensely 'internal' way of experiencing the world, brought change in its wake. It seemed to me then, that to acquire a new skill, the old one had to fade away. An ability you could draw on before was no longer available and it therefore took courage to move on.

Perception to me was a little 'deeper' than empathy. Writing my pseudo psychological articles on: 'loneliness; different kinds of love; girls who wanted to be in men's jobs; shyness, and so on', I interviewed so many young people (sometimes my own friends!) with a particular vision of helping people by getting to the depth of things.

We would sometimes ask a psychologist from the Tavistock Clinic to add his professional comment, and my interest in the field was enhanced. In retrospect I had the feeling that life had set it up in such a way that I got the experiences personally 'five years ahead', and could then offer them back. I still feel that!

I also wrote half-page 'think pieces', so my early yearning to 'have opinions' finally paid off. There was no doubt, however, that when Carol Sarler demanded that Terry promote her out of the fashion room to become a feature writer, it was she who shone in this particular genre.

Carol had strong feminist, socially radical views but, even better, she could really write. She wrote 'straight off' and fast. She left *Petticoat* before me, to do some broadcasting like *Start the Week* – and then to freelance for *The Sunday Times,* as her daughter Flyn went on to do. Despite our gaping differences, Carol and Andy (an art designer), Rick and I spent many good Saturday evenings eating stuffed peppers and made-from-the-packet creme caramel, at one or other of our homes in Tufnell Park (them) or Winchmore Hill (us). I'm sure, however, that our combined workload went down, since we talked so much at our desks!

Rick was in computers. Although an extremely skilled linguist – he studied French and German to honours levels at university – he decided to migrate from arts and retrain in this up and coming industry. When I met him he worked for Marconi and lived in Colchester. Quite soon he got another job with Remington Rand in the Euston Road and our first married home was a flat in Winchmore Hill.

Later we moved to a tiny cottage in the smart area of Totteridge Lane. To live there had been my dream since childhood. Since then I have never played safe by living anywhere 'sensible' or by doing the 'right' financial thing - despite what I came to recognise as my overriding fear of not being safe in the world.

I took it for granted that besides Rick, two other people loved me unconditionally: my mum, and Mary. My mum was my champion and as a child was my bedrock. I was born a sad looking sight, with excema around my head. At the age of two it turned into acute asthma, and for twenty-four hours every fortnight my eyes would sink into their darkening sockets as I heaved and fought for breath.

My mum tried everything available in those days: burning night vapours (which I once knocked over and burned my arm badly), and ephedrine, which made me twitch. My asthma lasted until I was thirteen and inhalers only came into use at the end. My mother never wavered, and fortunately I never knew you could actually die from an asthma attack.

I learned later that not all mothers love their children unconditionally, and that however angry I was with my mother's tough love as a rebellious teenager, I was lucky. My mother's life was spent loving her family and, alongside that, helping all and sundry around her when the need arose. It was my dad who caused me most grief.

I met Mary when I was twenty-two through her college friend George. Rick and I met George camping on a beach in Greece that year. Mary brought out the mothering instinct in me – as she did with most women she met. Some inner compulsion made me want to do things for her, and she was adopted like a daughter into my family.

Over the years she became more of an aunt to my brother's three children than I could ever be. And when my father died and I got married, she went to lodge with my mother for three years, which was a godsend to them both. It was also in 1970 that, on my persuasion, she applied for a PA's job at *London Weekend Television* – I made her a maroon

9

corduroy frock for the interview! She started in the difficult arena of live television on *World of Sport*, and during her career became extremely sought after for her ability to work on multi-camera live shows, particularly Opera.

Our depth of enjoyment and communication over literature, theatre and art has never been surpassed for me. I learned how to bathe and grow in the comfort of 'sameness', and in retrospect had been making a tiny, grateful step towards understanding how, at the time of women's liberation, the masculine and feminine energies within us were changing. Although Rick might have wondered occasionally why I wanted to spend so much time with Mary, on the whole they got on well. They would often decorate our various homes together while I cheered from the sidelines and made tea.

Although women have been true companions and champions in my life, it became clear that it was men who were destined to be the faulty, perverse, painful and enigmatic engines of it. Our lives have long since diverged, but Mary and I remain like sisters: we take each other for granted!

One morning, not too long after I joined *Petticoat*, a publicity handout, addressed to Janet Street Porter, landed on my desk. It was an invitation from astrologer Frederick Davies to draw up a free horoscope; an offer I couldn't resist.

It was Freddie's aptitude for publicity that led him to become the first well-known, well-paid newspaper astrologer, respected for his skill. Before that, as an editor once told me, it was probably the tea girl who listened to conversations on the tube and wrote the daily horoscope accordingly. Freddie led the way for other great astrologers like Patric Walker and Jonathan Cainer, before seeking his fortune in America.

Freddie's reading, which took place in his flat near Sloane Square, quite literally changed my life. It was the trigger that opened me up to the astonishing realisation that life is far bigger than we could ever imagine. It was as though from that day on I was caught on a thread, like Theseus drawn to face the Minotaur, and there was nothing I could do except respond to what felt like a 'call'. That one reading set the scene for a lifelong search for meaning.

Two things in particular struck me forcibly. First that 'someone, somewhere' knew more about me than I did. And, secondly, that I did not have to stay with Rick for life. As happy and content as I thought I was, I knew deep down and unexpressed that it wasn't right. The reading in 1973 was like a trapdoor I didn't know existed suddenly opened above my head, and I could expand in some way that I never even knew I wanted.

Carol left *Petticoat* to be replaced by Ros Franey. A Bristol university drama graduate, Ros was far too academically bright and culturally intense for *Petticoat*, but she was a real delight and very funny. Her mother lived in Stroud in Gloucestershire, which I had never heard of then, but I thought of Ros many years later when I lived in Stroud myself.

Ros was thirty and needlessly insecure because she was still single. A year or so later, around the time I was made features editor, she left, too, humping an enormous white holdall bag around Ethiopia for a year. It was there she met her husband Jamie, also a Bristol graduate, and eventually returned to edit *Shelter*, the magazine for the homeless.

During her year away, Ros loaned me her marvellous red VW Beetle, Guv, for the cost of its depreciation. Imagine my horror when I returned to Totteridge station car park one day and found a truck had sat on its front end. Unbelievably, the lorry driver had left his details and his insurance covered the repairs.

Terry Hornett, after setting up and running *Club* - a magazine for men - alongside *Petticoat*, left IPC to start his own company Carlton Publications, off Oxford Street, with financial and distribution backing from IPC. Our assistant editor, Colin Bostock-Smith -who also at the time wrote one-liners for the satirical radio show *Week Ending* - (and later devised the television sit-com *As Time Goes By*) became editor, and he appointed me assistant editor.

I had not been a good features editor, and was even worse as assistant editor. I had become bored with writing features and wanted promotion, but I had no natural zest for production and administration. I was a perfect example of the Peter Principle. To be honest, neither Colin nor I had our hearts in the job, and *Petticoat* started failing.

Eventually Colin was sacked and I had to carry the magazine until a replacement was found – a job totally beyond my competence. Bill Williamson – another IPC star editor – eventually took over and brought in Pat Roberts from *Rave* as his right-hand woman. While Bill and Pat ran *Petticoat* between them, I – virtually jobless and extremely low – had to carry on as though nothing had happened.

Bill also brought in Sheila Blick as feature writer. She had recently broken up with her motoring journalist husband, Kevin, and he subsequently lodged for several years with Mary. It was being in such proximity to Sheila that I began to explore, as best I could, what was happening for me, as my inner life began to take hold of me.

It was several years later, when Sheila herself had gone through Jungian analysis that she told me how difficult it had been to grasp what I was saying - despite the sympathetic resonance between us. Nor did I know myself that 'the call' I had experienced was an attempt by what Jung called 'the higher self', to become conscious. All I knew was that I had begun to sense things were changing and, through a felt sense of the ineffable, that life was not quite what I thought it was.

I was on a search for meaning, and with it came a knowing by early 1974 that what had worked so well for so long was floundering. I had begun to write a diary that year because I had this 'certainty' that the following three years would be important. (I remember interviewing David Hemmings that year and he felt the same. In fact he married his girlfriend Prue and left for the USA, where he found even more success as an actor).

My intuition was heightening but apparently it was more than that. Although I didn't know it at the time, I was entering the phase of my 'Saturn Return'. This is a period of roughly three years beginning around the age of twenty-eight, when Saturn returns for the first time to the place it was when we were born. It is a time of inevitable change and renewal and invariably marked by difficulties. True to form I was having problems on two fronts: work and home.

Lyall Watson's concept of 'the inspired failure' (like the fish that came onto land to escape their predators eventually evolved into human beings) was not known to me then, but in retrospect it is one that I adhere to. The increasing feeling of failure at *Petticoat* galvanised me into action. I had to find a way out.

I am a Leo and despite the underlying insecurity and shyness, like all Leos I obviously wanted to shine. When I studied astrology many years later I learned that those with moon in Leo (a high proportion of my closest friends over the years) rather than sun in Leo like me, are far more at home with 'kingship'. They assume that they 'rule by right' and that people will satellite around them. Sun in Leo people are merely aspiring towards it.

My ambition was always to be in television and clearly now was the time to try. The only person I knew on acquaintance terms was a producer, Roger Eckersley, a man on his third marriage, who I occasionally had drinks with. He worked for the BBC, but agreed to put me in touch with a local news director at ATV in Birmingham. At the same time I decided to write a proposal for a young magazine style show for television, and sent it to Bill Cotton Jr. at BBC Light Entertainment.

Some people, like Mary who has never been ambitious, find opportunities just walking towards them. I, on the contrary, have always had the notion that there is only ever one option out there for me, and that I have to write at least fifty letters to find it. This time, amazingly, both applications were in some measure received favourably and yet this only served to increase my anxiety.

ATV offered me a week's trial doing front of camera news reports, while Bill Cotton wasn't interested in my idea but expressed his acknowledgement of my initiative by inviting me to meet him. As a result, he suggested I apply for the job of researcher on *Parkinson*.

I wanted more than anything to do the reporter trial, but in the end I knew I couldn't. In those days, to leave Rick at home while I spent time in Birmingham would have signalled the end. That left *Parkinson*, which was still not an easy ride. Despite Bill Cotton's recommendation I was competing with hundreds of others. Firstly I had to convince producer Roger Ordish, and then, much more difficult, I had to persuade Mike.

If ever I needed empathy and perception, plus sheer willpower, guts and gall it was now. After my interview, Roger suggested I do two trial research interviews, and I contacted my chosen people.

Colin and Rosie Swale had become celebrities after a round the world sailing voyage with their two young children. They agreed to see me in their Norfolk home, even though there could be no promise of inclusion in the programme. The couple were later involved in a minor scandal when wild-child Rosie left Colin and her children to live with another woman.

In many ways this job was a downward move. Research interviews are the easy part of a feature writer's existence. But for me the lure of television was so great I put everything into my task.

My second interview was with satirist Alan Coren, who I met at *Mother Bunches* wine bar in Farringdon. To my horror Alan talked faster than anyone I have ever encountered, except perhaps Cliff Richard, and far too fast for my usually adequate shorthand. I was so worried I hadn't got it all that in the end I had to use a lot of information from cuttings.

Eventually, after several weeks, I was invited to meet Mike and Roger and the two established researchers, John and Graham, in the BBC bar. Mike took me aside for a chat. By then I assumed that Roger was on my side and that Bill Cotton had persuaded Mike to meet me, and the day before my twenty-eighth birthday, I was finally offered the job. I would start late August for the new series beginning in September: a team of three Oxbridge graduates and me.

Alongside these anxieties about work ran tensions at home. Rick's job was crazy. He worked for a small salary and then on commission. Computers were at a very early stage then. If he could sell one vast mainframe computer to one prospective buyer he made a million pounds. If not, he made nothing. For three years he had the *Bank of America* in his sights. He spent hours of his life with their charming representative, wining, dining and hoping. In the end, to our huge disappointment, the bid went elsewhere.

His sense of dissatisfaction and lack of fulfilment must have been overwhelming. Rick was so creative and accomplished in so many ways, and yet as my willpower went further into overdrive, Rick's seemed to diminish. Tensions between us came and went more often, and now more than ever I felt oppressed by Rick's constant need to hang out with the Crowd.

I disliked the phenomenon of the crowd. As individuals to me they were just like spoilt children: too rich and too idle, but boosted by the ethos of the crowd, they existed *en masse* as a powerful, sacrosanct entity, and Rick loved it. While I took part less and less, he would spend most Sunday lunchtimes in *The William* pub, and sometimes go to parties at 10pm, just as I was going to bed. Though neither of us dare admit it, we were now going along separate paths.

And yet we hung in. We still enjoyed meeting at the *Eliza Doolittle* pub near his office in Euston at the end of the working week, or in the sawdust darkness of *Mother Bunches* near my office, where the wine and pate were magnificent. It was here, with tears streaming down my face, I once tried to explain about the internal things that were happening to me, and the opening to 'something bigger'. He said he could see I was experiencing something important to me, but he simply couldn't understand what I was talking about.

I left *Petticoat* on Friday 9 August 1974, after five years. I still have the fabulous card – a pastiche of a *Petticoat* cover the art room made for me - and the little silver fish on a chain. After eight years in total I left IPC. The following weekend I went on a three-day break in Guv, to Maidencombe, near Torquay - the first time I'd been away alone.

On the Sunday, for no reason at all, I went to the service at the local church. Suddenly the truth and enormity of it all became apparent, and my experience of what Jung called 'synchronicity' began. The vicar preached a passage from St John's Gospel. 'To some of us the gifts are given... healing...wisdom...the gift of tongues...and the spirit.' Was that what I was meant to hear? I don't know, but it meant everything to me while I was there. I felt certain that one day I would know, and it made me want to cry.

The next day I returned home. I was fearful, yet with that was the sense that I was about to begin. I must let life take me, completely open, as I was from then on.

CHAPTER TWO

I don't think I was ever consulted on who the guests might be for *Parkinson*. This was the producer's domain with input from the established researchers John and Graham, who had the right contacts.

By the time I arrived in the office the schedule board was already filling up. It went without saying that all the *Lardies* (la-de-dahs – stars) had something to sell: a book, a record, a show, so the publicity companies were getting their celebrities booked early. But the commercial aspect never intruded.

The routine was established. Each week there were three guests, one per researcher, usually allocated through natural selection. The early part of the week was spent reading everything ever written about our chosen person, starting with the newspaper clippings in the cuttings library. And at some point we arranged an interview, and face-to-face we picked up the salient points, the amusing stories, and anything that might help Mike in his approach.

From all this we typed up the questions we felt would get the best responses, photocopied useful anecdotes, and handed it all to Mike on Saturday morning. We would discuss it a bit, but once Mike had established his questions, our only job on the day was to take the guest to the green room, make them feel comfortable, at ease and aware of the questions that would come. Like 'when Mike asks you about your time in Russia you tell him that hilarious story about the brown bear'!

To me as a journalist it felt too scripted, but of course it often veered off course and it was truly Mike's skill to go with what happened and produce a benign and interesting show. Perhaps his weak spot at that time was powerful women. He once interviewed woman politician Helene Hayman, and I ran out of the studio in embarrassment.

The programme was recorded around 7pm and went out around 10.30pm. After the show there would be drinks and celebrations in the green room – Mike's wife Mary sometimes came. And then I'd drive home in Guv to watch the recording with Rick. Although at some level it was just a job, and far less responsible and taxing than the one I'd been doing before - because Mike, not I, was on the frontline – I confess I did like to see my name on the credits.

My first guest on the programme was Charles Aznavour, promoting a song called *She*. Apart from the cuttings there was nothing much I could do, since he could only come in on the day. He was on the show with Edna O'Brien and afterwards I joined them all for supper, a rare occurrence. I was quite shocked when Edna was obviously about to disappear with one of Charles' minders.

It was around my second guest the following week that I realised Mike didn't yet trust me. On the Thursday I took the train to Manchester where Dave Allen was rehearsing his new show. The interview was grim. He hated a direct approach and dismissed any interest in his life and times. By the end of the session he could see how disappointed I was, and as he went off to supper suggested we travel back on the train to London together the following morning.

What a difference! The journey was lovely. He just chatted and made me laugh for two and half hours, with his life and times disguised within it. It was such a joy and relief, and back at the BBC I wrote my report, stressing that although he wouldn't cope with a normal interview situation, it could be done.

The next day the tension was mounting, as it always did, by 5.30pm, waiting for our people to arrive. But the evening, to me, was a disaster - because no one would believe Dave was petrified.

At his request I took champagne to his dressing room, but even then the transmission was held up to get him another glass on set. His nerve failed him completely when Mike's personal questions came straight at him – exactly as I suggested it would – and the interview limped along until they got onto safer ground. Later in the green room Dave invited me out to a future lunch.

The following week I took two days off to read two books by my next guest Lyall Watson. *Supernature and The Romeo Error* required a lot of concentration but with both books under my belt I spent Thursday morning deciding what I would ask when I met him.

I was already fascinated by what was subsequently called 'non-materialist science'. I had even tentatively suggested, with no response, that Colin Wilson might be a candidate for the programme. I was beginning to feel a link between what I was calling the ineffable, or consciousness, and what other more scientifically inclined people were trying to understand about psychic phenomena. People like Colin Wilson and Lyall Watson were amongst the first to introduce scientific investigation to enhance their theories. And it was later through my own interests that I looked for the relationship or resonance between consciousness and quantum physics.

Supernature had been a huge best seller for Lyall and his fame was sealed in 1973 when he first brought Uri Geller's spoon-bending abilities to the attention of the British public on the David Dimbleby show. Mike was clearly reluctant to have Lyall on the show because the subject was far beyond his remit. But for some reason John, and presumably Roger, were enthusiastic – and so was I.

Three weeks earlier, when I had first walked into the office and seen the interview board, it was like an electric shock. As soon as I saw Lyall Watson's name, I knew he would be my guest and that for some reason he would be important to me. A few days after I met him I knew that it was he I had come for, and he was the reason I had been led to the job.

I met Lyall at his publishers *Hodder and Stoughton*, and was introduced by his publicist Eric Major. A publicist's task is to be charming, of course, to make a journalist want to feature their product, but over the years I continued to feel an affectionate link with Eric, as I did with one or two other men in this field. One in particular, Chris Nixon, then a unit publicist for feature films who I first met in the *Fab-208* days was a friend for thirty-five years, until his death. (It was he who first called me Annie, not Anne, and it has stuck ever since).

My impression of Lyall was of a lovely, gentle man, his soft mid-Atlantic voice and casual way of dressing distinctive. Suddenly my head blazed with thoughts and questions. It was hard to keep to *Parkinson* needs; I wanted to talk so much. It was magic!

I rushed back to the office and wrote up the interview, then called Mary and asked her to meet me. I wanted to talk and talk about my conversation with Lyall, the excitement of knowing that 'someone knew'; someone else could touch the mystical side of life.

The next day, Friday, I talked through Lyall's interview with Mike, suggesting he concentrate on *The Romeo Error* rather than *Supernature*, which John was arguing for. And the show itself went well. Lyall was up front, followed by the more conventional celebrity guests. To Mike's surprise and my delight, Telly Savalas sparked with Lyall because he was also interested and knowledgeable in the psychic field. Actress Gina Lollobrigida was promoting a coffee table book of her photographs.

In his success – Lyall told some very good stories – I felt such warmth for him, and after the show he invited me out to supper. We talked about fears: his fears, my fears, his future, my future, his sense of 'new beginnings', and he invited me to meet him the following day 'by the tiger in the Victoria and Albert museum'.

Of course I went, because I 'knew'. But at the same time I began to be afraid of my hunches and convictions. When he turned round totally unexpectedly during our tour of the museum and said 'what would you say if I said give up your job and come to the Amazon with me on Tuesday?' I was so shocked I said nothing – except to explain that I was married, and had only just started this job of a lifetime.

I felt useless, unhappy and desperately tired, at this mystical meeting that was utterly pointless. I suddenly didn't know how to behave. At that moment I doubted my emerging attempts at abstract thinking could ever have value against his extraordinary intellectual abilities. My experience was infinitesimal compared to his and my knowledge practically nil.

At supper later I gathered back my confidence, and as I was about to go home Lyall asked again 'If you were single and didn't have a job, would you take a chance with me?' I said 'No'. He tried again. 'If we were both to give up everything and begin something new, would you then?' Why did I say yes? Why did I say, 'If you still feel the same in six months time, come back and tell me and I'll leave'?

The following morning I woke up relaxed, comfortable and very calm. Since it was Monday, our day off, I could doze and think and dream and wonder; my head busy with Lyall. I considered a letter I might write telling him my fear about finding the courage to leave my familiar surroundings, whatever the 'conviction' inside me. I dreamed all night about Lyall, as the only significant person on earth, who I had to get to!

The next day, the day Lyall was due to leave for his home in Bermuda and then the Amazon, was different. How could a three-day meeting have that much significance? Was he sane? Could my need for independence ever fit in with his life? Was I crazy?

Still not denying the possibility, the excitement was gone and best forgotten. But eight days later a letter arrived at the office from Bermuda. In a roundabout, literary and cleverly romantic way it was... the invitation.

My guest that week was Richard Burton, although his would be a pre-recorded afternoon show, to go out at another time. He wouldn't do a prior interview and the bombshell dropped on Friday that he might not turn up at all; he had laryngitis. In the end he did come, looking rather grey and pallid, a sadly broken man, yet still unbelievably charismatic with such warmth that I, too, was totally charmed. Though insecure and nervous, he wanted to make it work well.

We watched in trepidation as each drink went down. His hands shook and he smoked a great deal, which clearly worried his then partner Princess Elizabeth of Yugoslavia because he was officially 'on the wagon'. But the show went brilliantly, way beyond the carefully crafted, benign script: into his drinking, his love of poetry and Elizabeth Taylor. Mike did a fantastic job and he was thrilled with the result.

The evening show also worked well. Mike took it much more casually than usual. Harold Robbins – who I had met beforehand and produced some sketchy research – enjoyed himself, and Harry Secombe and Anita Loos were marvellous. I took a taxi home, my head splitting with tension and pleasure. I couldn't sleep with all those people dancing in my head.

My work life was always separate from my home life. With Rick's blessing – or at least his acceptance – I often went out for lunches, drinks or meals with friends and colleagues, men and women. I was never the perfect housewife, but in this job even less so. Rick's doting mother, and his Godmother – even my own devoted mother – felt sorry for him. In their eyes I wasn't looking after him properly.

Perhaps he knew at some deep level, as I must have done, that almost unwillingly but inevitably I was withdrawing. Rick was clearly unhappy. His lack of success at the job made him confused and depressed. His opportunity to record some songs fell flat, and the one thing that might have made him happy I couldn't give him. I just knew I didn't want children.

The 'search for truth' is a selfish road and I don't blame anyone who has distaste for the 'ME generation'. But deep down I forgave myself for what I did, at every step. I have never liked the loaded word 'morality', and despite how things may have looked, I have never doubted that my life has been imbued with a deep sense of integrity. The search for truth is also a devastatingly lonely and painful road that, as I often said, I would not wish on my worst enemy. But from the moment that trapdoor lifted off my head and I felt what I describe as 'the call', there was never ever a question of turning back.

Once again, I 'knew' in my bones that 1975 was an important year and that something big 'cosmically' was happening, not just to me. I knew that to follow it would take enormous courage. At one level it was a matter of waiting, and

I could sense myself 'clearing up my life' at home. Tidying things, throwing things away, keeping only the things I really needed. I knew, and I didn't know, I was leaving, and at the same time wondered how I could be so calculating and certain, how could I hurt Rick?

The show also went on. My guests included Ronnie Barker, Dame Thora McLeod of McLeod, Mohammed Ali (one of Mike's most popular shows when Ali got up and almost brained him!), Peter Sellers (incredibly tense, nervous and even more twitchy than Richard Burton), Andy Williams.

At the end of a momentous year, I prayed that God would guide me towards goodness for everyone. Because, above all, as painful as it would be to many people, and to me, I knew this journey was something about God, or rather, about opening up to spiritual awareness.

At the beginning of January Lyall wrote again. I discussed his letter, as alluring and clever as before, with Mary, and as ever her support and strength convinced me. Lyall was coming to London mid-month and I was to leave a message at his hotel if I would see him.

Of course I did. Talks were happening in the office about the next *Parkinson* series and although there had been moments of magic, the thought of just continuing appalled me. There had to be more.

When he called I felt like an adolescent again. But when we met for lunch at *Lacey's* a few days later I was mostly rendered into silence through panic, while he talked: about dolphins and his myriad other interests as a naturalist. We arranged to meet again on Sunday, which proved even more bizarre.

Lyall suggested we go to a party given by Lorne and Lawrence Blair, two startlingly dramatic brothers whose latest pursuit had been to put their lives in danger by making a film on the Bugis pirates of Indonesia. Again I felt insecure and silent in that milieu.

Lawrence's girlfriend at the time was Jenny Agutter, and to this day I wonder what her reaction was to the evening's entertainment: an 'experimental' film by a woman called Ann Bevensey on vulvas and vaginas. I'm glad to say Lyall had the grace to be embarrassed and apologetic.

That same week I went to a publicity lunch given by theatrical agent Theo Cowan. A lot of people sat at a huge round table and I know I talked to my neighbour. But when, two or three days later, writer/theatre director Ronald Harwood invited me to lunch for the following day, I had no idea it had been him. He explained he had felt compelled to contact me.

When I arrived, late and flustered, at *Don Luigi's* in the Kings Road, he told me he was concerned I might take this invitation in the wrong way, but he had told his friend and tennis partner, Harold Pinter, about me, and it was he who said he should ring me.

To my astonishment we talked for five hours – about me! He used the word 'considerable', and said he saw 'a power' about me that I must use. He told me that my job on *Parkinson* was demeaning, that I must go on and have faith in myself, believe in the energy I had. Could I write profiles, go in vision? What was I scared of? Fear of cameras, for example, would fall into place, he said.

We had tea and then we left and I have never seen him since. But somehow I understood. It felt as though he had come as a guide, to give me his wisdom, and offer me something like recognition. It added to the sense that I was being forced to take an opportunity that I felt was coming.

Life was conspiring but my heart was heavy and my mind was whirling. That same week Rick said he might have to leave me. His work just wouldn't take off and he was afraid of getting the sack. If that happened, he said, he would blow everything, take off – probably to America – and sink or swim. We talked blandly about splitting up.

I made the decision. I wrote to Lyall that I'd come. A week later a letter came back with a one-way ticket to Bermuda. He also sent a picture of the cottage 'which sits on the end of the peninsula beyond the bridge. My boat is moored in the blue lagoon behind it.'

I didn't live it lightly. The following days I couldn't sleep and I kept dissociating. I forced myself to watch television, or anything, to find a focal point for concentration. Yet a powerful dream of huge winds hurling through windbreaks confirmed that enormous changes were inevitable.

I couldn't get a handle on what was happening to me. I was afraid of losing my mind. But every day I was given experiences that added to the picture and gave it meaning. That week I went to lunch with an old friend Robert, who I had interviewed many years before for a feature on young millionaires. (It was through knowing him that I knew the millionaire lifestyle had no meaning for me.)

Robert had played too hard and lost his business, and in trying to chase it back his mind worked overtime and he had a nervous breakdown. When we met at *The White House* after all these years, he was a changed man and it frightened me. At some strange level we were communicating more deeply, more meaningfully – at 'higher revolutions' – than we had before. But by the strange notions in his head and the bees in his bonnet, I could see he was still mentally unstable.

I began to see that touching 'madness' and touching the spiritual realms was a question of degree, of what was and what wasn't a natural unfolding to 'faster' energies. I never doubted my sanity again!

The *Parkinson* season was coming to an end. One evening at the BBC bar Dave Allen recognised me and bought me a drink, and to my surprise was very attentive. He asked me if I would like to come to see his show on Sunday and suggested I meet him in his dressing room at 7pm.

It was a lovely, fantasy evening. Dave was complementary, we drank champagne and I felt a million dollars. Bill Cotton was there, too, as surprised to see me as I was to be there, and he took me up to the box during transmission. Bill then took Dave and me to supper at Pu Tong. I went to his show a couple more times and we had several drinks and lunches after that (most at the *Maids of Honour* in Kew). He was always an enigma but I guess we just liked talking to each other.

I booked my flight to Bermuda – for March 29th – and although I couldn't quite understand why Lyall's ticket had an add-on leg to New York. I presumed I was meant to go on to New York after Bermuda for some reason, and phoned the BBC New York office just in case. I couldn't believe it when the woman on the other end of the line, Elizabeth Farrell, said I could stay with her for a couple of days if I was stuck.

The last day at *Parkinson* was downbeat for the end of term, and although the food at the Portobello Hotel was wonderful, no one seemed in the mood for a party. Although a new producer was taking Roger's place and might not want me, we talked as though it was a forgone conclusion that the same researchers would be there for the next series.

CHAPTER THREE

My stated plan to Rick and my mother – and my true intention – was to go to Bermuda for a three-month holiday while we were off air. When they saw me off at the airport both of them knew and for some reason accepted that I had been invited by Lyall. And yet, despite that, and although nothing in my life was certain, I had a feeling I wouldn't be back.

The arrival into cloudy, warm, humid Bermuda was painless. Lyall was waiting with a taxi to his little white cottage across the island in Somerset Bridge. I had everything I could want; a double bedroom to myself, a log fire, bottles of wine, horsebox doors and an English country garden with a grapefruit tree.

My initial memories are random. I learned early on to identify the eight species of birds on Bermuda, and particular loved watching the ubiquitous kiskadee, and the white-tailed tropicbird cruising on the thermals overhead. I would trip across the dewy grass every morning in bare feet to pick grapefruit. Tiny whistling frogs camped in the crevices of the house and I stopped being scared of the lizards with the orange phalange, which ran up and down the inside and outside walls.

I was looked after completely. In the evenings Lyall and I would sit by the lagoon watching the sun go down, drinking wine and eating nuts beside the bay grape bushes. I listened endlessly to Captain and Tennille on ZBM89, the local radio station, and enjoyed the wind brushing sonorously through the casurina trees.

Most exciting was my pop-pop motorbicycle, the sort you start up by peddling. I went everywhere, sometimes with Lyall on his smarter yellow bike, but also exploring on my own. There were few cars and the three principle cross-island roads had a 20 mph speed limit.

Bermuda was an ice-cream island. All houses had to be painted in pastels and these melted delicately into the brightness of the blue sky against the miraculous turquoise sea.

On the beaches the black bodies of the local people shone like dark opals against this beautiful backdrop.

To explain Lyall is impossible even now, but I was certainly thrilled and captivated by the whole idea of him. I want to say at this point that the pull between us lasted eighteen years, although very few of those years were spent together. There is no doubt in my mind that we were destined to meet, that he was and remains a huge part of who I am. But our relationship was always impossible, like heaven and hell rolled into one.

Lyall was a loner, a true eccentric, disciplined, totally defended against his vulnerability, and self-sufficient. He was an Aries initiator with a will of iron in a softly spoken glove. I think, above all, he was a storyteller, and over time I realised that any truth could be stretched for a good story! I often heard our own adventures repeated in ways I would never have recognised. 'What is absolute truth?' he once said. To me it was everything.

Without doubt he was the brightest man I have ever known, his fund of knowledge inexhaustible. He had been a student in several countries, including his native South Africa (where he ran the Johannesburg Zoo for a time). He had a doctorate in zoology from London University, studying primates under Desmond Morris. I remember him being rather scathing about Jane Goodall who without qualifications (then) was studying chimpanzees in the wild, under the protectorate of Louis Leaky. (I would, however, like to say that I think she is amazing!)

But at that time Lyall's predominant field of interest was the paranormal, and when I arrived in Bermuda he told me he was just extricating himself from a group in Ossining, in upstate New York, who were involved in rather secretive psychic exploration.

In a nutshell, two scientists – Lyall and Andrija Puharich (who had written the book *Uri* on Uri Geller) – were working with two or three women psychics. One of these, Phyllis Schlemmer, was apparently channelling an extra terrestrial group called *The Nine*, who were planning to land on planet earth. The whole enterprise was being funded by British Baron, Sir John Whitmore, and continued to be so for many years. Clearly their work was sufficiently important for them to be bugged by the CIA, as I learned later, but everything in my gut said 'nonsense'.

Almost twenty-one years later, when the idea of channelling was more commonplace, Phyllis published her account of that time in her book *Landing on Planet Earth*. Many people have found it extremely helpful in their understanding of universal principles, but as far as I know *The Nine* did not land in terrestrial form, and at that time I felt deep down, and still do, that powerful men and psychic women create something sexual and 'off-centre'.

It was through Lyall that my knowledge and contacts and context for the world I was in began to grow and take shape. I realised over time that I was soaking up information and putting it into slots. He had thousands of books I could read, and when he told me things I listened. But the more he told me, the more I was rendered into silence. For one whole year I virtually said nothing. My inner life was vivid, my intuitive knowing was carrying me into the strangest realms, but when he pleaded with me to 'tell me things', I couldn't explain.

Lyall and I, in our own way, were both 'pattern-makers', trying to make sense of the world through linking processes and cross-referencing, but with totally different mental functioning. My friend Vlyn once described her way of gathering knowledge of life was like a snowball. The bits that made sense and added to the picture stuck; the rest went by the wayside, a brilliant description. I added to my snowball through feeling and intuition, Lyall's thoughts were academic and sequential - although even that is too simplistic.

Gifted psychic, Lilla Bek, told me several years later that at the age of five Lyall's third eye had stuck wide open through family trauma. 'He didn't know he was psychic and that what he saw wasn't what everyone else saw.' On the other hand, he always said I was more analytical than he was. But I began to recognise there was a difference between brain and mind, and I was beginning to give much more credence to the latter).

Three days after my arrival Lyall was due to leave Bermuda for a pre-planned, ten-day trip to New York and then to Washington for a parapsychology conference. He had decided to leave me to get my bearings in these first three days and not approach me, but inevitably we became lovers before he left.

By the time he went I was desperate for him to go and at the same time desolate that he had gone. With or without him I felt lonely and isolated; afraid it wasn't going to work and aware that both of us felt vulnerable, impatient, hopeful and ultimately impenetrable. So what was the point? We were a pretty good reflection of each other, but even after a week, returning to *Parkinson* also felt pointless.

For ten days, with all my reference points gone, I went into reverie, one day joyous, the next fearful. My mood changed as often as the atmosphere of the island changed. I biked in solitude to the local *Piggly Wiggly* supermarket; wrote letters to Mary and Rick, walked to the *Hitching Post* for newspapers; took the ferry to the capital Hamilton, and also sat at home and read. Carlos Castenada was a consistent read.

One of my favourites pastimes was to go into the garden and watch the planes stacking over the island, waiting their turn to land, which only happened at lunchtime. Or I would take my bike to the airport and experience the thrill of standing right under the vast jumbo jets as they came down onto the runway. Strange, since I hate flying!

One day I went to lunch with the family of an acquaintance in London. They entertained me on the premises of their family business *The Irish Linen Shop* in Somerset, which was fun and very different and rather 'colonial'.

I also contacted some local friends of Lyall: a couple with a young child who had opted for the purist yachting life, sailing on the seas and island hopping. Mostly they stayed in the British Virgin Islands. I wanted to continue the semblance of a freelance writing life, and I thought their story would be good for the monthly magazine *She*.

Lyall always wrote by hand on golden yellow pages and I remember vividly sitting on the floor with a sheet of that paper, writing down the title for a book: *A Spot to Stand*. I kept that page for years, but the promise has taken all this time to fulfil.

I was glad when Lyall came back and so was he. We talked about going to the Amazon, and about spending time, maybe a couple of months, sailing his boat *Samadhi*. This took us way beyond my expected time with him, and the excitement affected us both.

The days went by, glorious and unbearable by turns. What had begun as a holiday had become too 'weighted'. We had created an intensity between us that couldn't possibly sustain itself, yet we were uneasy when it wasn't there. What he wanted to see in me was strength; what I wanted to see in him was vulnerability. Neither of us seemed able to oblige.

We went snorkelling by Somerset Bridge and in the lagoon in front of the house. It was my first experience and I loved it – until we saw a small but ferocious baracuda shark in the water with us! We biked to the pub, or to the *Lobster Pot* for a supper of Bermuda rockfish. If we went to the cinema in the daytime and saw two films, we would still attend a concert in the evening. He teased me and left me silly notes and gifts. He was also a talented cartoonist. Lyall's capacity for enjoyment and interest was rapacious.

One adventure remains in my mind – which I used as an idea many years later in my novel *Shadowplay*. Hans Esser, the Director of Mental Health for New Jersey, occasionally came to Bermuda – to Hall's Island in Harrington Sound. He was overseeing an experiment about male dominance, with a social group of gibbons. One evening he and his wife invited Lyall and me to dinner, and then organised a visit to the site.

The day-to-day running of the experiment fell to Terry, an American postgraduate student. He picked us up from the shore in a small dingy and motored us to the island. Gibbons look small and golden and gentle, but Peter, the dominant male, looked extremely menacing at every terrified step I took. I was glad when we left.

I loved my time in Bermuda, but ultimately it began to feel parochial. Remnants of a certain class of Englishman and a few Americans who indulged successfully in commerce, with a black community that was set apart, in the end made it feel strangely sterile. To Lyall it was a good, private place to write, and he had already told me he needed to be alone to write his next book *Gifts of Unknown Things*. I now knew why I had the add-on flight to New York. There was always the assumption that I would go!

We talked about me joining him in September for his trip to the Amazon, and in stronger moments I felt confident that these were our plans. But not once in my relationship with Lyall did I feel he was making a commitment to me, and whenever we parted I was never assured that I would see him again.

In part it was my fear that was driving me even further into the unknown. I phoned Elizabeth Farrell in New York to say I was coming on 5th May and arranged to stay with her 'for the first few days'. After that I had no idea where I was going or if I was coming back. And yet I did know.

Lyall and I spent our last evening at *Dennis's*, a hidden-away restaurant with a cafe atmosphere, where we ate green turtle steaks and shark. I left the following day, aching with a sense of loss and futility.

Liz Farrell, a Brit living in New York and working as a secretary at the BBC, was an extraordinary woman. My two-day invitation became an extended stay, and as confused and lost and sad as I was, my first experience of New York was amazing, thanks to her. Liz unconditionally opened her apartment, her hand and her heart to me, as she did to any stray BBC contact that came into the city.

Liz was divorced from her American husband Bill and supporting their four-year old daughter Stephanie (Tuffy). In her own way Liz was as lost and confused as I was, but when I went back to see her three years later, she had re-met and was about to marry another American, fifteen years older than she was. He was Vice President of a paper making company and had first met Liz in England when she was five, through her father's own paper making business.

Liz saved my life. She simply took over in my obvious distress and disorientation. She listened as I talked endlessly about myself, was practical and immeasurably helpful in her unsentimental, down-to-earth way, while I tried to make sense of what was happening.

Apart from everything else she was a brilliant cook, and was always trying new recipes. She also introduced me to the delightful ritual of a glass of chilled Ernst and Gallo Californian white wine and nibbles every evening. I remember one dinner party when a lobster crawled across the floor before it went into the pot.

There seemed to be no past or future just a continuing present. The only life I had was here. What I did know, however, was that I would write to Bill Cotton to tell him I wasn't returning to *Parkinson*. I was reading *Pilgrim at Tinker Creek* by Annie Dillard. Her poetic prose touched me deeply, and as I read I understood more and more that there was no turning back. And this was nothing to do with Lyall.

For several days I mooched about in misery, or went to see Liz at the BBC. I remember seeing Alistair Cooke recording his weekly *Letter from America* and being hugely impressed that he didn't use a script. Sometimes I helped Liz by taking and then collecting Tuffy from school, and occasionally took her to McDonalds because she liked to watch the cartoons there.

Tuffy was a fabulously brash New York kid, completely the opposite of Liz with her contained Britishness. I adored her. Some years later she told me in confidence that she would rather be called Stephanie not her baby name, but she didn't want to hurt her mother by telling her.

New York was, and presumably still is, a high-energy city. If you were in the whirling vortex, part of the speedy and glamorous action, you were fine. But if you weren't you could feel and look like a loser. Much later, when I discovered that

New York was built on granite - the hard quartz-crystalline rock that enabled them to build so high – I understood why the city had the strange effect it did on me, and why there were so many 'weirdo' people walking the streets.

It was as though my speeding mind was resonating with the high energy of the crystal quartz. Some days I felt so 'high' it was as though I was walking above the buildings not beside them, and there were moments I did feel I was losing my mind.

It was at this time that I met up with Chris Nixon, one of my warm acquaintance publicist friends from *Fab-208* days. He was in New York trying to sell a film script. He would never know how timely his visit was, or how much he helped to ground me during the week he was there, simply by offering something stable and familiar to hold on to.

I had been in New York for only two weeks. Lyall had already phoned and written a couple of letters saying, in his cartoon way, that he was missing me. But it took me completely by surprise when he said that *The Nine* group: John Whitmore, Diana Becchetti, Melanie Toyofuku and even Tony Morgan (who was, in fact, a BBC Governor and by coincidence an ex-business colleague of my ex-millionaire friend Robert), were coming from Ossining to Bermuda, and I must be there. The ticket arrived next day.

I was booked for an evening with Chris and his friends Tracey and Murray Garfield. Chris had worked with Tracey on a film in Britain before she left show business to marry Murray and settle in style on West Central Park.

By coincidence I knew Tracey (Vivienne Crisp as she was then) from my days before journalism, at eighteen. We both worked for a cosmetic company in the Burlington Arcade where she was the stunning telephonist who became a model and then an actress (even in a Bond film). It was Vivienne who had introduced me to the music of Barbra Streisand.

The next day I was in Bermuda, wondering if I would see New York again. For a while Lyall and I felt estranged but gradually we moved closer again. But when his visitors came the following day and talked non-stop - in a warm and familiar and cohesive way - my confidence slipped again. None of my experience seemed to fit this situation.

My sense of inadequacy in Lyall's company lasted several years, despite his best efforts. His energy simply overshadowed mine. His brain, with its voracious appetite for the natural world, for books, for movies, and collecting information, stored everything. I felt I knew nothing. So what did he see in me? Did he ever really need anyone?

When the Ossining group had gone Lyall made it clear, yet again, that he needed his space to continue writing. My ticket back to New York was booked for the following Tuesday. We talked about going together to Cape Canaveral for the last manned launch of Apollo in July, and being in New York for my thirtieth birthday, and still nothing felt certain. The September Expedition to the Amazon on the *Lindblad Explorer* seemed fantasy, too, even though he persuaded me to buy some suitable clothes.

Back in New York with Liz, our fairly social life went on. People continued to come by and stay. Since I first arrived I had tried to make contacts and written two or three pieces to send back home. I actually interviewed Dr Atkins before anyone had heard of his diet. He made the observation that although every single food in the supermarket had a diet equivalent and everyone was slimming, most Americans stayed fat! He said it was a ploy to keep Americans eating.

One of my stranger contacts and friendships was with Jock Manton, a retired ABC News director who lived in a tiny apartment on the West Side. Born Archimedes Giacamontonio he trained as a classical sculptor in Italy and during his life he was commissioned to make statues of such luminaries as the Shah of Persia and Eisenhower. He still sculpted in his country home in Sparta, New Jersey. I did stay there once, but it was a bit creepy.

In my rudderless state I was always praying that something would turn up to make me feel real again. When Carol and Andy came to New York it was lovely to see them, but the distance between us was now too great. When I

35

bumped into Georgina Mells, a colleague from IPC who was also travelling, I felt comforted by the coincidence.

Liz had contact with other British media and occasionally we met them for a drink in *Charlie O's*. (I only once went to *Harry's Bar)*. When Dermot Purgavie, New York correspondent for the *Daily Mail*, told me there were three weeks' work in August - as office manager at the *Daily Telegraph* - I knew I wouldn't be going home: at least, not for some time.

Lyall arrived in New York on 10 July and stayed at the San Carlos Hotel on East 43rd Street. He did not suggest I join him, though we did see *Jaws* together. A few days later we flew to Orlando, Florida and hired a car.

The last manned flight of Apollo, launched to meet up with Soyuz, was on Tuesday 15th July 1975. We drove to Cape Canaveral from *Disney World*, where we staying. As usual Lyall and I were cool and distant and hurting, but the event itself was amazing. We walked past a spent booster rocket, which gave us a sense of the immense size of the project, and took our place on the wooden stand. The three-hour wait was worth everything: the red fire, the lift off, the noise, the movement. At the last moment I decided to watch it through my binoculars to make the event last longer. Now I wish I hadn't – like Lyall.

Back at *Disney World* – much smaller than it is today – we saw as much as we could. The next day we drove to the Florida Keys, stopping in Sarasota to watch pelicans dive on the sea, and an ibis on the beach in the beautiful morning sunshine.

Miami Beach, Coral Gables, and the Everglades, where we walked along two boardwalk pathways, over a tropical swamp with pelicans, buzzards and alligators. We arrived in Key West, the southernmost city of America with its Greek, European, Spanish Colonial styles, and its drifting community.

For several days we sat and watched the spectacular sunsets blazing over the sea. We ate conch fritters and key lime pie in *Tony's* bar, and drank (my first) ice-cold lagers. We swam and bicycled and talked crazy, exploratory talk, or just went ominously silent.

The day before my birthday we woke early and caught the plane from Key West to New York, changing at Miami. We were both ready to go back. On the morning of my 30th birthday, I left Lyall at the San Carlos Hotel and went back to Elizabeth's to check my birthday mail. Two of my letters were from Rick – and then he called me.

The evening of my birthday I collapsed with a terrible headache. My guilt over Rick was immense. But still I couldn't stop. Lyall and I spent the evening in his room high up in the San Carlos. I felt good in my simple, long green cotton dress and my hair up – which he liked. We ate delicious things and watched the magical full moon over Manhattan from the balcony. Finally we had found something special – and inevitable - together.

I did not deceive Rick lightly. It was never ever simple. Until the night of my birthday I did not know for certain that I would leave Rick. Yet everything I did, as this extraordinary pull went on and on, had a sense of rightness and meaning. There was no question deep down; I had no choice. I knew that in following my heart I was being led by my soul. For what purpose I didn't know.

I had no illusions that I would be happy. In fact, part of me was certain that ultimately Rick would fare better than I would. I was terrified of letting everything go: my job, money, home, security, with no promise whatsoever of a safe landing. Lyall was willing to support me while I was with him, but he would never make a commitment.

In the middle of my tedious and uneventful three weeks at the *Daily Telegraph* (except for meeting their Weekend Magazine editor, John Anstey, who was on his way to Jamaica) Rick came to see me, in the ninety-seven degree, humid August heat. He, too, had been travelling and came via San Francisco and Connecticut. With Elizabeth's unerring kindness she suggested he stay with me.

The following day we spent six hours walking around Manhattan, talking, saying it all, and saying nothing, unable to help ourselves, or each other. I never believed it could be so frightening and so final.

When eventually a few days later he left, vulnerable, empty and alone, I prayed with all my might that he would make it. I knew that if this was right for me, it had to be right for him. (In fact, the young woman who within a week he had invited into our house to be his lodger eventually became his wife. They have two children.) We had been together for eight years.

So a new era of my life had begun and it left me feeling sick, dizzy and incapable. I felt like a traitor. On 21 August 1975, overwhelmed with gratitude for Elizabeth, I left Manhattan and flew to Bermuda. And for the next two years it felt as though I was clinging to the cliff-top by my fingernails.

CHAPTER FOUR

The one fantasy Rick had was to 'chase bullfrogs up the Amazon'. It is ironic that it is I who fulfilled his dream. Lyall had returned from London, where *Gifts of Unknown Things* had been accepted enthusiastically by Hodders, and in September 1975 we left for the Amazon on *The Lindblad Explorer.*

Lars Eric Lindblad was an extraordinary pioneer. He built *The Explorer* as an Antarctic expedition ship for tourists, in such a way that it would reach parts no other ship was able to do. It had a flat bottom that allowed it to enter shallower waters, and then Zodiac dingys were used to transport people further into the unreachable places.

The Explorer was unique for its time. Wealthy people, mostly Americans but not exclusively, paid a great deal of money to travel in first class conditions to the wildest regions of the world. When it was not in the Arctic or Antarctic, the ship sailed into warmer waters, and Lyall (who didn't like the cold) was Expedition Leader for many of these.

These trips were true expeditions, and well-known naturalists clamoured to come aboard to lecture because it was also the opportunity of a lifetime for them. Prince Philip and Prince Rainier had been amongst the guests, and while I was on board – during several different trips – Sir Peter and Lady Philippa Scott and Ron and Valerie Taylor (who shot the sequences of the great white shark for *Jaws),* were amongst the experts.

It was Lyall who taught me to travel light. The enormous amount of luggage I had brought to Bermuda was now whittled down into one small, cream *Samsonite* suitcase. In fact this case lasted twenty years! In it was an array of suitable clothes. In every way I was dependent on Lyall.

The Lindblad Explorer was a pretty ship with a red hull; much smaller than a cruise ship. It took seventy-five passengers and an equal number of staff. The officers were Swedish (Hans Hasser was Captain and Ammi, his girlfriend, the Purser), whilst the rest of the crew was recruited along the way.

The big, cheerful Tongans were the most fun. The hostess, Ruth, who spoke five languages, was Swiss, and deep in the bowels of the ship was a real Chinese laundry, because all towels and linen were changed every day. It was a luxurious way to travel.

Lyall was in charge, and played all the roles perfectly: the naturalist, the expert, and the social director. I was the girlfriend and fell further into silence. Although he offered me the chance to lecture, to feel involved, I couldn't do it. Apart from collaborating on the writing of the ship's log, I went gauche.

As luck would have it we set sail in a hurricane! For eight days I, and many others, lay flat on our backs feeling like death, despite the reassurance that it could have been worse, because at least the ship had stabilisers! To keep on the edge of the hurricane, we zig-zagged through the Leeward islands and stopped at St Lucia where dolphins danced at dawn, and at Trinidad, where in the twilight we watched the vivid scarlet ibis coming home to roost, like lights in a Christmas tree, in the *Caroni* swamp.

At last, at Belem, at the mouth of the mighty river, the rocking and rolling stopped, and despite the insecurity of living 'without any life ties or promises' as Lyall was quick to point out, the most amazing adventure of my life began. Through Lyall I had a taste of the Wilderness that I could only have dreamed of, and through his eyes I learned how to look and see.

By lunchtime we were entering the narrowest part of the delta, and quite soon we were in the narrow channels of the Rio Para. It was lovely to be on deck. We passed the tiny settlements where survival had been simple for two hundred years, through logging, fishing or rubber tapping. We waved at the children as they paddled furiously towards us in their dugout canoes and laughed with them as they played on the bow waves.

At sunset the world changed. The macaws and parrots began to fly overhead, the low sun outlining their breathtakingly strident colours. Such a big sky: high black mountains of cloud with sweeps of blue and pink below. Then a dramatic peak of black cloud ringed with light against the setting sun, breaking off into a deep chasm of red, like an inferno with rays of sunlight streaming through.

The first morning we woke at 4am, when the air was cool and beautiful and there were no mosquitoes. The six zodiacs were in the water by dawn. The world was wonderful in this first wakefulness. I didn't know how lovely it would be: the quiet, the shadows; the sounds of the birds, the sweet smells, and the light itself.

The Amazon may be teeming with life, but it is surprisingly subtle. A tree is a tree, and the trees along the Amazon, predominantly cecropia and inga, seemingly unchanging. Yet, to me, as my gaze intensified, they always looked different as I watched them each day, in light or shadow, in mist or clarity.

We went past a small settlement and turned into the narrow Boca Da Aquiqui tributary, moving slowly along pastureland with herds of zebu cattle. As we passed a small bend, water buffalo were being herded through the water up onto a wooden ramp and into a pen built on stilts at the water's edge.

There was lots of activity already. Canoes passed us with old men and small boys. People piled together on their front verandas and waved. It was cool and comfortable, no bugs. We saw the tucuzi dolphins, the big primitive, pink river dolphin that looks like an alligator with two large 'eyes', coasting through the water. We saw young hoatzin birds, which shoot straight down into the water, horned screamers and an Oriole-like bird, the troupial.

We came back for breakfast, slept after lunch, and by 4pm were back on the river.

The afternoon was hot and in the channel of the Guajara our local guide Moacir, and Soames Summerhays, a British naturalist, threw nets to show us small 'laughing' catfish, yellow piranha, golden cyclid, and elongated hatchet fish. Of course they put them back.

Behind us the sun was setting, and ripples of gold washed up on the shore from the bow waves. Ahead of us, the reflected blues and pinks shone in the shimmering pools of muted shot colour, each surrounded in pure gold dancing light. A profusion of bright white clouds exploded high into the sky.

Most days after breakfast we had debriefings, and each evening after supper one of the four or five naturalists gave a lecture. After that, for those who were still awake, there were drinks in the lounge and socialising. Lyall felt obliged to stay up, but I usually went to bed. Even in the best-run ship there will always be occasional rumblings of discontent, and on the first night one or two people were unhappy because 'they didn't expect the Amazon to be like this: so much water and lack of activity'!

The next morning we were out on the river well before sunrise and into the wonderful swamp area filled with water birds at the mouth of the Rio Curua. It was startling to cross the well-defined line between the coffee brown waters of the main river and the black of its southern tributary. Dragonflies danced around us, and we passed small islands of arum lilies.

The afternoon was different again the bright green waters of the Rio Tapajos. The ships anchored opposite a long white beach, a short way from the boomtown of Santarem, then the topmost point of the trans-Amazonian Highway. A zodiac shuttled from ship to shore all afternoon, and we swam in the clear green warm water. In the evening we had a barbecue on the beach and sat in the firelight watching the stars.

The next day we docked at the tiny town of Obidos, sleepy in the mid-day sun. Here the river was at its narrowest – one mile wide. The people seemed to accept us, and just stared or smiled and shyly followed us around. Hundreds of faces stared at us, too, in the Brazil nut factory: a Dickensian scene, where rows and rows of people in an ill-lit room worked with simple equipment, cracking nuts one at a time. Women and tiny children then piled them into panniers, paid by piecework.

Several days later we reached the halfway point, Manaus - much hotter and more humid - where we witnessed the fading opulence of what was once the centre of the rubber boom. When the rubber industry crashed in 1914, Manaus began to degenerate. Yet even then the exploitation of resources and the ecological damage done by the Highway was causing ecologists concern.

Lyall was vociferous about this long before the eighties drive to save the Amazon rainforest, and on my return I wrote an article about it - thanks to my fortuitous meeting with John Anstey in New York. It was published in the *Telegraph Saturday Magazine*, and although he didn't run the article until 1979, I know I was one of the first to bring it to public attention.

We visited the incongruously sumptuous plush red velvet Opera House, originally opened in 1896 and recently restored. Then Lyall's passion for food led us to the 'best Feijouada in Manaus', at the airport, where four of us staggered through a huge pot of pork and beans each with farinha and rice. We returned to the Opera House in the evening for a ballet performance by a Sao Paulo company.

One morning after breakfast we took the zodiacs to the Boca das Guaribas (the place of the howler monkeys), for our first walk in the forest. This was not original primal forest, which is almost impossible to find, but secondary forest. In most places the tall canopy trees were split and broken with the light shedding through, which made it difficult to walk. It was tangled with lianes and fallen tree trunks.

Above us we saw green-winged macaws, crimson-crested woodpeckers and huge iridescent blue morphos butterflies. At our feet large parasol ants marched along fallen branches carrying huge pieces of green leaf back to their nests. A giant one-inch soldier ant stood over the workers. And finally, we not only heard but also saw the red howler monkeys. We never did see an anaconda!

Most of the bigger craft like ours turned round at Manaus. The Explorer, however, with its low draft, could navigate the shallows right up river to the end. At Tabatingha on the Brazilian border we anchored offshore to wait for customs clearance, and an hour later we sailed in the twilight into the rowdy, frontier shantytown of Leticia, on the border of Peru, Brazil and Colombia.

Lyall and I walked into the town up the main street slope with tiny shack shops on either side, lit by candlelight. There was loud music in street bars, but we walked to the end of town for our beer to the recommended 'good place' - the brothel! There were girls in enormous platform shoes and tiny frocks and plenty of sailors, including ours!

The whole town, it seemed, was run by our local agent Mike Tsalikis, an extraordinary Greek American incomer. The next morning most of the passengers toured Mike's zoo. There was still a great deal of illegal trading in wild life and he was probably responsible for most of it, but after our lecture the night before on Salvador Benevides and his one-man fight against trafficking, no one would have dared to bring an ocelot skin on board

In the afternoon the Tsalikis guides took us to a Yagua Indian village. The guides were young American students or postgraduates who wanted to travel. Mike had discovered the village about five years before. Apparently when he found them, a young Indian girl was suffering from a rifle wound and Mike took her to Leticia hospital and then to Bogota. The village moved closer to be near her and he now brought them food and took care of them when they were sick. In exchange they allowed him to bring tourists like us to the village.

We waded through mud to meet this beautiful community of tiny people: one family of twenty men and women and minute children. The men wore thick grass skirts, the women, bare from the waist up, wore tiny red cloths. They kept pigs and chickens and were hunting not planting people. They showed us how they used their blowguns with remarkable precision.

A couple of days later we reached Yanamono, a tourist complex, and walked to a Yagua village, which felt slightly less authentic. The women were sitting on the ground with their youngest children making string bags; there was a communal house and a witch doctor's house, and two men making thatch. Later that day, after three weeks on board, we zig-zagged slowly into our final destination, Iquitos, along the alarmingly shallow river.

Before we set sail I had written to Annie Dillard at Western Washington State College where she taught English, saying how much I had enjoyed her book. I told her about the Amazon trip, in case the link might one day lead her to coming on board as a naturalist. She had replied enthusiastically saying that she had toured the Napo River in Ecuador by outboard motor and dugout canoe, sleeping in tents. It had been 'wholly strange and wholly home'. She told me that by the time I got back from the Amazon 'you will have no nerves, you'll be a polyp - a happy one'.

Sadly I was not a happy polyp. At that moment I was in such a crisis of confidence that I forced myself into a heady display of independence. I told Lyall that since the ship was now taking a new group of tourists on board for a two-week round trip, I would leave the ship here with the rest of the outgoing passengers. I would find my own way to Cuzco and Machu Piccu and return in two weeks to be picked up when the ship came back to Iquitos.

I sat like a terrified zombie in the foyer of the *Hotel Touristas*. The town was the most unkempt we had experienced so far. Dusty streets with enormous potholes, beat-up cars, terraces of tumbling plaster houses, and one generator for the whole town so electricity was on ration. Everything was tatty and tumbledown and as depressed as I was.

But by the evening I was fine, except for the vast cockroach that crawled across my hair and into my bed, and kept me awake for most of the night as I kept the light on. The following day I took a plane across the spectacular Andes to Lima.

Lima, the City of Kings, had a Spanish colonial elegance, although the shantytowns on the perimeter were a shock. The Pan American Highway runs along the Peruvian coastal desert, through hills of sand with oases of fertile valleys at intervals, served by river water from the Andes. Nomadic Indians with herds of goats lived in makeshift huts of grass. I booked a bus to Pisco for the following day.

Pisco was an incongruous town, a mixture of colonial style, balconied homes, alongside crumbling brick, unfinished, unroofed houses. *The Embassy Hotel* (with cold water only) was comfortable in the sparse environment, and the following day I shared a taxi with Ursula, a Swiss girl I had met on the bus, to the Paracus Peninsular. We walked for two hours over the mountains of sand marking the necropolis (pre-Inca burial) site. We then hitched backed to town and booked our bus to Nazca

From Ica the landscape changed from flat desert sand to bare mountain, with changing rock colours and flat green valleys between. The famous Nazca lines begin to appear in the Pisco valley but are concentrated into the five valleys of Nazca. Although you could see the outsized birds, whales, spiders from the ground it was better to see them by air, as Ursula did.

Nazca was warm and gentle by day and cool at night. We walked through the town and across the river to the foot of the mountains where, on the first slopes, were the ruins of the old pre-Inca Nazca. Later we walked to an ancient Inca aqueduct, where women were washing clothes. No one knew then how the water got there, but the Incas must have understood about water and soil to set up such intricate systems. Two days later I caught the bus from Nazca to Cuzco.

I must have been mad! Bumping over the Andes for thirty hours, the last ten of which were hell, the bus became more and more crowded, standing room only, with people, chickens, and bags. I was jammed in my seat in an agonising position with my small white travel bag, now filthy, on my knees. Every few hours my handbag tipped upside down and I lost everything on the floor. I was dusty and exhausted.

The last hours were a nightmare. A seedy, fumbling man sat next to me and throughout the journey made me uneasy; he even asked me how much it would cost to sleep with me!

When we arrived in Cuzco at 1.30 in the morning, only he and I got out into the deserted square. I was terrified.

I rushed for the only waiting taxi, asked the driver to find a hotel, and was dropped around the corner at the *Hotel Touristas.* My heart sank when I realised it was closed, and imagined at best walking the streets all night, at worst being attacked by the awful man. In desperation I hammered on the hotel door and to my intense relief the night porter came out. At last I had a bed and a bath.

The following day I saw the hotel was quite grand and comforting, not the austere place it had seemed the night before, and it was a relief to be with other tourists. Cuzco was a magical city: the 'place of the heart' where the Puric people of the Incas lived on a metaphysical plane and 'knew' about the spirit. After four hours sleep I was up at dawn, refreshed, and I walked and looked. In the Cathedral the many chapels had candles and beautiful flowers, there were many arum lilies. The Indian women sitting along the walls selling ponchos looked marvellously colourful, where yesterday they had only looked dirty.

I moved to the simpler *Hotel Ollanta,* and decided the next day to find the ruins of Sacsahuaman. Here, on a hill on the northern outskirts of Cuzco, the stones were reputedly bigger and better than at Macchu Piccu. But by the end of that day I wondered whether my terror in Iquitos had been a premonition!

That morning I thought I was taking the path to Sacsahuaman when I walked along the bed of the river. At first I passed Indian women washing clothes and gold panning old timers shaking out their baskets, but gradually as the riverbed got narrower and became deserted, I started to climb along the bank with only two boys and their dog behind me.

For some reason I put my passport and some dollars inside my jacket. If they stole my bag or purse at least I would have that. But it was only a fleeting thought. As the boys passed me I asked 'Sacsahuaman?' They nodded yes and said they were going too. We smiled and nodded and I felt safe that there was a dog.

I was behind them as we climbed a sort of path, and then we walked together. The older boy, about seventeen, was kind and asked me if I was alone. When it got difficult to climb he helped me and carried my bag. We chatted easily in gesticulating language, since I don't speak a word of Spanish.

It was hot and getting hotter as we climbed for about an hour and a half. We had to be nearly there. We rested on a ledge and I washed my exploding face in the cool falling river water. We walked on and I gave them my pens because they had been so kind. The older boy cut up a cloth as if to put it round his head in the scorching sun. But, it wasn't for that. Suddenly he grabbed me and launched the cloth over my face, my mouth, my eyes, my nose, and pulled. I have no doubt he intended to kill me.

When you are going to die it's too shocking to hurt. I just thought, 'no, not after all this. I can't die here because no one will know where I am.' I also knew in that moment that I had not completed what I came to do. I tore at the cloth in desperation, while the other boy tugged at the watch on my wrist. I struggled with a strength I don't have and shrieked each time the cloth came away from my mouth; until eventually they had to give up. They took what I had and fled.

My mind was calm. I knew I couldn't return the way I had come in case the boys were still there. But if necessary I still had eight hours of daylight to go all the way round the valley. I grappled and hauled my way up the mountain, and slithered and slid on the downs. My fingernails snapped off; my face was on fire and my arms were grazed, but there were no paths or houses to guide me. I just prayed I would eventually come down on the opposite side of the river.

When I did finally reach the river again I ran, and kept running, through the water, round bends, over rocks, until I reached the road and found my way back to the hotel. Only then did I start to shake. Once I let go I cried as though I would never stop, and throughout the night, when I eventually got to sleep, I saw crowds of grey people with hoods and cloaks and deathly faces walking across my vision.

When I woke I was still shaking. I was scared to walk to the station. On the tourist train to Macchu Piccu some charming English men tried to be friendly but I flinched every time anyone talked to me. By the time we reached the beautiful pale green water of the Urubamba river, rippling white over the enormous boulders in the canyon, everyone around me felt threatening. A minibus took us up the vast hairpin bends to the city and I walked the steps and terraces alone for two hours. I know I could have enjoyed it more, but it was good to have been there.

I flew from Cuzco to Lima and then back to Iquitos. I was waiting on the riverbank by the time the *Lindblad Explorer* came into view. Lyall was on the gangway when I arrived at the dock and I could tell he was as pleased to see me, as I was to see him. The passengers, due to disembark the next day, later assured me that Lyall had been 'frantic' that I might not be there.

'Wholly strange and wholly home'; what a relief to be back in the gentle familiarity of those murky waters! Of course that relief couldn't last long. It was as though I was living on many different levels and they couldn't all be at rest at the same time. But three weeks later, the third and final trip was over, and on November 23 we sailed into Rio de Janeiro where we left the ship.

A day or two later, on our own again, we took three flights, via Sao Paulo and Curibiba, to the spectacular Iguacu Falls. The plane circled the Falls for full effect before landing. The Falls make clouds, and one morning at sunrise, two magnificent rainbows fell across the path – and I saw an armadillo.

The three flights back to Rio nearly shot my nerves. However much flying I have done I still loathe it, even now. And my head ached with tension, knowing I had one 'last chance' to go home. But, of course, despite my anxieties, I didn't.

On 5 December we flew to Johannesburg, Lyall's university town, and hired a car. We drove through the burnished, autumnal bronze of the flat high-veld, and on to Barberton in the low-veld, where avenues were aflame with flamboyant trees. Here we met David Hughes, a long-time naturalist friend of Lyall's. Then out into the thorn forest, the real Africa, with flat-topped umbrella shaped acacias, and into Swaziland with rolling hills and rondavels made of wattle tree frames, filled with stones and mud.

We stayed near Ghost Mountain and went at dawn into the Mkuzi game reserve. The following night we stayed at the Umfolozi game reserve and spent two hours watching more birds, more animals, before sunset. My diary has pages and pages of what we had seen, but while Lyall continued to tell me things, I still stayed silent. I wasn't unhappy; I just didn't exist any more.

I read as much as I could: *The Lions of Tsavo*, *The Plains of Camdeboo* and *Out of Africa*. I began to wonder what people did in life if they didn't watch birds! And although my heart was in my mouth when we were confronted in our small VW Beetle by a herd of fearsome Cape buffalo, the thrill of seeing a leopard was unsurpassed.

From South Africa we drove through the granite bubble landscape of Zimbabwe – Rhodesia as it was then. Our plan was to spend ten days at Christmas with Lyall's immediate family, at Wankie National Park near the other spectacular, Victoria Falls, on the banks of the Zambesi.

For the first time since we met I relaxed. His family: mother, father, brothers Drew (Andrew) and Craig (Buster) and their wives and five young girls were charming. Our safari lodge was the perfect setting, and I shall never forget Christmas day, eating steak sandwiches and from our balcony watching elephants rolling in the saltlicks.

Mary, Lyall's mother, suffered badly from osteoarthritis; his father, though the tyrant of Lyall's life, was always warm to me and we corresponded for several years. When Mary died a few years later I was hugely touched when Doug gave me a gold necklace that had belonged to her. He subsequently remarried.

With Lyall's brother Andrew, who later became a well-known and respected healer, I had a warm if occasional friendship, particularly when he and Diane moved to London. We corresponded about our respective spiritual journeying, and it was through Andrew that I met Ian Gordon-Brown. Ian was the pioneer of Transpersonal Psychology and it was he who at last reassured me that my inner experiences had validity.

(Andrew's elder daughter Katherine was then eight years old, and many, many years later, on Lyall's death I heard completely by chance, a presentation by Katherine about her uncle on BBC Radio 4's programme *Last Word*. She mentioned her first captivating meeting with her uncle at that very early age and then described his girlfriend in very warm terms. Could that be me?

I felt compelled to track her down in Brisbane and - by then forty years old and a playwright - she confirmed that it was! We emailed warmly for several months, during which time I sent her grandmother's gold necklace. It had been returned to its rightful place).

1975 had been the most extraordinary, significant and progressive year of my life. Did I thank God – as Alistair Hardy's *Biology of God* would suggest? Or did I accept Lyall's belief that there was no 'plan'; that each of us has to work and produce by our own random efforts? Whatever, I did thank God.

In January, Lyall and I flew to Malawi for a few days by the lake, and then on to Nairobi. We drove along the escarpment of the incredible Rift Valley, one of the most beautiful views in the world, looking across the savannah ranch land to the Longenot and Suswa volcanoes; and to Lake Naivasha, where the flat-topped fever trees turned golden green in the fading sunlight.

On our journey towards the coastal town of Mombassa we stayed at Taita Hills and then at Salt Lick Lodge. This was a village of rondavels built on stilts and designed to look onto three water pools from wherever you were, and the game came to us! From Mombassa we drove north to Malinda and there took a small plane up the wild northeast coastal region and over to the ancient Arab Swahili island of Lamu.

Lamu then was unspoilt by tourists, untouched by progress. We stayed for several days in the small white hotel set on romantic Peponi beach, at the end of the island on the southeast sand dunes. We liked to watch the dhows as they came up the coast on the trade winds or walk to the main town of Lamu with its narrow streets of coral stone houses, wooden shutters and fabulous, locally-crafted wooden doors.

Some time later, back in London, I wrote an article on Lamu for *Vogue*. Unlike our weekly magazines – as far as I am aware – the glossies sometimes tailored articles to advertising, although it was new to me. It became apparent when *Vogue* asked me to mention East African Airways in my article, because with so much free publicity on Kenya the airline was being asked to advertise.

To my immense surprise, a week after it was published - several months later - East African Airways not only sent me a personal thank you letter for mentioning them, but also offered me a first-class return ticket to Nairobi, or the equivalent in money!

It didn't occur to me to turn it down. I had left Rick owning virtually nothing, and after one depressing visit to the benefits office, on my return to London, I knew I would never apply for the dole. I had chosen this path willingly and I trusted its rightness, so no one else need pick up the tab for that. This ticket was another example to me of synchronicity - it had come unasked for - and I asked for the cash, which they sent me immediately. Three months later East African Airways went out of business. I hope I wasn't responsible for its demise.

Our last days in Kenya were spent in Samburu National Park, in the semi-desert land of the Masai warrior people, and then on to the cultivated savannah grassland hills of Meru National Park. On 29 January 1976 we left Nairobi for a thirteen-hour flight to London and arrived at Heathrow at 7am in a glorious pink sweep of dawn.

After almost a year of twenty-four hour a day togetherness Lyall did exactly what I most dreaded he would do; he told me he had a book to write in Bermuda, and without even a 'see you around', he left me standing.

CHAPTER FIVE

It was an ignominious return. I took a taxi at Heathrow with no idea where I was going. The only thing I could think of was to 'go home'. But when I knocked on Rick's door at 8am and asked if it was convenient to come in, he said no, it wasn't. I got back in the taxi and went on to Mary's. The next days, back with my mother, were a daze of tears. I didn't know what to do. I had lost everything.

My enduring friend Chris Nixon had a friend in Kew with a spare room and within a couple of days I moved in with Jock. I lost weight because I couldn't eat and when Rick invited me to take things I wanted from our cottage I cried again, imagining myself in that beautiful space.

I read Teilard de Chardin and Laurens van de Post and saw solicitors about our divorce. I met many old friends, which was nice, but when I left them I felt alone. I took up – and then gave up – both tap dancing and transcendental meditation. I realised quite early on that I didn't need to meditate because this was what I was doing every second of the day anyway! I have never meditated since, except when expected to do so in groups.

I also contacted magazines like *Vogue* and began to write one or two features from my travels. Although I became freelance from that time, the insecurity of the 'hustling life', as Lyall called it, never quite suited me. And yet I have loved the freedom.

She took an article on Peru, and John Anstey expressed an interest in 'something on Manaus' for the *Telegraph Magazine*. Most days I went to Kew Gardens (which then cost 1p at the turnstile) and mooched around the tropical houses, gazing at the Amazonian bromeliads. I was hardly in the real world most of the time, destined to be melancholy, up and down in a purposeful/purposeless existence.

Four weeks later, though it felt like a lifetime, Lyall finally wrote to me. He had drawn one of his cartoon characters looking as though he missed me! He said he wasn't as good at 'this living alone business' as he used to be. And at the end of February a plane ticket arrived. We were to meet in Miami at the end of March and sail from Fort Lauderdale where his yacht *Samadhi* was now moored. Somehow, deep down, I had known.

Far from being happy I was even more tense and anxious, as I concentrated on the extra research for my *Telegraph* piece. Even Mary was worried about my 'self-obsession'! It was Socrates who said *'Know Thyself'*, and in those dramatic years of searching for a spiritual identity, I and others like me, knew there was no other way than to obsess about 'Me'.

Work was no longer my life. My life was my work, and I remained convinced that even the most forward-thinking, non-materialist scientists would never understand the evolving universe until they knew themselves, and what it means to be human. Eventually, through the unfolding process, the internalised absorption stopped and my life became calmer and less cluttered, but when I recognise it in my clients I respond with great sympathy. It is not an easy choice.

I was, of course, my own worst enemy. When Lyall and I met at Miami we were thrilled to see each other. But when, there and then, he made the commitment I yearned for and asked me to marry him, I laughed. To him it was serious, but to me it felt wrong: like another of his projects.

I understand now that this was a defining moment for him, and although I didn't know it then, at some level, though passionately loving and decisive about us being together, he never again thought seriously about committing to me. Ironically, just for a moment I knew what it was to love someone enough to want his child.

Yachting, unfortunately, was not my *forte*. I'm not sure it was Lyall's either – despite his dream of owning a yacht. We made Fort Lauderdale our base and enjoyed *sorties* on our fold-up bicycles, but once we were on the move around the Florida Keys, the accommodation felt a bit too cramped and, more than that, I found the mechanics of sailing difficult.

I loved seeing Key West again, but in the end we gave up the idea of sailing into the ocean sunset and planned instead our next *Lindblad Explorer* journey in August. At the end of April I was back in London looking for a flat for us to rent for three months. After a false start living (for a week) in the flat above the *Spaghetti House* in Knightsbridge – my choice – we moved to a service flat in Draycott Avenue, Chelsea – his choice.

As usual Lyall took over everything: shopping, cooking, organising, but at least I had my first introduction to mozzarella cheese from the Food Hall in *Harrods*. So the style of our relationship: lurching from elation and misery went on!

Supernature and *Romeo Error* were everywhere and Gifts *of Unknown Things* went quickly into the *Sunday Times* bestseller list. His American publisher even considered it better than Carlos Castenada, which delighted him. I was frustrated by my envy of his success and worried that despite my luxurious life I only had £30 to my name! I wanted to be independent, and when John Anstey offered me a job as the writer for a proposed new diary column on the *Weekend Telegraph,* I was pleased.

It was a complete disaster. I was not a natural 'gossip' writer, and I left after two or three weeks because I couldn't get it right. They spiked an item on Colin Wilson, but at least I'd had the opportunity to meet Colin at his home in Cornwall – something I had always wanted to do. He told me that he had married his wife, Joy, because she was the only person he knew who had also read James Joyce's *Ulysses*!

When I came to write my own book *The Wise Virgin* a year later, I was thrilled that Colin asked to write the foreword. But because Lyall, too, wanted to do that, Colin wrote the 'strap line' on the back cover: '*At Last the Female Outsider!*' His own 'angry young man' bestseller, written when he was twenty-five, was called *The Outsider*. It was the best accolade he could have given me.

Back in England I could discover in more practical ways what was going on in my inner life. It was the early days of the mind, body, spirit movement, or New Age – if it even had a name then. Reflexology, acupuncture, healing, transpersonal psychology and astrology were virtually unheard of, and those who were being drawn to these disciplines held them in a holistic, spiritual framework, which is not necessarily the case today.

It was an exciting time to be within a small sub-culture, and as a celebrity in the field, Lyall opened doors I could never have imagined. Though rendered into silence when Lyall was holding court at private parties, I met people like Brian Inglis and Arthur Koestler. But on my own I enjoyed talking to others like Kit Pedlar (author of TV's *Doomwatch*) who I met at a debate between Lyall and other scientists at the Royal Society. I was also reading copiously.

If I had known about Jung's Four Functions, or about Neuro-Linguistic Programming it might have been more obvious why Lyall and I never 'heard' each other. It was a comfort to me that Lyall's brother Andrew was having strange experiences of his own and wanted to come to London to explore them. He was a 'feeling' person like me and at that moment more in need of guidance than I was.

Lyall recommended Andrew talk to Professor Markus from the spiritualist society and to Matthew Manning, already a healer by then. He also attended a Psychosynthesis group held at the Wrekin Trust by Diana Becchetti - now Sir John Whitmore's wife. Diana had trained in Italy under the founder of Psychosynthesis, Roberto Assagioli, and after he died set up one of the two main schools that exist today.

The Wrekin Trust, which only closed down in 2017, was the brainchild of Sir George Trevelyan, the acknowledged 'father' of the New Age movement, whose adult education courses became a beacon of light for spiritual seekers. Andrew and Diane were also early visitors to the Findhorn Community.

Eventually it was agreed that Di would go back to be with the children in South Africa, while Drew would remain in London for another six months. It was obvious to everyone that Drew was experiencing the confusing energies that would eventually make him a gifted healer.

At the end of July 1976, Lyall and I left London via Moscow to join the *Lindblad Explorer* again, this time in Japan. Although we spent a fabulous ten days before joining the ship, and I particularly enjoyed the old Shinto town of Kyoto, I didn't quite take to Japan. We joined the ship at Yokohama, and until Lyall got back into stride and all the old doubts came crowding back in, it was a sweet return.

We visited several Japanese islands, including Iwo Jima, the centre of America's Pacific campaign - because it had an airport - and Guam where the American planes carrying the first nuclear bombs left for Hiroshima and Nagasaki at the end of the war. We then set sail in bumpy seas for the islands of Micronesia.

Sir Peter Scott and his wife Lady Philippa were on board. He was to be the fish expert (with waterproof illustrations for underwater viewing), because for him Micronesia was unexplored territory. Ron and Valerie Taylor were there for the sharks. Valerie was a stunning, beautiful blonde, and the subject of all Ron's underwater films. To my relief, Robbie Fernandez and Soames Summerhays, naturalists I knew, were still on board.

We snorkelled on uninhabited corals reefs of the Mariana Trench – the deepest trench in the world - while the more adventurous went scuba-diving into the dark – and scary - chasms beneath us. On other occasions we swam in the open sea looking for sharks because Ron and Valerie assured us they were never dangerous – except the great white shark in Australia.

We sailed into the lagoon at Ulithi atoll in the Carolines and anchored off Mogmog. We landed on the beach, anxious to observe protocol. We must not whistle, pat children on the head, shake hands or ask personal questions. We were invited by the chief to enter the men's house, a long rectangular building of corrugated tin on a latticed wood base, and then to watch six increasingly energetic dances.

Another afternoon on the tiny island of Map, in the Yap group, was wonderful. I subsequently saw a documentary on the dilemmas of tourism there now, but almost forty years ago it was unknown. We were shown the Map money, like small millstones, situated all round the island, and then sat outside the men's house to watch their dances.

Three weeks after leaving Japan, we heaved over the confused waters of the Lombok Straits (the Wallace Line between Asia and Australia) for the passengers - and the Scotts and the Taylors - to disembark at Bali. Later that afternoon the next group arrived and we set sail again. For some reason that I can't now remember, Soames became Cruise Director, not Lyall, who poured his enthusiasm into just being one of the naturalists. Also on board were our Indonesian experts, Lorne and Lawrence Blair.

Lyall's book *Gifts of Unknown Things* was a factional story set amongst the 13,000 islands of the Indonesian archipelago. I was reading it now, and thanks to the zodiacs we were able to visit islands that at that time were difficult to get to. There were so many, and these are just a few:

We sailed through the Paternoster Islands and anchored a mile from the island of Sailur Besar. We went the rest of the way over the shallow coral floor by zodiac. The people from the Mandar coast of Sulawesi had not seen anyone other than Indonesians since the Japanese occupation. They rushed towards us along the beach and clamoured for us to take photos.

Very few people then had visited the island of Komodo; the habitat of the notorious komodo dragon. It was a magical island of soft light and miraculous colours, very dry with only one village because there was so little fresh water. In the afternoon the ship's doctor set up a clinic for the locals in front of the chief's home, while the rest of us went in search of dragons.

We walked through the pale dead grass amongst strangely dead looking trees. The interior of the island was much more lush. We reached a ravine where, a few feet beneath us, the bait had been set. A wild boar was already snuffling around with other pigs but eventually a three-foot 'dragon' came and ate beside it. Fifteen minutes after that a big seven-foot dragon brushed cautiously through the undergrowth and finally tore at the mauled goat. It was an awesome sight.

Savu was the most special island. Every island had dancers but these were the most graceful. The girls wore 'tubes' of the local cloth, the most rare of what were soon to become familiar Indonesian designs. Three couples, the Ledo Hawu dancers, did several dances. Then we heard chanting from the plantation behind us, and slowly, as the sound grew, the wonderful, rhythmic *Pedua* dance began. Twenty-nine men and women - with baskets on their ankles to give the 'shuffling' sound to their dance – swished and rattled in unison.

At Mai, an uninhabited island in the Luci Para group, we beached the zodiacs far from shore, along the huge fringing reef shelf, which dropped into the depths of the ocean. We looked into rock pools and lifted coral heads to see the wealth of life beneath them, without the need to snorkel. We walked across the coral to the sand shore where sadly five men were catching turtles to sell.

The men agreed to forfeit their catch that evening for us to see the *arrivada* of the turtles on the beach, but it was only on our return voyage that we saw its full impact. On that trip we watched, spellbound, as hundreds of heaving, sighing green turtles hauled their way up the beach and gouged out deep holes in the sand with their back flippers. Then, with tears streaming down their faces, as though crying with the effort, they dropped fifty or sixty eggs before covering the hole and laboriously crawling their way back to the sea. It was one of the most magnificent sights I have ever seen.

We sailed on into the Banda Straits in sight of the glorious Gunung Apil volcano. We visited the Spice Islands, Banda Neira and Banda Bezar, where the Dutch forced the monopoly of nutmeg production. The dancers here were different, and the first we had seen who laughed with enjoyment. The others were all very serious.

At the village of Amasekaru on Manawoka island we had a strange experience. The *kris* bearing dancers led us dancing from the shore. Dark Papuan faces swarmed behind us and the crowd milled and ebbed like a swirling tide, which was a little alarming. At the chief's house we were seated on a veranda and the performance began.

One elder went in and out of trance until he cracked two glasses and ate a few large pieces. Then, small boys in a line were each offered a piece to eat, which they chewed and swallowed with enthusiasm. Then the little boys were sewn together with needle and cotton, most through their ears but some through their cheeks. Afterwards they showed us the boys - no holes, no blood. This magic was part of their tradition and religion, they said, and all the young people could do these things. They assured us there would be much more magic after Ramadan!

We went from the Aru Islands across the shallow water of the Arat Fura Sea, to the coast of West Irian. We sailed slowly into the Lorenz River from Flamingo Bay and anchored at Agats, the mission station town of the stone-age headhunting Asmat people. These were unsmiling people; ferocious-looking men with long serious faces, and furrowed brow, centred towards the bone piece in the nose.

Almost everyone there was in western clothes because the mission had persuaded them this was correct, but the following day was different. We were up at dawn, ready for the three-hour, eleven-mile zodiac journey into one of the tributary channels. As we turned into the inlet they came: twenty-three war canoes with six or seven grand and beautiful Asmat warriors in each, shouting their low war cry. Most wore government-issued khaki shorts but some had orange and white painted circles or streak over their naked bodies and wore only the bones through their noses.

This was only for show but also a little alarming as they closed in and circled the two zodiacs and continued to chant. But what happened next was for real. The canoes escorted us to the two villages we were to visit, one zodiac party to each.

61

We knew the first was the village suspected of killing Michael Rockefeller Jr. who had mysteriously disappeared a few years earlier. What we did not know until we arrived was that the chief's son of our village had just that morning been killed by people from the other village while gathering from sago trees.

We knew headhunting was 'moral law': a head for a head, and not indiscriminate killing, so we knew we were safe. But despite the dancing welcome and the determination to be normal for our visit, the atmosphere was taut with tension. A man was carving the *bish pole*, the ancestor pole that marks a death. And when the balance is disturbed the people *papish*, where women offer their breasts to be suckled by all the men. Soames got caught in an embarrassing situation! (And, yes, he did!)

It was an enchanting, alarming, fascinating day, to touch such a culture. But as we left the village and were joined by the rest of our party from the village further up the river (where a revenge killing had already happened), the villagers couldn't contain their grief any longer. The eerie, agonising wail that set in along the riverbank was monstrous.

The passengers disembarked in Darwin, so I can claim to have visited Australia for the day! All available staff was needed for the quick turn round, so I was given the task of meeting the next group and taking them on a half-day tour of the termites' nests in the Northern Territory. It was good to have a role and the passengers continued to believe I was a member of staff most of the voyage back to Bali.

Bali is Hindu, unlike all the other Indonesia islands, which are Muslim. It was charming then, and perhaps it still is. Lyall and I left the ship here. We stayed ten days and hired a motorbike to explore.

It was only when I met Lyall that I realised the pleasure of living the same part of the day as my partner! Rick was a night owl but Lyall and I both preferred to rise at dawn and go to bed early (I still do). I remember one morning I had the most memorable sight of all: a duck herder herding his ducks along the bank of a stream in the soft, golden light of dawn.

62

We returned to London via Bangkok in early October. I heard that Rick was to marry Carolyn on 23 November. Once again I was on my own. Lyall wanted space and went to a hotel; I went back to Jock's. A week later Lyall rang to say he was off to Germany and I, once again, was left to cobble my life together.

I wrote letters with feature ideas and took a typing test for some temporary secretarial work. I was offered a job taking down shorthand notes for a two-day conference at a hotel in Heathrow. I buried myself in Assagioli's *Act of Will*, and also saw quite a lot of Andrew.

I waited for Lyall to ring again. When he did he told me he had bought a terraced cottage in Oxford and planned to spend his winters there. Also that he was going to Africa soon to research the *strandlooper*.

We met to see the film *Picnic at Hanging Rock*, and at dinner at *Laceys* I tried to adopt an unreal version of me who was strong, removed and in control. We went back to the *Belgravia Hotel* and he said he loved me, but when he showed me the plans for his house, with no space for me, the persona collapsed.

Lyall then took another flat in Draycott Avenue, Chelsea. He talked of me 'spending time there', or 'going down often to Oxford', but it felt too difficult to play it his way; I just wanted to feel he wanted me in his life.

I'm not sure when I knew that the only way out was to write a book. I had just received the money from East African Airways and an actress friend from the Rick days, Heather Wright, had offered to lend me her cottage in Somerset for three weeks over Christmas. Heather had starred in a film *The Belstone Fox*, filmed in the Quantocks and had bought her weekend home because of that. I decided I would go to Heather's and DO something.

In the meantime the universe conspired to help me. I was introduced to Aida Svendsen, the Danish girlfriend of Lyall's friend Tony Buzan. She was teaching Tony's *New Learning Methods*, a system of learning through 'mind mapping', which became well known through his book *Use Your Head*. Aida was the first person on this crazy journey that I really felt in touch with. It was she who eventually introduced me to the most important contact for my book, Isobel McGilvray.

The most important person for my instant sanity, however, was Ian Gordon-Brown. At that time Ian still worked as an industrial consultant and I met him at his office. He was a marvellously intuitive man, with a background in the Alice Bailey teachings and connected with the *Lucis Trust*. He seemed to understand exactly what I was saying about the unstable confusion of my 'knowing'. He spoke comfortingly of what he described as 'breaking down to break through.'

I was so excited that I was determined in the New Year to do the courses he and his partner Barbara Somers were running. Within a year or so, Ian and Barbara took the plunge to set up full-time their *Centre for Transpersonal Psychology*, and trained many of the first-class people who are qualified in the discipline today. What they gave me was the language for my experiences and I shall never forget that. I also went to see Sir George Trevelyan at his home in Ross on Wye, and we had what he reassuringly described as 'rich conversation'.

I stayed with Lyall in Sloane Square for much of November, seeing friends, typing notes, while he went about his business. In early December he drove me to Somerset via Wallingford in Oxfordshire, where I wanted to interview Nora Weeks who ran the Edward Bach Centre. Already in her eighties she continued the life's work of her mentor and partner, ensuring the purity of his flower remedies until her death a few years later. We then drove on to Holford and once I was settled in Heather's cottage he left.

I was determined to sit, completely alone, for three weeks, meditating until I got the sense of my book, an inkling of what it was really about. But Holford had other ideas. I had never lived in a village before but I soon found out. Since I was a friend of Heather's no one was going to let me be alone at Christmas. On day one I had so many invitations there was no chance of staying home!

Heather's cottage was attached to Lady Charles' cottage and on Christmas Eve I went for a drive with her cousin Betty, also down for Christmas. I had lunch with them both, walked the dogs up the combe, and in the evening had drinks with various ladies, one of whom, Mrs Bunch invited me for Christmas dinner. Despite our differences in age and history (she was nineteen years older), Vlyn Bunch became the most consistent person in my life over the next fourteen years. Our friendship was absolute, and no doubt karmic!

On Christmas morning Sylvia Cave and her mother Oenone, who lived across the road, invited me for an amazing breakfast, and then Sylvia and I went for a four-hour walk across the moor. We talked about 'religion'. She said she was deeply religious but that 'here' was her religion. She loved to paint trees because she felt a special communion with the trees here. She felt her religion in the spirit of the moors. We liked each other and both felt invigorated by all our talking.

Christmas dinner with Vlyn and her husband John seemed like a meeting with the 'nobility' of Holford. Apart from Lady Charles and Betty, and the couple who lived in Doddington House, the most important character I met was the truly unique and eccentric Rev Peter Birkett.

Peter was deeply, intuitively spiritual, which made his Christianity feel alive, and his Saturnian attractiveness added to his incredible charisma. His passion was to be a cowboy and he would ride across the Quantocks dressed in *bone fide* stetson, boots and chaps. Several years later he fulfilled his dream and went as a working cowboy to British Columbia.

The first time I saw Vlyn, before I got to know her, she was walking to church in a flowing blue cloak, singing at the top of her voice. I guessed she was a 'one-off', but I have no doubt now that it was Peter who made her heart sing. There was a sense of creativity and excitement between these two unusual and attractive people, and the spark between them was plain for everyone to see – including her husband John, who was a shyer more retiring man. But for both of them, for their own reasons, it remained just a spark, which brought its own painful ramifications and misunderstandings.

A few days after Christmas Sylvia told me about her childhood; that she had been sexually abused for many years by a family member. Eventually he was sent to prison and the family had moved to avoid the scandal. Sylvia had hidden herself in intellectual preoccupations until ill health brought her back from America and she was forced to relive and exorcise the experience. As a result, her life's work as a botanical artist was beginning to emerge.

My connection to Vlyn and to Sylvia over the next three or four years was hugely meaningful to the story of my life. It was the time when, as Andrew once described it, 'my molecules were rubbing together' faster than ever before, or since, and the excitement and fun of rich friendship and psychic drama was at its height.

CHAPTER SIX

Despite so little time alone in Holford, the intuition I needed to begin my book had arrived. The idea of 'triggers and tools' had come to me with a certainty. The trigger to my own 'call' to the spiritual path had come through astrology. Once the call had come there was no option but to give up everything that was safe in my life and follow that call wherever it took me.

All my life I had willed myself to 'get out of the paper bag' of my background, and by the age of twenty-eight had miraculously achieved all my material ambitions. But then, to my chagrin, had found that the security of the glamorous job, good income, dream cottage and marriage, had no meaning.

It seemed to me that once the trigger was set there had to be a totally different 'tool', or means of expression. In those days the mind, body, spirit ethos was in its infancy and weird disciplines of holistic health and healing were almost unheard of. Those who were drawn to them were yearning to express this new sense of connection to the spiritual aspect of themselves.

I wanted to write my own truth, but there were two problems. A first rule of journalism is that you don't include yourself in the story. The second difficulty was that I felt I had no authority to say what I wanted to say. Why should anyone else take me seriously?

I was devouring books by Jung, Assagioli, and Rudolf Steiner, gathering language for my experience and sources to corroborate it. Yet deep down one of the key certainties I had was that this journey was something to do with a conscious understanding of 'the feminine', which was the way I described the ineffable realms, and was being led by women.

In the end I decided to use the one technique I knew. I would write about other women who were having similar experiences to me and who had already found their alternative practice. To be frank I planned to encourage them to say what I wanted them to say, to express it for me. Then I could leave myself out of the book completely, yet take it where I wanted it to go.

When I returned to London I went back to Draycott Place. Lyall was away in Africa, and I started my search and research. It wasn't easy because I needed a 'felt sense' of who would be right. The new age movement was a small sub-culture in which everyone knew everyone else. I was surprised that some obvious choices didn't work for me. Some powerful, impressive women in the field disappointingly 'lacked substance' or didn't feel right.

I remember naively attending an 'intuitive massage' weekend with Anne Parks - who had been a respected leader in the Growth Movement on the west coast of America - not thinking that this meant you had to be naked! During the weekend we worked our way towards ever more threatening and intimate parts of the body. When my worst intuition came true and a particularly sleazy man asked me to partner him for the last afternoon's 'upper front' session, I fled!

A firm rule in the new age business is 'discernment', which was often an excuse for being judgemental about people you didn't care for. The Growth Movement of the Seventies certainly had the key psychological ingredient of looking at blocks and difficulties, but I began to feel this was not necessarily spiritually based. I realised that many people who did gestalt and primal scream therapies at the age of thirty, were looking at the same emotional junk I had looked at when I was eighteen or nineteen. I felt I was looking at something else.

My gut feeling was that what some people called 'spiritual experience' was actually psychic mediumship, and understanding the difference has always been of paramount importance to me. I felt that the purely psychic realms were based in the materiality of matter, the 'lower chakras' of humanity and were open to misuse of power.

I was looking for women whose experience of the super-conscious connected to the integrity of our divinity. I wrote then that 'the spiritual is necessarily psychic but the psychic is not necessarily spiritual.' Eventually, after many stages of the journey, I had the confidence to teach the difference.

Of all the disciplines I tried and workshops I attended, I felt most comfortable with Ian and Barbara's Transpersonal Psychology approach. (I even met trained Jungian analysts who I 'knew' had no personal experience of the super-conscious realms despite this being the foundation of their work).

Throughout my six months of research, my friend and mentor and fellow enthusiast was Isobel McGilvray. With her moon in Leo she sat like a goddess in her home in Hampstead, gathering towards her those of us who were struggling to make sense of this extraordinary time. If we touched base with Isobel, we knew we were in touch with each other.

Isobel was more than just 'one of my women'. She and I sped on the wind of our flying minds, to unfold the book together. Her journey had led her from New Zealand where she was a nurse, to train in the Alexander Technique, and subsequently to take this as a basis for her own form of healing. Eventually she and a colleague set up their own Alexander School, but she was always courageously different and experimental with the many new ideas that came to her.

We spent wonderful evenings together in her flat, eating exquisite things she prepared and hurtling around the cosmic reaches of our minds in a weirdly charged and heightened way.

One of the newly discovered 'laws' of individuation, as Abraham Maslow described this phase of human evolution, was that once on the right path the 'carrots would dangle', and Jung's synchronicity abounded for me. Meetings were miraculous – many acquaintances came and went but many friendships remain to this day. Books jumped off the shelves, inspiring avenues opened up, like the weekly 'Mythology in Literature' class I found at the City Lit, which added poetic ammunition to my arsenal of research.

Over the weeks I found and interviewed my five wise women - amongst them was Diana Becchetti - although even this process was not without pain. I recognise it now as the creative process, but for every one day of exciting new vistas and insights, another followed of such abject depression and despair, that I could not get out of bed.

My life was taking such frightening leaps into randomness in order to tell a story, not of the intellect but of the intrinsic being. It felt as though the kaleidoscope of my life was constantly rearranging its colours and patterns. And this was the first of two times of struggle in my life when I finally let go to 'let God', and said 'all right, I'll do it' – whatever that meant.

And, as always, when Lyall came back I felt unbearably undermined. Nothing I did had relevance without him, yet I could do nothing of relevance when I was with him. My project about 'being' seemed to slide away beneath me in the dynamics of his 'doing', as his busy, successful, eccentric life went on as usual, without reference to me. He let go of Draycott Place and in June 1977, ready to begin writing, I went back at the invitation of Vlyn and John, to Holford.

For a manic month I pounded on the typewriter 'like a rattling train above their heads', they said. Once I got through the barrier of 'where on earth to start' it just gathered momentum and I was oblivious to everything else. When I'd finished I took a short break back in London and then returned to Holford to edit for the next eight weeks.

It was fun with Vlyn. One of our greatest successes was our celebration of the 7th of the 7th, 1977. We announced our intention of driving to Danesborough, the local mystical place, at 7am for a morning meditation. As far as we knew we were alone as we lay on our backs contemplating the magical moment. But later that day Peter and his guest, a Coptic Priest, and Dick Snell a local friend, all told us they had ridden over to try and find us!

In July, for my birthday, Lyall sent some money from Arizona to 'take yourself and Vlyn – and the vicar – out to a birthday dinner on me, with lots of wine and the best food in Somerset.' We did, and after that our 'Man of the Year' dinners – between our birthdays (Vlyn was also a Leo) – took on majestic importance, and lasted seven years. Our designated men charmingly recognised themselves as part of an extremely exclusive club!

We were irreverent in our pleasures. Our most lasting venture was *The Out Group Society (TOGS)*. A particularly disturbing newsletter arrived about the New Age 'separating the sheep from the goats' in terms of those who were part of the leading edge of consciousness and those who were not. This led us to downgrade ourselves from The Elect, to join the sheep – or was it the goats? We gained several distinguished members over the years, the names of whom were written on the back of the picture 'The Elect Reaching into Heaven' in Vlyn's home.

Over the years Vlyn and I spent many hours on her leather sofas in front of the fire, drinking tea and talking astrology. She was the first person I knew to study the art and I learned the language through her, almost by osmosis. I studied astrology myself later, firstly on the psychological level through the pioneering work of Liz Greene (one of my original Wise Women), and then on a more mundane level, through the Company of Astrologers in Queen Square. For many years it was a powerful tool and map of consciousness for me, as well as a shorthand way of communicating with several of my friends.

In this heightened time in Holford, strange things happened. The ancient oak woodland in the Combe seemed to hold secrets. One morning on our walk Vlyn and I seemed to cross through space-time into another world. At other times, walks on the moor held tangible echoes of the past.

By default I was learning that landscape held resonances that were possible to sense into, and sometimes the energies of Holford were oppressive and claustrophobic. This seemed to be mirrored in Vlyn, who was always possessive of me and sometimes seemed to energetically invade my privacy. I was often glad to get away, but I always came back.

A letter from Lyall suggested that we meet on his return from America in September and stay together at the *Belgravia Royal*. He was en route to his new, academia-accessible terraced house in Oxford, which I unkindly called his 'isolation hospital' (mainly but not exclusively because it clearly didn't include me.)

As always, excited to be seeing Lyall and simultaneously wary of the inevitable hurt, I took my precious pages to show him. I sat silently and nervously on the floor with a bottle of white wine, while Lyall read through the whole manuscript in one go. When finally he put it down, he turned to me and said to my intense pleasure and relief, 'I didn't know you knew such things. It's terrific'.

In the following days he edited the text and made suggestions – mostly about personalising things a little more. And then on his suggestion I sent it to *Hodders*. Within days Eric Major had responded and although he regretted the book wasn't right for them, suggested I send it to Alick Bartholomew at *Turnstone Press*. Turnstone was virtually the only New Age publisher at that time and Alick, who became a close friend, was a true pioneer in his field. He agreed to publish *The Wise Virgin* for 1979.

I had achieved my ambition to write a book by the time I was thirty-two. I felt I had captured in words, just for a moment, a framework for the ineffable experience of consciously linking with what Jung called *the higher self*, touching into a tacit way of 'knowing' through the higher mind. I might now describe that experience as *'Gnosis'*.

The book had taken everything I had. I felt totally empty, and it took a year to fully fill up again. And then, only gradually did I begin to realise that my gruelling seven- year journey into 'spirit' had merely been the precursor to the real purpose of the journey and the 'other aspect' of the feminine principle: the descent into the darkness of matter:

In early January 1978, while Lyall settled into Oxford to write, I went via *Laker Airways* to New York, clutching my manuscript in hopes of American interest. I talked non-stop to my neighbour all the way. Jonathan Pertwee – who turned out to be the nephew of actors Bill and Jon - was a horticulturist. Several weeks later he invited me to visit his nursery in Essex, and it was the first I heard of cloning, an experiment he was then pioneering with plants.

I stayed briefly with Liz Farrell who was as welcoming and kind as ever, and I repaid her as best I could by child-minding Tuffy, who was now seven. Several publishers expressed interest, but nothing came of it, and most of that month I spent on the Greyhound Bus - an experience I would not have missed but would never do again!

To keep down costs my precision planning allowed me to travel overnight on the bus on alternate nights (I could sleep at the drop of a hat in those days), and book into hotels for the rest. I would arrive in the most ghastly downtown areas at four or five in the morning and drink tea until dawn rose and it felt safe to venture out.

I went south, firstly to New Orleans, and then to Austin Texas to visit Lyall's ex-wife Vivienne - they had married in South Africa, post-university. She was an academic and at that time waiting for tenure as a full professor at Austin university. Surprisingly we got on well. I had come to know that intellect and intelligence were not the same thing. I gathered my understanding from somewhere within and, apart from with Lyall, could usually hold my own.

My next stop was just outside Tucson, Arizona, to stay with Bill and Peg Speed, two elderly friends of Lyall's who had been passengers several times on the *Lindblad Explorer*. Their property was set in a large amount of desert – roadrunner and rattlesnake country – amongst tall sequoia cactus. In the distance were the mountains, which shimmered through glorious stages of pink and apricot at sunset. My love of the desert and its wonderful changing moods began here.

Bill and Peg were attentive and charming hosts. They introduced me to Merv Larson who ran Tucson zoo and his wife Peg who had written a book about the desert for the *Sierra Club*. One time I met her she had a broken leg after dropping off the edge of the cliff she had been climbing, in shock at coming face to face with a rattlesnake.

Peg Speed was a gifted sculptor and general enthusiast. When I left she gave me several local crystals, which introduced me to the idea of collecting stones, and later led me to the idea of recognising and experiencing the 'energetic resonance' of crystals.

On my return to England, wondering and worrying as ever where I would live and how I would earn my living, I spent time at Beaumont Buildings, typing Lyall's book *Lifetide*. Towards the end of March we celebrated our books one evening at the *Elizabeth Restaurant*, and that night I woke up with the world '*HEALING*' screaming in my brain.

The following week Malcolm Lazarus from the Wrekin Trust came to see Lyall and mentioned a weekend course to be given by healer Bruce McManaway. I had begun to feel sensitivity in my hands working with Isobel, so perhaps I could now believe in a new direction. Research into healing would bring me into the matter of the body.

The weekend was a revelation, with two important synchronicities. At one point a participant suddenly felt unwell, and two people unknown to me then, Ann and Tony Neate, stood up to give her healing. What touched me most was their way of working together. The other significant event was meeting Baroness Edmee di Pauli, eminent networker and doyen of the New Age, who some weeks later offered to rent me a room in her sumptuous house in St John's Wood.

Bruce's instrument of intuition was the pendulum and after the weekend I was swinging away with my moonstone ring on a string. I used it as a point of reference for healing purposes for several months, especially after an anxious follow-on training week at Bruce's home in Scotland, which I left feeling a total fraud.

I had first learned to use a pendulum at a Psychosynthesis workshop with Diana Becchetti. I soon realised that, since you could easily influence it yourself there was no point constantly asking if Lyall and I would be properly together! I did, however, trust it as a tool for healing and especially for dowsing such things as vitamins.

While Lyall went back to *The Explorer*, to the Galapagos, I went home to mum, yet again, and tried to make sense of my life.

For many years Lyall had been concerned with the over-hunting of whales, and was particularly incensed by the attitude of the Japanese. He rather dismissively felt that agencies like Greenpeace did not achieve much, and by August that year, 1978, in his own inimical way he had persuaded the government of the Seychelles to appoint him as their delegate to the International Whaling Commission and to designate the Indian Ocean as a whale sanctuary. His goal was to fight for a worldwide ban.

In order to meet the Japanese delegation head-on that October, he decided to spend the following three months in Japan, learning how to think and behave in Japanese society. He also suggested that I attend on his behalf a Jojoba Conference at Stanford University in California. (Jojoba was the suggested alternative to sperm whale oil). He would meet me there at the end of the seminar and then return to Tokyo.

I am sure I fulfilled my brief at Riverside Drive. I attended the lectures and collected notes, but basically, as always, I waited in suspended anxiety and excitement for Lyall.

The first signs on our meeting were good, but the following morning I saw a basket of flowers on the hotel desk, addressed to him from someone, a woman I guessed, in Japan. I finally flipped. Whether it was a misunderstanding or not I'll never know, but I can see myself now, striding through the departure gate at Los Angeles airport in a haze of purpose and pain. I was leaving Lyall once and for all.

CHAPTER SEVEN

At the end of 1978 I moved into Grove End Road. My 'studio' was a small room with pull-down bed and a table to act as a desk. I had the use of the Di Pauli's kitchen, which I tried to do just once a day, early in the morning before anyone else was up. It was only several weeks into my tenancy that Graine, Edmee's osteopath daughter, told me I woke her up by creeping around on the creaking floorboards above her head. She lived and worked in the self-contained apartment underneath!

I felt changed. I loved my room. I lived at the front of the house and I loved looking out of my window at the trees. It made me miss the trees in Holford and although on Liz Greene's advice Vlyn was spending time in London doing some Jungian analysis, I also went to stay with her regularly in Somerset.

In Holford, Vlyn and I took to thinking about energies and leylines around the area and set up a huge contoured map on a drawing board in her kitchen. It stayed there for years! We also explored the idea of Templars and Cathars.

But the most significant and fortuitous meeting of that time at Grove End Road was with Lilla Beksinska – later shortened to Lilla Bek. Soon after I arrived Lilla, who was then forty-seven, divorced with three children who lived with her husband, came to the Di Pauli's house to take a weekly yoga class. In a chance remark she mentioned she wanted to write a book. And when I said that I, too, had the sense of writing a second book now, we decided it was too great a synchronicity to miss. We set to work.

One day a week for a whole year we met for a glorious rice-based fry-up or tea and cream cakes to tease out her book on colour and yoga. Although I was always hesitant about the yoga part, I was fascinated by the healing power of colour and had already attended courses by pioneers Lily Cornford and Theo Gimbel.

It was a fabulous trial by fire way of learning. I did my job of pushing and pulling and shaping what she knew, and more importantly what she didn't know she knew. In those days Lilla's thoughts were quite unstructured, and when I came up against a barrier through my own perception, I'd push even harder. I wrote everything down in shorthand and spent the rest of the week shaping the book.

Lilla was unique in her field. Yoga had been the trigger for her and as her extraordinary psychic gifts began to unfold she read everything she could lay her hands on to try to verify what was happening to her. She had a scientific aptitude and was always keen to be tested in that arena.

Her way of working with clients, present or not, was to 'read' their signature. Through this she 'saw', interpreted and diagnosed through the interplay of colour in the auric field and the chakras, which included a resume of past life influences at the crown chakra.

She was also one of the most down to earth people I ever met. 'When I see visions of Christ and the Virgin Mary I know I'm not using my energies properly', she said once, despite being a Catholic whose church canonised people for just such experiences.

Once when we were both staying with Vlyn in Somerset and we all went for a walk, she lagged behind to 'talk to the elementals'. When I said how much I envied her she flicked her hand dismissively. 'Oh, you used to do it in another lifetime; but you're lucky not to do it now. They're so talkative, they take up so much time!'

One of my most important lessons came through the topic of the *Masters of Wisdom*, who Lilla often said were in the room. One day, pondering on where and how she saw those things, and wondering if our 'seeing' was simply a difference in language, I suddenly felt an energy that was deeply familiar to me. In a flash I recognised, 'so that is a Master'. Although clairvoyance looked overtly more impressive, energy could be accessed in myriad ways.

Another day we were talking and I suddenly shivered. She told me Lyall was there, and that her friend John often visited her in his 'higher self' to tell her things that his consciousness couldn't say.

I could feel Lyall's anger as she 'talked' to him. He said he was not so much angry at my rejection, but at my lack of understanding of him. When he offered me everything he saw my 'cup' so over-full with myself, that anything he poured in would just pour away. How could there be love with no understanding.

Suddenly there was a change in the atmosphere and I felt sadness and compassion for him. He said, through Lilla, that his peripatetic way of life was a means of running away from himself. He needed other women in bed so he would not be with himself. It did sound feasible, and completely natural. I could feel he was unhappy.

Lilla said that to be in contact in this way sometimes is the relationship. I had communicated with him at a deeper level than anyone else and therefore we were still linked. Clearly he blamed me for the distance between us, but foolishly perhaps it made me cling on to hope.

In another of her throwaway gems she said, 'I was talking to Gurdjieff the other day and he told me Jung didn't always see the sub-personalities he thought he was seeing. Often they were entities.' There was no answer to that, except a lasting gratitude for such a genuine, sensible and humble (as well as fun) introduction to the unseen world.

There were things in the realms of the psychic of which I was and still am completely unaware. My own journey (which incidentally Lilla never seemed to find interesting or inspiring!) had so far been a psychological/spiritual one, and my pursuit of understanding the difference between the psychic and the spiritual has been a vital part of my journey.

Although the 'descent into matter' was to include some terrifying astral and psychic experiences, there were aspects of the psychic realms that I knew were irrelevant to my journey: astral travel for example. I learned more about that through an upsetting incident with Sylvia Cave in Holford.

Sylvia meant a great deal to me. I loved her awkward independence and creativity of spirit, and the hint of dark secrets that lured you into her botanical paintings. The depth of our friendship touched parts of me that were continually nourished and changed. I loved our rare walks and conversations, but what I didn't know until much later was that we were unwittingly walking into a past life drama.

Earl and Countess Beatty - David and Annie - were local friends of Sylvia's. I had met them once at a dinner party, but since I had no conversation about *avant garde* films, I had felt rather out of place. Staying with Vlyn several months after that uncomfortable evening Sylvia told me that David and Annie had since split up and that she was now going out with David. It was natural then that we should spend a couple of pleasant, gentle evenings '*a trois*', talking of poetry and music.

Certainly David was attractive, but never to me, not least because he was the partner of a friend I valued. When, on my next visit, Sylvia said she was too busy completing a painting and insisted David and I go for an afternoon walk in Snowdrop Valley, I went reluctantly. And at supper that evening, as the conversation ebbed and flowed, I could somehow feel I was being 'set up'. She suggested I meet up with David in London and it felt rude to say no when it was clearly what she wanted.

I could never understand why David came to Grove End Road, several times. Admittedly we could talk for hours at a time. We ranged high and low, dipping and soaring in our intellectual minds, cross-referencing, cross-matching, and interweaving our widest expanses of esoteric knowledge. The conversations were enjoyable in a warm kind of way, but they never touched me in any meaningful, connecting sense. My relationship was with Sylvia and I was doing my best for her.

When David began sending letters and poetry, some written especially for me, the friendship began to take on a depth and quality it didn't really have. I had the overwhelming feeling that unconsciously manipulated by Sylvia, I was taking part in a cosmic play.

I was reluctant to go to Holford because the energies were so strange, but when I finally did go, with Lilla, all became clear. Sylvia told me that months earlier David had told her he was attracted to us both; that we were like opposite ends of a pole: light and dark. Through the utter terror of losing him, her plan of action was to put us together. No wonder I felt manipulated.

The following morning Lilla told me that she had stayed awake all night (we shared a room at Vlyn's) in order to protect me from the 'cats' Sylvia had sent psychically to attack me. She had also astral travelled to visit Sylvia to reassure her, and when we saw Sylvia that afternoon she told us she had seen Lilla and appreciated her coming. None of this was apparent to me, but I shall never forget Sylvia's shining ethereal beauty that day, which Lilla told me was 'the elementals looking after their own'

What I did come to know, through Lilla's intuition and Vlyn's astrological insights, was that David, Sylvia and I had been reliving an Atlantean past life, in which the task of the dark and light feminine polarities were used to initiate male priests. It confirmed what I also knew, that the inner integration of the 'split feminine' was my task in life.

I have seen the same drama enacted several times since There has always been pain and separation and invariably the man ends up without either woman, as David did. My overwhelming sadness was a sense of betrayal, as I perceived it, that Sylvia could go so far to sacrifice our friendship. Of course I understood, but I've always regretted that we never saw each other again.

Lilla's book took a year to write. To earn my £15 a week rent, plus food, I took a one-day, sometimes two days, temp typing job with a wholesale garment manufacturer near Oxford Circus. For some reason I enjoyed it there, working with the other secretaries Vivi and Amanda, and became quite a dab hand as a telex operator.

But my great excitement in 1979 was the publication of *The Wise Virgin*. I was thrilled with the cover chosen by Turnstone – the androgynous angel in the Leonardo painting

Virgin of the Rocks. Sylvia had taken the photograph for the back cover and Lyall had written the foreword.

This was my *magnum opus*. No one was yet talking about the significance of 'the goddess', and I was told that *The Wise Virgin* became a 'reference book' for the transpersonal psychology movement. I received many letters of gratitude and appreciation for 'saying those things' (plus one or two that were not so polite!) and was asked to hold workshops (which I was then too terrified to do).

Although it is now long ago and virtually forgotten (though thanks to Amazon still listed – under my maiden name Annie Wilson), for many years women – and later men – would tell me how much the book had influenced their lives. I was even recognised by the librarian of the Jungian Library in New York – from my back cover picture!

A couple of months later for some reason I decided to send a copy of the book to Unity Hall, my old editor on *Fabulous*. She was now woman's page editor of *The News of the World*, and also wrote brilliant spreads for the newspaper on celebrities such as Britt Ekland. She suggested I go to see her and when she knew I was writing another book, she offered me two days work a week initiating a new slimming column. It was typical of Unity to look after 'her girls'.

I was elated and nervous at the same time, since I hadn't written features for such a long time. Work began at 10am, a late hour for me. I shared a room with Unity and her incredibly glamorous secretary and friend Sandy Lamming, who smoked forty cigarettes a day and made passive smoking an obligatory part of the job.

As always the journalists got the oldest typewriters, while the secretaries had up-to-date golf ball models. I shared my typewriter and flexi-time with Amy, another of Unity's old colleagues, and later also with Pamela Townsend, a *Fabulous alumnus*.

Newspapers were very different from magazines, and Unity was still an exacting taskmaster. The most difficult writing jobs I've ever had were on *Fabulous* and *News of the*

World, both demanding a 'jargon' style that I obviously did not find easy.

In early 1979, once I had finished Lilla's book and could do more days, she put me on to women's features, which she made me rewrite endlessly. This was all the more depressing because the sub-editors always changed them out of all recognition anyway – or spiked them.

But at least I was earning a living, and it was a nice life, once I'd got the hang of expenses. My first job was to research an article on instant coffee, but when I submitted a claim for £2.64 for bus fares, Unity gasped in horror. 'You'll have to do better than that', she told me, 'or you'll get us all the sack.' After that I travelled first class, took taxis and stayed in good hotels.

Back in the office, most lunchtimes Unity would send Sandy to El Vino's to buy a bottle of champagne. I had not drunk coffee or alcohol for a long time, but I couldn't refuse; it was part of the camaraderie. It took me at least three hours to recover from just one glass, so I'd get back in focus by about 4pm. Fortunately, it was a flexible timetable and we just stayed until the work was done.

Unity was the fastest writer I ever met, and in her spare time she wrote racy romantic novels under the name Jane Summers (the surname of her ex-husband Owen Summers). Thanks to a new agent she had just sold her latest novel by auction for a vast sum in Britain and America and one day she offered me the manuscript to read overnight. I left it to the morning and decided to skim through it on the bus to work.

I was riveted. How did she imagine such things? Could she? Would she? I was so engrossed in her amazing sexual gymnastics, that when I looked up again the bus was in the depot! I did catch a glimpse of where it might have come from when she once offered me a room in her house (which I didn't subsequently take). Her only stipulation was that I had to be out on Mondays – obviously the day her long-term lover came to call.

In fact, while she was there she began a relationship and finally married the paper's deputy editor, Phil. They were an unlikely but devoted couple until her tragic death – after months of total paralysis and coma following a heart attack – in 1992. There were many of us at her memorial service at St Bride's Church, Fleet Street, who mourned her in gratitude for the profound influence she had had on our lives.

In early 1979 I did leave Grove End Road. The year before, Lilla had taken on a flat in Stamford Street, Waterloo, when Isobel's friend Marian had gone on a long-term visit to America. For some reason, we now decided to swap homes. Waterloo was slightly scary, mainly because of Cardboard City, the hangout for the homeless in the underpass, but apart from that I loved it. I particularly liked walking across the bridge to work.

After some rewriting – and to my relief putting the yoga section at the back – Alick took *What Colour Are You?* for publication in 1981. Some time after that he sold Turnstone to a subsidiary of Harper Collins, which was just moving into the New Age market. It was good for us because distribution was better and the rights were eventually sold into four other languages.

The *News of the World* was a tacky newspaper – and was proved to be even more so over the years – but working on the woman's page was separate and different. Somewhere down the corridor in other offices women reporters plotted to lure the unwary into some unsavoury exposure, then 'make their excuses and leave'. But for months it never touched me.

In fact, I met and interviewed more caring and unconditionally loving people who moved heaven and earth for their loved ones and families, than I ever met in the New Age movement at that time. I learned a lot.

Living in these two worlds was fun, but as so often happened in those years of my life, running alongside the adventure was a terrible fear and blankness. I was crying inside for the loss of meaning that being with Lyall gave to me. The withdrawal symptoms were unbearable.

But far worse, I was beginning to lose the connection to my 'knowing'. I couldn't feel where I was, and was mourning something irretrievable. I was going into the dark, and the hardest part was to trust.

At Easter 1979, a week's conference at Dartington caught my eye. Its title *Education and the Self* sounded exactly right. In the event, it was more about education than 'the self'. It was so intensely intellectual that my head was stretched by the endless lectures and virtually no sleep. On the last day I heard a blood vessel go bang in my eye and I left the conference with conjunctivitis!

Yet this was another extraordinary turning point in my life and I met people who became true and valuable friends and acquaintances for years to come. Like Mark Braham, Professor of Education, who was running the conference. Although I didn't get to know him then, he featured prominently in my life for the next seven years.

His friend, Lt Col. Tom Welch, a gifted networker and tireless trustee of many organisations, including *Findhorn*, made a bigger first impression – as he did with many women! Over the years I watched in fascination as his charismatic charm beguiled women into believing they were 'the special one' to him. Although I did visit him once or twice at his home in Devon, we were never more than warm friends. I introduced him to Vlyn and he came to Holford. He was our 1980 Man of the Year.

I also met David McCauley, a tutor at Kingston Polytechnic and saw a lot of him in the next few months. We drank wine and ranged far and wide on the meaning of life. These men, like Alick Bartholomew, were charming and older, and were only ever just friends. The New Age brought many easy friendships and 'recognitions', but it was important not to confuse these with love, as many people did. In any case, I was still loyal to Lyall.

In fact, my most important contact at the conference was Malou Hatt-Arnold, who had come from Geneva to give a children's workshop on *Eurythmics*. This was a method of working with music and movement, originated by Jacques Dalcroze and approved in Swiss education.

Malou, trained by Dalcroze, was now his leading exponent, and I shall never forget the impression the workshop made on me. She played the piano in varying moods, which gradually drew out the children to express themselves through movement. When at last one painfully timid child began to stomp himself into existence it made me weep. As a result I got up early each morning to do the adult class, and I spoke briefly to Malou.

If I hadn't met Malou, I would have ignored a letter I received on my return from the conference, from an Austin Hatt-Arnold in Geneva. He wrote that he had read my book *The Wise Virgin* and wanted to meet this 'new kind of woman'. He was coming to England for a school reunion in August and would I have dinner with him. I was so taken by the coincidence that I replied, telling him I had just met his wife and agreeing to meet him. His letter by return told me that he and Malou were separated.

In July Lyall came back! We went to dinner at a local restaurant, and for the first time since we met I did not feel diminished by his presence. When we got back to Stamford Street, he asked me if he could now matter in my life, but I didn't understand what he meant. He told me he always felt as though I was 'passing through' on my way to some unseen goal, and that he was always just a stepping-stone on the way.

My heart ached with the misunderstanding, but I could also see what he meant. I was driven by a sense of a journey and a 'task', but to me what he saw just wasn't true. The moment I said I knew he mattered, he told me it was too late, and he left. My heart went into paroxysms of despair, and then there was calm. At least, after five turbulent years, I did finally know it was over.

A week before I was due to meet Austin Hatt-Arnold I could no longer stand what felt like the violation of the mucky energy at *The News of the World* and gave a month's notice. I had no idea what I was going to do, but my life had to change.

On 15 August 1979 I met Austin at the *Britannia Hotel*. He was tall and slim and public school attractive, fifteen years older than I was. His father Sir Eric Arnold had been a Trade Commissioner in Burma and then, when the Japanese came, in India. His last posting was Canberra, Australia.

Austin, brought up in India with English schooling, was a Cambridge economics graduate. Too sensitive for commerce and with a burning ambition to work for developing countries, he had pioneered with four others the International Trade Centre, an offshoot of GATT, and was now ITC's Chief Evaluation Officer – a D5 level post that merited diplomatic status (CD plates on his car).

We had a charming, polite and 'British' sort of dinner with a little too much wine and then he took me home. He was on his way to a school reunion and then to visit Iona. In the middle of the week, on his way back to Geneva via London he came through on Unity's phone and asked me again to dinner.

This time we went to a Brazilian restaurant in Covent Garden. I was never able to find that restaurant again, and the energy around us that evening was so strange, I'm not even sure it really existed! We talked about the Seven Rays, the spiritual laws in the teachings of *The Tibetan* (the Master of Wisdom Dwal Khul), channelled through Alice Bailey in the early part of the 20th century.

Austin, like Ian Gordon-Brown – who turned out to be a friend and fellow Bryanston Old Boy – had been a student of the Alice Bailey teachings for many years. Although I knew little about it then, I discovered this intellectual, esoteric, hierarchical approach to spirituality appealed to many people I knew, particularly men.

Austin began to explain the meaning of each ray, but as soon as he came to the second ray 'love-wisdom', I suddenly seemed to drop downwards out of my body and 'disappear'. As he went on talking I was fighting to regain my composure. He also told me that if he weren't already married he would ask me to marry him!

Two weeks later he came back to England for the weekend. We drove to Canterbury Cathedral and again the energy went haywire – it was as though my third eye was activated and I became totally disoriented. We then went to the Isle of Sheppey and walked through what can only be described as 'shit'. Suddenly I doubled over in acute pain, to the extent I couldn't stand up for fifteen minutes.

Something was definitely happening between us! I could monitor the energy flow between us with my hands. His long-term interests: Alice Bailey, Francis Bacon and awareness of 'spirit of place', matched and excited my own emerging interests: the Templars, and 'redeeming the dark feminine' in relation to the 'Magdalene' energy, through the physical body.

At the end of the weekend Austin suggested I come and live with him in Geneva. It had a quality of madness but one I recognised. It was the same madness that Lyall had presented six years before. To let go again, to cut all ties, to trust I was still in the pursuit of goodness and truth. It all felt inevitable.

About that time another friend Linda Larson was also planning to go to Switzerland. I had met Linda at Grove End Road when she briefly took a room in Graine's flat in the basement. Linda was American but had studied voice and drama in England and was now studying Rudolf Steiner's movement, Eurythmy, at Emerson College in Forest Row. In September she was leaving for Dornach, the Steiner headquarters, to continue her training.

Linda had also talked about a well-respected documentary filmmaker at the BBC, who had made films on the most relevant cultural and free-thinking figures of the day. Since my dream was always to find a way of bringing alternative ideas into my work life, I had written to Hugh (before I met Austin) without much hope or expectation. We arranged to meet for lunch in the BBC canteen, end-August. It was one of those moments, but the wrong moment. He was just about to get married and move to the country, and I was off to Geneva.

In the few weeks between, Austin and I wrote highly charged letters and had sleepless nights. Isobel helped me clear

Marian's flat as she had decided not to return to England. Lilla said she saw Austin and I 'corded on all levels', and felt it right for me to go, but unnerved me by saying the relationship was not forever. (Going into a relationship that 'would last three years', did not help our first two years together!)

Austin told me he was eliminating activities and ties to create a vacuum for me to come into. In reality this included releasing his social connections around Alice Bailey and Bhagwan Shree Rajneesh. He and Malou also instigated divorce proceedings. And on 16 September, six weeks after we met, I went to live in Geneva.

PART TWO

GENEVA

CHAPTER EIGHT

Our first social outing on my first weekend was to Austin's friend Vivi at Schoenek castle in Germany. The experience was profound for its heightened beauty; like the gold red chestnut tree with bright green fruit; and swirling mist in the dip of its contours. I felt the need for simplicity, to forget 'the spiritual' and absorb the reality of the earth.

I spent my first six weeks in Geneva cleaning Austin's tiny three-bedroom apartment – my way of making it right for myself. 19 chemin Pre Cartelier was within walking distance of the UN building – though not so close to Austin's office at ITC – and belonged to M Rigataux who lived downstairs.

Our sitting room faced onto a park with a view towards a glorious oak tree. Just beyond the kitchen window were two spectacular redwood trees. One of these had a 'face' in its huge trunk, and in darker moments that tree was my friend, a point of stability.

I would sit each day watching the trees changing in mood and colour in the hazy autumn sunshine and listen to the birds. My senses were coming alive and the energy that flowed through me and out of me, including my hands, seemed to confirm that I was indeed 'earthing the dark feminine through the physical body'.

I realised that I could work on Austin's auric field, and facilitate a process of change. My consciousness of his body was growing through my hands, which seemed to be 'told' where to move. The energy would raise my hands and make circles and then seem to dip down to places I must touch. He said it felt like a hosepipe of directed energy.

And as Austin opened up to me he began to 'see' in the astral sense and through him my consciousness of colour was also heightening. It is not surprising that our moods oscillated daily. As Austin put it 'the joys were so intense and the despairs so profound'. He knew that 'somehow your conscious/unconscious playing on mine is forcing me to deal with undealt with things. A deep cleansing of the Augean stables is going on.'

At times of crisis something from 'outside' would come in to help us. For example, Austin was an enthusiast of Gildas' teachings, channelled by Ruth White, and often her words would touch the spot. 'The most important and lasting lessons of life are learned in the blackest depths, and it is the jewel brought forth from the darkness which is the eventual strength of the individual or nation.'

On another occasion it was the words of Alice Bailey's *Esoteric Healing* that restored my heart to the connectedness of meaning. I yearned for the opportunity to learn and understand about healing.

When I couldn't find my bearings, or felt I would never learn French, or was bored, I would catch the plane home several times a day in my mind. But invariably when Austin came home from work it was fine again.

Austin went several times to Confignon, his family home. He went alone because Malou was unable to face me. I felt for her distress and wished it could be different, but I know the pain of separation never left her. I met his children: Blaise, then nineteen, and France (Titi), seventeen, who I liked enormously. She had such a clear, open face, bright eyes and Pre-Raphaelite curls. Malou's son Didier, by an earlier marriage, was also a delight but always more distant.

According to Alice Bailey, Geneva was 'the heart centre' of the world. It felt to me like a bowl into which I had sunk – into lethargy. I had been told that thirty per cent of people in Geneva went into the mental hospital at one time or another, and a book *The Ion Factor*, suggested that because of its positioning between the Jura and the Alps it had a high ratio of *serotonin positive ions* (as opposed to healthy *negative ions*.) The electrical activity of the winds, the *Foehn* of the Alps, the *Bise* and the *Mistral*, also affected the health of Geneva. I heard they didn't do heart operations when the *Bise* was blowing.

My whole time in Geneva was spent countermanding its soporific atmosphere – I even took up drinking coffee again, after five years, just to 'get to ground level' each morning.

My picture of Geneva as the perfect mirror for the 'descent into matter' only came gradually, yet it was rich in symbolism. For example, the long tunnels of the CERN nuclear particle accelerator were close to, and possibly under, the city. And the 'dirty money' of unnumbered bank accounts was awash within it. Dark matter indeed.

It was a relief, then, after my first month, to visit Linda in Dornach for the weekend. It was good to experience the shapes and colours of the village built according to Steiner principles and to witness the Goetheanum.

Linda is unique and her style has changed many times over the years I have known her, but at that moment what concerned me was that the women all looked similar; somehow too 'ethereal'. Eurythmy, with its diaphanous veils, takes you into the ethers, which felt slightly odd at a time when in my view we were 'meant' to come down to earth.

It was here that I first talked to one of her friends about the Cathars, who espoused a belief in 'dualism' and 'gnosis', and were exterminated for their heresy by the Catholic Church at Mont Segur in 1244. The Cathars and the Templars were beginning to figure strongly in my 'search for truth'.

Meeting American artist Rowena Pattee, through friends of Austin, was a delight - and daunting. Her creative output was astonishing, including paintings 10' high for a film *Tree of Life*, and a set of paintings for her own *Woman's Tarot* pack.

When she talked about the descent from light consciousness in order to bring the light right down to earth – which she called the compassionate stage – it related to my own sense of descending through the animal, plant and mineral kingdoms to redeem the earth. But to 'work with the light and be aware of how that affects the body' were new terms to me.

We talked of the transit of Pluto into Scorpio in two years time, as the 'real descent'. The light had touched the earth, she said, but the important stage was the redemption of the earth in the next twenty years. To Austin and I she felt light years ahead, but I still felt we had our part to play and it was enough to touch the groundswell of recognition with such others.

In November, Austin went 'on mission' to Egypt and I went with him. At first, on our free weekend, Cairo felt heavy, which matched a kind of emptiness that had arisen between us. But something changed in the Queen's chamber in the Giza pyramid, as though my body could relax and the heart open and the energy flow through the whole body. I was able to commit myself more fully in some way.

While Austin evaluated the results of ITC's project in Egypt I walked for hours in the dust and bustle around Cairo. I began to like the activity and movement of this chaotic, sandy city with its veneer of sophistication over underlying poverty. I had coffee in the famous *Groppi's*, then still a pinnacle of ex-pat chic, and by comparison Geneva felt inert and sterile.

I loved the Egyptian museum where I scoured the images of the Old, Middle and New Kingdoms for clues and recognition. I liked the opulence of the precious stones and was intrigued to feel the energy of the pink granite in my hands. I was particularly fascinated by the depiction of hands – my new place of cognition - in the imagery. I noted the temple women touching the Pharoah with flat hands, and scenes where the sun's rays were pouring into the women's hands.

At the end of the week we plunged headlong into crisis. Austin had been invited to a country house for a lunch party with various Ambassadors and dignitaries. I was excluded because I wasn't his wife, which upset him. He asked if my reluctance to marry was because our relationship might only be a catalytic one and would 'finish when the work was over'. He had hit on the one thing I had kept to myself throughout our continual communication: Lilla's prediction that our relationship was finite.

I couldn't reply, but it made me think. Did I want to marry someone fifteen years older? Would I one day want a child and family after all - which wasn't an option in this situation? Once again a relationship was making me feel separate, and out of control of my destiny, and this became a central part of my life with Austin. We moved closer in and further away by turns and yearned for some stability between us. But neither of us could give up on our relationship.

After two weeks' work in Cairo (with one day in Alexandria) Austin took a third week as holiday. We flew to Luxor, and sitting on the East Bank of the Nile, looking towards the shadowy, etched sandstone hills above the narrow strip of greening fertility where the shadows of the trees shimmered on the water, I was happy. The rest could take care of itself.

We walked in the early morning in the Temple of Karnak and sailed in a Felucca on the Nile at dusk. We walked from the riverbank in burning heat, through a sugar cane village where women and children stared at us from doorways, to Queen Hepsephut's Temple and over the ridge to the Valley of the Kings.

On 19 November we flew to Aswan, where the pink granite bubbles of the landscape reminded me of the powerful sense I had had in the Cairo museum. The stone was mined here and presumably the temple altars were carved in this material because of the 'high' energy in the crystalline structure.At Abu Simbel we saw the Temple of Hathor dedicated by Rameses II for his wife Nefertari. Hathor, Goddess of love, beauty, music and dancing, was a vibrant symbol for this feminine journey. The idea of 'spirit of place' was growing. Egypt had been intense! Did every place we travelled have to have meaning?

Back in Geneva we needed time to earth it all. We had asked for a reading from Ruth White and a letter on our return was reassuring. Healing and karma could mainly be worked out via relationships. It was essential to try and relate honestly on all levels, including the sexual level; neither under-valuing nor over-valuing one level or another. We could only accept each day as a gift for the work we had to do and not limit the relationship by any expectations of ourselves or the other person.

I seemed destined for these 'karmic' relationships, but they would never be easy!

We had come a long way, but in December, isolated in the below-freezing cold with Austin away in New York, I fell down another gloomy hole. When Austin came back there was such a chasm between us that I panicked and began to dissociate. So much so that I booked an earlier flight than planned for a trip back to London.

The day of my going was odd to say the least. Austin was at work and I was due to leave the house at mid-day. At ten o'clock the doorbell rang and Austin's Yugoslavian (later Slovenian) friend Marko, who I had never met, was at the door. He told me he had been sitting at home the previous night and had had a strong intuition he should come to Geneva to 'protect Austin and me'. He had travelled all night, via Venice, to get here.

We sat down and talked about leylines, and particularly about Nikolai Tessler's *aquastats*. These were lines of energy in the earth that converged to one great point and could be affected, healed and manipulated. Marko was a sculptor and built monuments to the partisans along his home valley, following these energy lines. He had also designed a village on these principles. Amazingly the communist authorities were open to such unusual ideas, as long as they were earth based and didn't involve God!

I told Marko about Holford and laying out his map, which marked the connecting energy centres, he used his amethyst pendulum to tune in. Where before he had only 'seen' Glastonbury, he discovered a new line for him going directly through Holford! This line, he told me, connected the 'feminine centres', and was a line from Egypt, through Venice, Geneva, Holford and Iona.

The dark force 'Ijababa, which had cursed the feminine energy in Atlantis – and was in some way connected to the masculinisation of Christianity – was directed at Holford!

Apparently a second dark force was sitting on Geneva like a dark cloud, and by unconsciously linking to Egypt, Geneva and then Holford I had set up forces against me! He told me his job was to find 'five points' that would effectively stop this force, which was why he had felt so strongly to come today.

My mind boggled! When I talked to Austin from London later that day he said he had listened to Marko too, but could not feel for what he said. I couldn't dismiss the synchronicities so lightly, but I think I realised then that we all interpret our experiences differently. I was not inclined to 'dark forces', but I knew I had been afraid of something intangible, and that I had felt I was being 'driven out'.

Much of what happened during my time with Austin felt like taking part in a drama – with 'men and women merely players'. The further away from Marko, the more implausible his ideas seemed, yet at a Frances Bacon Society workshop on my first weekend back in London, Peter Dawkins suggested that the current planetary line-up was the most chaotic and extraordinary for thousands – even millions – of years. Uncertainty and change were inevitable, and participants talked of living through several incarnations in a short space of time, to be ready for these challenging and exciting times.

Francis Bacon (who according to enthusiasts was the founder of the mystery school responsible for writing Shakespeare) had synthesised all that was relevant in the Ancient Teachings and presented them in a form that everyone could acquire in 'ages to come'. Peter whose theme that weekend was humanity's movement from the lesser mysteries to the higher, also told us that a particularly amazing planetary configuration would occur on 21 December – as Marko had.

Although I couldn't fit my own stage of development into Peter's 'Initiation Chart', any more than I could resonate with Marko's 'dark forces', it was comforting to be with people for whom the old rules did not apply. Over the years I have learned – painfully – to hold my own truth and not continually negated or thrown into insecurity by other people's intellect or certainty.

The words of one woman I met at there, Egyptologist Ann Bowman, were particularly welcome. She confirmed that the rose granite had powerful magnetic radiations, that the Goddess Hathor was mother of Horus, the Christ Child, or the Grail flame, and – best of all – that the hand movements in Egyptian pictures did represent certain meanings, as etheric energy was beamed in.

Like Lyall had been, Austin was known in the circles I moved in – he was a regular visitor to Findhorn, for example, and again I felt under scrutiny. People seemed to feel free to make comments, which were often hurtful. Edmee once warned me to be careful, implying Austin had a reputation with women. Lilla said he 'depleted my chakras'.

In many ways Austin was naive but like everyone else he was doing his best to work for the good of humanity. In fact, he was financing several East Europeans, like Marko, who otherwise could not have come to the West.

All this was nobody's business but ours, and it made me want to withdraw. With my Capricorn moon I have an intense need for privacy. But I was learning something about judging and being judged. Also, that although psychic experiences were not my territory and I should not go looking for them, touching the astral and the psychic planes were part of the descent into matter. Looking at the inner darkness was part of the feminine journey.

Austin came over to England for Christmas, and after time spent with Vlyn we returned to Geneva. When Tony Judge, a brilliant intellectual friend working on an international directory, came to visit Austin and talked of 'disintegration before integration' I knew what he meant. I realised my analytical mind was losing its focus, in order to work from a different part of my being.

Another overnight visitor was Claudine Brelet, a friend of Austin's and coincidentally a name given to me by a friend before I left for Geneva. I knew Claudine had written a book about her own experience of painless childbirth through acupuncture, but what I did not know was that she was now translating into French Lyall's book *Lifetide*! Claudine had a fairly inflated view of herself, but on that first meeting her dynamism highlighted my own inactivity. She told us she was 'a leader in Paris' and that a psychologist had once told her he could not help her because she was a 'shaman' and must find her own way. By the time her comment 'when I was at your stage' came, I was jangling with irritation.

The next morning was better. We both felt Geneva was a place of transition, a place to push the boundaries. She was looking for a way to leave her husband and home in Carcassonne in France – where she had felt connected to the Cathars – and to support her two girls through permanent work in Geneva. I finally decided to stop worrying that my creative life had dried up and the next day was offered a three-week typing job at UNESCO.

Early February 1980 was cold, crisp and gloriously sunny. I enjoyed sitting in my office in the *Bocage* – a cream coloured house with bottle green shutters, doing virtually nothing. I read *North-South – the Brandt Report*, dry and plodding yet full of idealism and optimism that a fairer share could be had by all.

It was Austin's friend Rene Wadlow, editor of *Transnational Perspectives* who said one lunchtime that it was a privilege to work in Geneva. Being here one had a 'duty', and you had to wait until your particular duty arrived. I certainly felt I wanted to contribute yet I wondered whether 'another element' was required. Wouldn't 'the North' - the developed world – have to move into a new moral order?

I was still doing my 'healing' on Austin. I had discovered that the completion of any session was marked when my hands were guided into a figure of eight movement, and that no session lasted more than a few minutes. This is still the case today.

Austin was immensely sensitive and could pick up other people's energy and identify too easily. I realised he would even carry the distress of a film like *Ghandi* long after we had left the cinema, so we had to chose our movies carefully. In many ways his watery nature made him very receptive and feminine. On the other hand he was also extremely stubborn, which stood him in good stead against my will. He simply took no notice!

Geneva continued to exert its strong downward pull towards inertia. Even Austin began to realise how soporific it was. Someone once told me she had come to Geneva for a year and had been there for twenty-eight. It didn't surprise me. Geneva was a place to get stuck in.

Someone else I felt was trapped by Geneva was Austin's stepson Didier. Didier, who was twenty-seven when we met, was a gifted theoretical mathematician and musician, but throughout his life he suffered crippling bouts of depression. His three-year old brother had died when he was very young, and then his father died in a tragic climbing accident on Mont Blanc. Although Austin did everything he could to make Didier feel comfortable, he never quite accepted Austin as his father.

At the end of my stint with UNESCO, and a few days after he had completed some work in Cairo, I met Austin on mission in India. Our hotel *Claridges*, was colonial and crumbling with a slightly tatty, faded elegance; the women were elegant in their beautiful saris. To me Delhi at first sight was wonderful, the scent of the frangipani exquisite. There was a gentle slow warmth in the air, a new and immediate experience to vanquish the lethargy of Geneva.

On the first morning Austin had left for work by the time I woke up. I walked along the tree-lined road, aware that in New Delhi I was seeing less poverty than in Cairo. Emporia abounded. The Indians were not passive; they were selling! But soon I realised that the growing sense of emptiness and 'superficiality' was of New Delhi itself. A place created to be seen not felt. Clean, organised and heartless, without depth or soul.

How different to Old Delhi and the teeming Chadni Chouk, crammed with people, rickshaws and market stalls. Our sumptuous meal with UN officials at the Taj Mahal restaurant further juxtaposed the wealth and poverty of so many developing countries.

The ITC desk officer for Delhi was Zabolc Piskolti, a rather formal Hungarian, brought up in Austria. His wife Liz, originally from New Zealand, became a good friend when they returned to Geneva soon afterwards. They welcomed me warmly as Austin's partner although I knew Austin was still a little embarrassed we weren't married. While the men worked Liz took me around town.

There was so much to see. The Ghats – the memorials to Ghandi; the Jama Masjid – the largest mosque; and the *son et lumiere* at the Red Fort, which touched the imagination and brought Mogul history and its sophisticated Court acutely to life. But I was pleased to go alone to the Ghandi museum, the house of his martyrdom. I wanted to sense into the spirituality of the man and absorb it in my own time.

While Austin stayed in Delhi, I decided to travel further by bus for three or four days. I wanted to catch a glimpse of a more realistic India. On the road to Jaipur there were tents, huts and hutches huddled along a patch of green and irrigated land. People squatted at the roadside, watching the brightly fronted lorries that plied the roads.

In Jaipur itself – a magnificent red stone town – cows wandered the streets, bullocks were harnessed to carts and camels pulled buggy loads of stones. Bicycles teemed in the streets alongside motorised rickshaws. I felt ill at ease, an intruder in the misery of a woman and child lying filthy on the roadside. The Taj Mahal in Agra, of course, was stunning: also the caves of Elora and Ajanta.

During the month we were in India, the feeling of discomfort never quite left me. Back in Delhi I also felt irritated by the incessant wheeler/dealer attitude. We could never walk out without someone wanting us to go somewhere or buy something. I didn't feel faith or spirit, just greed; even the beggars were organised. India is such a Mecca for so many people, yet I have never wanted to return there.

One of the highlights of our stay was meeting Austin's Californian friends Param and Milana, with their friend Anananda. It was my first experience of what was to become a common occurrence, whereby devotees of an Indian Guru changed their names to something appropriate to that faith.

Perhaps my dislike of India stems from my inherent distrust in the Guru phenomenon. My own journey of the feminine and spirituality within matter envisaged a new male understanding of non-paternalistic leadership. So the idea of giving away power to a male patriarch who preached cosmic spirituality was opposite to everything I believed. I have never adhered to any one school of thought.

Paramilana (the couple) were delightful. I was not so sure about Milananda (the triad!) They said they were 'compelled' to India and were 'clearing old energy lines to make way for the new'.

This idea of working with leylines and chakra points in landscape was to become familiar to me. Pilgrimages to mystical sites around the world are now commonplace, but then they were new. And yet I had already begun to understand that my own travels to 'significant' places were a kind of unconscious pilgrimage. I knew that visiting past life experiences in this way was a means of clearing the old memories, personally and collectively, and as Paramilana said, making way for the new.

They, too, talked about the spiritualisation of matter and there were so many other points of agreement and synchronicity that shivers of recognition kept washing through me. At our breakfast together, when Austin was already at work, they told me how special Austin was to them, and how unconscious he was of his ability to tune into things so acutely.

At the end of Austin's mission we took two weeks extra to travel. Our first stop was Khajuraho to see the extraordinary 10th Century Hindu temples, carved on the outside with bestial sexuality on the lower friezes, celestial nymphs in erotic poses on the higher. Spirit in matter at the deepest sense - perhaps. I had bought *The Tantric Way* to read, but again, for any practical purposes Indian philosophy continued to baffle me.

We travelled on to Varanasi and in the afternoon took a bicycle rickshaw to Sarnath where in 500 BC Buddha gave his first speech after Enlightenment. The old ruined part felt peaceful and the sacred Bodhi trees with climbing parasitic plants were special. And then came a surreal event that shook us.

We were wandering on the Goddgaya, where the Buddha was Enlightened, when an Indian introduced himself as a Professor of Astrology at the Hindu University. After a while he invited us to dinner. Neither of us would normally respond to such an approach, but I was captivated by a hint of learning something about Vedic medicine, and Austin, too polite to say no, accepted.

Mr Gupta sent his car to our hotel at 7.30 and we drove for half an hour out of Varanasi. We were shown into a room with a bed, table, chairs, a few files and several books on subjects like 'gem therapy'. Two men – a bank manager and a business man – were already in the room drinking whisky and it became apparent that Mr Gupta was a gifted palmist with an amazing skill at administering Vedic remedies.

When Mr Gupta finally came into the room the two men left, and he began to lecture us on the mystical number nine, the Om, the endocrine glands, colours and gems. I was riveted because he seemed able to put some of my current thoughts into perspective. (He was obviously playing me as the gullible one, and later Austin told me that he had responded to my questions by giving me the answers I wanted to hear).

He then told us that the sun came into the body at birth through the hands, and that the baby establishes the body in sequence, with all the genetic characteristics included. He then told me lightly what my disease inheritance would be, and I went cold with fear. Un-stated was also the message that his method of healing could cope with these genetic inevitabilities.

At dinner he told us that the King of Morocco had paid him £100,000 to hire Hindu and Moslem religious people to chant for a year (we had heard some chanting earlier). This was to magically persuade his enemy Algeria to sign a treaty. Already through meditation there had been an earthquake in

Algeria, which had killed a million people. I finally began to feel uneasy.

After dinner he came to the point: my diagnosis and how much it would cost! Mr Gupta said he would need £50 to take enlarged palm prints and then make the diagnosis. When I turned to Austin for advice he said it was up to me to make the decision. But eventually, when I pushed him to tell me what to do, he then said I must say no, and we asked to leave.

Back at the hotel he told me he had felt 'bad vibes' all the way through. But I was surprised when he said he had been calling on all the protection he could muster! If I had offered my palm print, he said, I would have given him something to have influence over me. To me it was a question of stupidity, a lesson in being caught through the blackmail of fear.

Darjeeling, the most northern part of West Bengal, was reached by a six-hour winding taxi ride through mountain villages and hillside tea plantations. Here in what Alice Bailey described as a latent planetary centre, the delightful people were different. They were quaint and courteous with friendly open faces.

We did what people do in Darjeeling: we were taken by jeep to watch the sunrise over Tiger Hill at 4am; and on a walk up from our hotel saw the flags left on Observatory Hill, an especially sacred site for Hindus and Buddhists. We were aware, of course, of the influence of the large Tibetan community, since it was to here that the Dalai Lama and his followers first came when they made their escape.

But whatever the meaning of its powerful essence, Darjeeling left us with a feeling of anxiety and sadness, an intrinsic loneliness. We were glad after four weeks away to go home.

CHAPTER NINE

Back in Geneva there were several letters waiting for me and I picked up Lilla's first. Our book was about to be published, which was exciting, but her words consumed me with distress. She hated the cover, she said. The sales literature negated her as a yoga teacher, and since everything around it was being directed at me, her friends and family thought I was exploiting her! The next letter was from an American woman who three years on had decided to tell me that *The Wise Virgin* was 'crap'. I was desolate. Why had this happened? The doubts crowded in. If this could happen what value my work? I never wanted to write again; never again wanted to set myself up to be knocked down. I would surrender to the inertia and allow it to swallow me up.

In fact, Lilla later wrote to apologise, and came to like the cover, which represented a symbolic idea of chakric colour not the accuracy of science. *What Colour Are You?* became a best seller in its own way. It was translated into four other languages, had several editions and engendered royalties for eleven years.

Our circuits crossed little after that, but Lilla went on to be well known and successful, not least through the success of our book. We met two or three times over those years, with great affection. But the incident served to sever links even more with my old life. I had no certainty any more. Austin suggested I should sink right into the inertia until I found its dynamic.

I took up another G3 temporary typing post, this time at the *World Health Organization*, and Austin and I began our hiking life. With our boots and backpacks we periodically took a train to the Valais on Friday nights and caught the Postbus to a small hotel in our chosen location. The following day we would walk from one valley to the next and find somewhere else to stay and we came back on the Sunday. I loved this part of our life, the beauty of the mountains, and the sheer physical tiredness.

We also began to work with massage and I still found my hands were telling me where to touch. I saw that massage could jog a memory lodged in the body and help remove the block. The body had a mind of its own.

In March, Mark Braham from Dartington, who turned out to be a good friend of Austin's, came to Geneva to give a series of lectures on his brainchild *The Association of Integrative Education*. I grew to love Mark over the years, but I always found his intellectual espousing of esoteric understanding a little heavy.

Mark's *Association* eventually brought him to live in Switzerland, but although he interested many significant people in his ideas, it never quite got off the ground. Mark had a very fixed vision and I think his lack of flexibility eventually put people off. Like many others he was also hooked on trying to raise large sums of money to 'set up a centre'. It became increasingly clear that this was never going to happen.

We spent Easter in the Alps up and away in the snow-capped heights. We walked in meadows of white crocuses and along pine clad paths with waterfalls dripping with icicles. The pure fresh-air breezes were such a contrast to Geneva that it was all the more depressing when the womb-like energy closed in on us the minute we arrived back. In fact a short while later Christian Schaller, a medical doctor who also ran *Soleil Diffusion*, a foundation that 'mixed the intuitive understanding of the body with the academic', told me that a lot of people felt caught up in 'the womb' of Geneva.

At the end of May I went with Austin on mission to Greece. With a few days to spare it was good to visit Delphi and Epidaurus and the Corinth Canal, but I found little resonance with classical Greece. The older Mycenean and Cycladian cultures, on the other hand, were bursting with life. In Mycenea itself we stayed at the hotel where Virginia Woolf had stayed and drank *Hercules Blood*, the deep purple wine of Nemea.

Since Austin had to work we agreed to meet a week later on Crete. To fill the time I took a ferry to Milos and a couple of days later went on to Santorini, where I was captivated by the extraordinary volcanic stratas in the rock and the burning hot black pumice beaches which reflected back no light.

There was a sense of beauty and depth about Oia, the small town huddled into the hillside on the north end of the island, very different to the main town Fira. But I had no idea that I would make a significant return there nine years later.

From Santorini I took a ferry to Crete and met Austin at the airport. We saw all there was to see of Minoan culture, which everywhere seemed embodied in Crete: in the mountains, the caves, the crumbling red rock; in the gorgeous yellow and pink of broom and oleander; in the cypress trees and olive groves; even in the eating of ripe sweet tomatoes and feta.

On our return to Geneva I devoured Arthur Guirdham's *The Island,* a far memory of 1250BC on an island off Crete, since disappeared. It affected me so much that I felt a new kind of frustration. He was saying so many significant things, in what seemed like fantasy form.

He talked of the Mother Goddess and the feminine creative principle behind the goddess. In his view evil was inherent; it existed. Paternalistic religions relied on a 'goodness and reward' idea and cults that taught 'transcendence' were using the same escapist notion. We must face the tragedy of life as it was, he said.

Lethargy set in again and I slept a lot. One night I dreamed I was swimming against the angry tide. At first I needed help but finally I managed to swim against the odds and make it. On another lazy afternoon I dreamed I was being eaten by a dog. My hands were being chewed up while a girl looked on passively recording it!

I felt I had had my fill of books on inner journeys, ancient wisdom and consciousness. My head was overloaded with mind excitement when I should have been 'coming down'.

My journalist friend Pamela came to stay, and in her inimitable way she brought me back to earth with a bump. She reminded me of the sensible life of pensions, insurance policies and mortgages that I had given up to follow this path. 'It's all very well, but what do you actually do? It's all so wishy-washy'!

I groped for words of justification, trying to defend my New Age crankiness, most of which I was critical of myself. If it wasn't cranky it could certainly be deluded. I also told Pamela tentatively of my growing awareness of healing, and then had to assure her that I was not imposing my will on someone else. The body had an endless capacity to self-regulate, I said, which I was simply 'allowing'.

We didn't really disagree but she was stronger on logic – and confidence. We talked about an independent force for evil. She was worried about people 'using power for evil purposes' – something that she as a woman with a powerful mind, was aware of in herself.

Despite my recent negative psychic experiences, I felt then, and still do, that the collective accumulation over all time of fear and negativity pushed down into the bowels of the earth and into the unconscious was what people constituted as 'evil'. I felt that 'consciousness' was the way to recognise and release our personal and collective negativity, and above all the will to power.

In August 1981 I went to England. It was good to mind-hop with Isobel and Andrew, and also to visit Vlyn in Holford. Although I had no real knowledge of astrology then, it had already become a useful language. Isobel and I talked about the significance of Pluto, heavily represented in both our charts, and the experience of dying to one thing in order to gain another. And it seemed significant to the depth of inertia I felt in Geneva. I came to see my 'cosmic/spirit' phase as Uranian, represented by Lyall, and this 'descent' phase with Austin somehow a Plutonic one.

Austin joined me and we went to Iona, en route to Findhorn, which until now I had avoided. New Age community didn't appeal to me at all, whereas for Austin Findhorn was a real spiritual home. A lot of misunderstandings took place in the name of the new age, as people experimented with newfound abilities to manipulate energies, whether consciously or not.

Recognising someone from a 'past life' was also a hazard, and separating what was 'real' from what was 'old' was often confusing. Sir George Trevelyan once said that the New Age was wonderful because it meant you could kiss the girl on the first date! Many people, husbands and wives included, got hurt.

I met Nirvena, focaliser of the Great Hall at that time. She was a Yugoslavian girl who Austin had sponsored to do a three-year course in dance in Britain. Much to Malou's fury he had given away a £15,000 inheritance to do so.

We had tea with Eileen Caddy, co-founder of Findhorn, and got the impression that the community was in transition. They were hoping to attract older people with more staying power and more skills. I was glad I had been there but did not feel the need to go again.

Back in Geneva I joined a three-week summer school at the university to improve my French. My written test put me into a top-level conversation class, but when the conversation passed me by, I demoted myself into a normal learning class, which immediately I regretted.

Later I did a regular evening class with the original conversation teacher, Danielle, and we became good friends. Sadly my French never quite made it, and it was only when I went to live in France several years later that I realised how much I had taken in over the years by 'osmosis'.

Austin and I were so telepathic I began to wonder who was thinking whose thoughts. I was also interested in the symbol of ill health. Why did I get a sudden bruise on my right foot? Why the pain in Austin's stomach? Why was my friend Marjorie always falling and breaking bones? Ruth White had said illness was a present symbol of past karma. So what had to be done?

In September we went for a weekend to Limoux in South West France for a second visit to Austin's friends David and Celia Inayat Harper. Celia was the daughter of the last White Raj of Sarawak, Anthony Brooke. David was the grandson of the man who brought Sufism to the west, Hazrat Inayat Khan, and nephew of its then leader Pia Vilyat Khan. They had married when she was twenty-four and he sixteen, to the disapproval of both families. They had a daughter, Sura, then thirteen.

David and Celia had a vision. Convinced that they should start an alternative school, they had set off in their 2CV from Paris and arrived completely penniless in the South of France. They found an old ruined shack on a hillside with no access road and no utilities, and built it up to make it fit to live in.

When I met them they were beginning to build another house, stone by stone, and make the hillside their home. To survive David sang in cafes in Carcassonne and Celia passed round the hat. A few years later Anthony paid for a tarmac road.

My contact with Celia was an instant delight, and David certainly had a special presence. Sura was sulky like any teenager. After several visits to her wealthy family in Paris she had resolutely refused to eat meusli, because 'it's what poor people eat'.

Like many people at that time they were fighting against the odds for their beliefs. The school in a dilapidated bus was an eyesore on the land, but at first they did attract a few local children and the occasional dropout family.

The area was already calling people from far and wide. The book *Holy Blood, Holy Grail* had a huge following, depicting the fascinating story of a 'treasure' connected to the church at Rennes le Chateau (just over the valley from Le Metairie Blanche), and the true bloodline of Christ. The conclusion of the book was that Christ had married Mary Magdalene and they had had a child, whose direct descendant was alive today, through the line of the French monarchy.

Although I loved the book I felt that the authors had reached the wrong conclusion to their painstaking an exciting research. Or at least, if true, they had missed the point.

When I began to put symbols to my own journey of consciousness, I felt that Christ and the Magdalene were living examples of the universal principles and polarities of spirit and matter; masculine and feminine; love and death, and that the integration of these aspects within human consciousness led to the birth of the innocent, wholly creative child within us all.

Over the years Rennes Le Chateau became a *mecca*, and Celia in particular felt a responsibility to, and a guardianship over the land. Even though the school quite quickly petered out because no one had any money to pay for it, Celia's enthusiasm never wavered. For years she continued to hold the dream for her land and her school, despite the terrible circumstances of her eventual break-up with David.

Pir Vilyat Khan and his wife Mary occasionally spent time on the land, part of which was handed over to the Sufi's for their annual summer school. Eventually they used a wood-frame glasshouse built on a nearby brow of a hill by another couple. When this couple split up, the wife continued to live there alone.

When Sarah and I were introduced the first time, my guard went up immediately. I instinctively did not trust her. So it didn't surprise me when, a couple of years later, I heard that she was the cause of Celia and David's marriage break-up.

This woman was caught up in an inflated view of her own power, the disturbing outcome of these new psychic perceptions that were becoming available to so many people at this time. No doubt touching into past life resonances in the land, she considered herself a priestess. It was apparently her task to 'initiate' all men, and Celia's David would be amongst them.

Whether or not he was I don't know but far worse was the fallout from a visit to England made by Sarah with her nine-year old daughter, and Sura. Whatever 'rituals' or ceremonies took place Sura came back from London an emotional wreck, her fragile ego shattered. For months afterwards she had terrible psychic terrors, and Celia spent the next years trying to find schools and institutions that could help restore Sura's mental stability. David could not take the strain and left.

In October, Austin went to the Caribbean and I went back to London (on my regular trips I stayed mostly with my mother or Mary). This time I was bowled over by a *Touch for Health* weekend and its practitioner Natalie Davenport. Applied Kinesiology – muscle testing for body imbalances – is common now, but then it was new. The idea that the body knows when it is out of balance was exciting.

Marko came through London and I introduced him to Vlyn, who at that time was working as a superior kind of nurse/housekeeper to a member of the House of Lords. The job didn't last too long when the wife realised Vlyn had a knack of bringing older men back to life through her lively personality, and soon decided to come back to London to take up care of her husband again.

I met Austin's mother Mary, up from Worthing, for tea at her club in St James. We had already met and liked each other a lot. Mary was a one-off. She resembled Margaret Rutherford: confident and powerfully set, from colonial days, in her class and convictions about 'the masses', yet eccentrically fresh and unconditional about 'the young'.

Bhagwan had once told Austin that he was afraid of women, and, "if you are afraid of women you are afraid of many things. You will be afraid of love; you will be afraid of death; you will be afraid of life, because the woman is all this. It is something to do with your mother and you will have to work on it or it will persist. With fear everything stops. Trust is a great changer. If you can trust someone, a thousand and one burdens simply disappear".

In my work on the Feminine I was greatly interested in the idea of the 'controlling mother' and the disastrous power women had over their sons. But I always felt 'I could do business' with this kind of spirited woman.

Mary was a powerful force in Austin's unconscious life, of course, but equally in his waking life. She was hugely critical about almost everything, and over the years her relationship with Malou had become a prickly one.

Malou preferred Austin's stepmother, Lady Jacqueline, so there were jealousies and preferences expressed. It was a huge source of sadness to Austin and he credited me with reconciling him to his mother, simply by virtue of me liking her so much. I met Jacqueline and his half-sister Charlotte who were both very nice, but somehow it wasn't the same.

Before I left for Geneva a conversation with my oldest friend Olga seemed to sum everything up. I met Ogi when she was sixteen and I was eighteen, when we both worked for a cosmetic company in the Burlington Arcade (at the same time I met Vivienne Crisp). Her family had fled the 1956 Hungarian uprising, but it was thirty years before I learned exactly how terrifying that ordeal had been.

She trained as an illustrator and like her older two brothers and sister was a talented artist. We later worked for IPC together and she sometimes drew illustrations for my beauty pages on *Fabulous*

At the age of twenty-eight Ogi had a child by a married man who let her down badly. She struggled for years to bring up her child in difficult conditions, and took up various educational training programmes to try to support them both.

Jeannette now has a PhD in chemistry and is a much sought-after research chemist – thanks to the support of John who married Ogi when Jeanette was twelve. But at that time Ogi, aged thirty-four, had been struggling with her inner demons, connected of course to the hardship of her life. But through her own psychic capacity she had seen that collective humanity needed to recognise the deep, dark, underlying 'other part' of ourselves.

"The darkness inside us appears like a horrific monster," she said. "I've never experienced anything so horrible, but at the moment I surrendered because I had no resources left, the 'something' that has always been there since I was a child, that I've always known as a 'guardian angel', took over, and it was gone.

"When I came face to face with my shadow it was not frightening at all. It had been like walking into the house of horrors, a distortion, but this 'other part' was really very small. I stopped struggling with all my fears and the blurring suddenly clarified; there was no segregation of my feelings and other people's. I felt one with myself and what I was feeling".

Although at that time my own experiences were less dramatic and 'psychic', and I still had some way to go, I recognised it fully as part of the descent into matter. Her view, and mine, was that humanity had to face this fear, this negativity, and that the level of fear in the collective was rising.

CHAPTER TEN

In early December I went with Austin on mission to Central America, again unconsciously treading the lines of ancient footsteps. He always took scheduled flights to move more flexibly, whereas I often went charter. Since Austin had arrived earlier he met my late night flight into Guatemala City with a colleague. It was very dark and I noticed an armed guard on the roof as I came out. The terrorist situation had made the country increasingly unstable, and the American government had forbidden its nationals to go there.

To say I was scared is an understatement, but one Frenchman from Miami and I braved the local bus tour. 'No problem', said the tour guide, showing us a map of where the guerrillas were in the country, but he did admit that 'they shot two Japanese tourists here last week!'

At the well-guarded Presidential Palace we saw a row of stained glass windows blown out by terrorist bombs. The 'peace' window had gone! The guide told us the native people were in turn rising up against the terrorists because they made them give up the produce from their farms – which the army did as well. But the Swedish Ambassador, who invited Austin and I to dinner, told us that Indians were in fact rising up against the right wing government, too, because their conditions were so bad.

The following day I walked from my hotel to another hotel across the centre of town, just for a cup of coffee. The place was deserted, except for two or three women sitting at a table speaking English – about medical astrology of all things.

They turned out to be wives of First Secretaries at various embassies. We chatted for a while and then they warned me not to take a bus, or a taxi, or to walk back to my hotel because guerrilla activity was so dangerous. That didn't seem to leave many options! So I walked back the way I came.

Austin and I had planned to see the Mayan temples in several of these countries, so from Guatemala City we took an internal flight for an overnight at Tikal. The guerrillas had been there too, it seemed, in September. 'They didn't shoot anyone,' we were reassured. 'Just knocked down the airline office.'

The remarkable 'late classic' Mayan structures (700 AD, and more recent than I had imagined) rose out of the densest jungle. The temples had been discovered when the people came looking for the chewing gum tree. It was good to see the ceiba, the national tree, again, a favourite of mine in the Amazon, and to know that the rowan tree seed was still made into bread, as it had been in Mayan times.

Back in Guatemala City they talked a lot about guerrillas. 'Too much', said Annette, the wife of the ITC desk officer. Their son Eric had recently had a car crash near their home and a gun thrust into his throat by three guerrillas who said 'it's your fault'. They had taken him back to his house where Annette, home alone, was forced to agree they would admit liability.

Annette was serene and beautiful, with two beautiful children; content to be the wife of a UN official and make her life wherever he went. I began to realise how resilient and splendid these UN wives were. While their husbands always had a job to slot into, the wives, starting from scratch, set up libraries or social projects, or managed to find their niche in whichever country they were sent to.

In El Salvador I felt slightly less apprehensive, though the guerrilla situation until recently had actually been worse. There was a feeling that the up-coming elections might make the difference. In the capital San Salvador there had been a great deal of shooting and the guerrillas would stop cars, turf out the drivers, and just take them.

Austin's contact point, the UN Development Programme office, was still locked against invasion and armed soldiers spot-checked cars for guns. For the two days we were there I decided not to go out of the hotel at all.

Honduras is surrounded on all sides by mountains, and my enduring memory is the rocky approach to landing at the airport through a scary wind tunnel. Poorer than the other countries we visited, Honduras 'spread its poverty better'. They treated the beggars kindly.

We took a bus to Copan, another site of Mayan temples, through countryside from pine to pasture, to heavy woods, then cornfields and tobacco plantations. There were settlers in evidence at the sides of the roads but no one in national dress.

I was disappointed to see how much of the 'pyramid' had been restored, but there were parts that had been left, mostly in original stonework: the Ball Court and the Acropolis, both with intricate carvings of hieroglyphs and priestly figures, even more wonderful than at Tikal.

Costa Rica was a beautiful country; like Switzerland without the snow. At that time there was an economic slow-down and a recent devaluation. The ITC man, Herb Jacobsen, said the UN didn't realise that however much expertise they sent, the economy did not have the resources to use it. The only way was co-ownership with outside investors.

I liked Herb. His philosophy that 'Life (God) is a bad joke, and the only way is to defy it', suited my mood just then! A good, old-fashioned chauvinist, he said that Costa Rican women like his wife Marie-Theresa could seem cloying. The fact that she spent all her time concerned for his welfare and comfort; 'I can't even get my own coffee in the morning,' could become a bit too much after a while, he said.

Herb took us to meet Marie-Theresa on her coffee plantation. Costa Rica had the best coffee in the world, they told us, and hers was the best. They also invited us to their club for lunch. It was the first time I had seen women whose fingernails had been painted in mosaic patterns.

I made a point of visiting the Black Madonna statue at Cartago, the old capital of Costa Rica until 1823. This symbol of a different aspect of the feminine, which was beginning to connect to Mary Magdalene for me, was becoming a potent icon. And the Jade Museum was spectacular.

Before returning to Guatemala we went briefly to Panama City, which was unbearably hot. We saw the Panama Canal and finally understood its rationale; that it saved ships twenty-one days at sea. Then, Austin's work completed, we flew to Mexico City where my friend Louise Kimber joined us from England.

I had met Louise in London a few years before at an evening class in public speaking. As capable as I was at one-to-one encounters, speaking into groups of more than two or three people – including at dinner parties – still scared me. I had hoped this might help.

Louise was ten years younger than me and born in Kenya. She was attracted to the kind of conversations we had on alternative ideas, and somehow it was planned that she should come with us to spend Christmas in Mexico; ten days on the Yucatan Peninsula exploring more of the Mayan temples.

For me the threesome didn't work entirely, especially when occasionally we all had to share a room to make the cost easier for Louise. Despite Austin's attentiveness to me I could see she was a very attractive woman! Later when Louise came to stay with us for a month in our tiny apartment in Geneva – with a view to taking a job there – that wasn't easy either. I wonder whether we were linked karmically in a particularly difficult way, and our visit to Mexico could certainly have been an indication of that.

Tulum, the Mayan ruins by the sea, was a truly mystical place. While the many tourists were given the story of the moment, I sat on a rock over-looking the sea. The bay grape and turquoise water reminded me of Bermuda, and I remembered the certainties and expectations of my time with Lyall. I caught glimpses of the intensity and vitality of that time. I missed my optimism and longed to be effective, creative and alert again to every moment.

I was sad to leave Tulum. We went to 'gubernatorial' Uxmal, ancient Coba - where we spent Christmas. But it was at Chitchen Itza that Louise experienced her greatest drama. We were climbing the steps of a very tall temple when she suddenly went rigid with fear. I helped her back down and later she said

117

it was a though the bottom was crumbling away and she was 'escaping' to the top.

It was some time later that I discovered that in this culture young women were chosen as sacrifices to the Gods: they were given drugs by the priests so they would go out of body, and beyond a certain step they knew they would not return to this world.

Austin and I, however, had to return to Geneva. At the end of 1981, aged 81, Austin's mother emigrated to live near his sister, Sal, in New Zealand. Sal was a wild creature, divorced from her husband Kit and living a languorously creative lifestyle with her two sons Doz and Nick. Despite her heritage, Mary managed to live with the 'looseness' of the culture in great style and lived to be ninety-seven. We went to visit her for three weeks that Christmas – Austin via work in the States, me on a charter from Geneva, via Iceland, New York, Denver, Los Angeles and Hawaii. My present from Sal was a silver necklace with a moth pendant. 'I am the butterfly' she told me! After our visit we returned to Hawaii for a short break on Maui.

By this time I had written two or three articles for *Resurgence* in the UK (including one on Marko), and had done several short-term typing contracts. My last job had been with the Mental Health Division at WHO, where I had told someone I was a journalist and I was now presented with the possibility of a contract to write features for the Division, to clarify its activities for the lay public (popularising). Without a degree I was not technically allowed to take a P (professional) grade job, but in the first couple of years several G3 posts led to P jobs, and as a short-term P3 and P4 consultant the problem of a degree never came up.

The pay – even for typing – was fabulous, and for a professional job it was brilliant. My tax-free earnings were far better then than they have ever been since! Austin's (at D5, then D6) were even more stupendous. With such crazy differentials (especially when we were working to mitigate the hardship in developing countries), it made nonsense of living life solely to 'earn a living'. Money could never be the sole criterion (and hadn't been for a long time); we could only live life as we were destined to live it.

I had started attending a movement class with a Genevoise girl called Genia, whose Sufi name was Sybillah, and we became good friends. I was excited to understand that energy will do what it is meant to do; that the body could move you to dance. I experienced energy from the feet, or the elbows, 'dancing' to their own tune, and witnessed the strength of that energy once it was allowed to move.

It was an amazing revelation that I could concentrate my mind on my body, as once I had concentrated on my emotions. It *was* my mind. *I* was my mind. In letting go I could be the *nuances* of my mind. I began to perceive a change in my body that all the 'trying' to change could not do.

At the end of January 1982, thanks to Mark Braham, I went to work. He had managed to talk himself into a job, setting up a Documentation Centre for the UN High Commissioner for Refugees (UNHCR), and one of his first productions was a nicely produced bi-monthly publication called *Refugee Abstracts*. He employed me and Piers, another Englishman, to write short abstracts of all refugee documents and books.

Working with Mark and Piers was fun, if chaotic – Mark was never the most organised person – and I loved having to get on the bus every day with somewhere to go. I was still agonising to find an alternative way of contributing, because I was convinced the world must change, but it was wonderful not to be bored!

When the work slowed down I went to London for a month. Austin was often abroad and that year was in Nairobi, India, Afghanistan and Peru and I went back to the UK several times each year. I enjoyed catching up with my friends, particularly Vlyn, Isobel, Ogi, Mary and latterly Linda Larson.

While Linda was studying Eurythmy at Dornach, she came to Geneva each summer for a temporary typing contract at WHO. At first she stayed with us but later found

Anthroposophy contacts to lodge with. When we were both working we had many canteen coffees together. But when she graduated and got a job as Eurythmist at the Totnes Waldorf School, I would stay with her in Devon or meet her when I visited Vlyn, who also lived in Totnes for a time.

I had a small amount of money put by, and thanks to Austin was also able to save anything I earned. By the end of 1982 I had enough money for a deposit on a tiny flat in Chalk Farm in London, which I immediately rented out to pay the mortgage.

If Austin had not helped me in this way I would never have survived the future vagaries of my life. Although his own mother kept telling me I should marry Austin 'for the security of his pension' I could never do the completely 'safe' thing.

At the end of April Austin and I invited Vlyn to Geneva, and the three of us went by train to visit Marko at his home in Sempas, Yugoslavia. It was fascinating to see that, notwithstanding Marko's skill as a sculptor, equally creative behind the scenes, was his wife Maca. Maca made beautiful things out of wood for their home; not least the magisterial seat that covered the earth closet loo! She once made me a cardigan from hand-dyed wool spun from her own sheep, which I wore for twenty years!

Their two daughters, Ira and Ana, who both went on to become healers, were a delight. Ana, then eight, proudly plink-plonked a tune I shall never forget on the piano, and we were taken to see Marko's monuments to the partisans in the valley. The level of passion the family showed in using art and creativity as an expression of 'the new direction of this energy', made me feel that the real artists, craftsmen and dancers were the way ahead.

Marko came with us to Venice, to show us the city through his eyes – he was writing an intuitive guide to Venice. He also introduced us to his friend Daniel, a composer originally from Argentina, and co-creator of the Ethos School, which saw Venice as a prime place to transmit the new energies, predominantly through art. Daniel's wife Maria showed us her artwork: a mandala representing the various aspects of life at the highest level – but within the base chakra. She was a woman after my own heart.

After this gentle time, we were not prepared for Florence! Vlyn particularly felt claustrophobic, fearful and disorientated, notably in the Medici Chapel. Austin told us of the Florence Conference a few years back, which brought together key New Age people, and had ended in chaos.

Two years later, when Austin and I returned to Florence for a Business Network meeting - invited by Ed Posey and his girlfriend Liz Hosken - we left feeling extremely sore about the divisive nature of the meeting. (Austin had earlier passed on his idea for *The Gaia Foundation* to Ed, and this ultimately became a beacon for ecological thinking through well-known people like Sting.) Although shortly afterwards Vlyn returned for several weeks to study painting, Florence has remained somewhere I would rather not be.

Back in Geneva I decided to do some bodywork and began massage with Sybillah and also with Ann Duvigneau, who later worked with the Peter Brook theatre company. I made a brief entry into Tai Chi, and Austin and I both did a form of movement with a Japanese expert, Tsuda.

Austin's bodywork of choice was Rolfing, and eventually his daughter France did a year's training in Rolfing in Boulder, Colorado. I remembered 'touchy-feely' Boulder (and 'arty-crafty' Santa Fe) from my time with Lyall, and I felt confident to recommend she go there. Now married to filmmaker Jean Daniel, and with two daughters, France recently set up her own health clinic in Geneva).

Through these things I began to see the possibility of a renewed relationship to life: one that emanated deeply but through the body 'downward', not through the mind 'upward'. It was a confirmation of connectedness but different and deeper.

At last, two years on, and to our utter relief, the focus moved away from the unmitigated intensity of our relating. And after three years at Pre-Cartlier we moved to La Rippe, a small village below the Jura, just over the French border and twenty miles out of Geneva.

Our landlord at La Rippe was Monsieur Luthi, a 'noble *paysan*', a smallholder, and the acknowledged leader of the village. One of our neighbours, Mr Dalziel from Ireland, had been in the village for eleven years. He told us that only this year had he put his foot on the bottom rung of the ladder (literally) when the village Christmas tree was being erected. It was in M. Luthi's gift to bestow this honour, and we felt fortunate to be his tenants.

Our house was part of a lovely old-style farmhouse, left to M. Luthi by his parents and converted almost from derelict into three rentable properties, although the third was not yet completed. We loved it and Austin insisted we furnish it throughout with Ikea (which was very new and daring then). He did not want anything of his old life (the antique formality of Malou's home in Confignon) to impinge on our new life. The fact that Austin couldn't change a light bulb and I did all the construction, says everything about the brilliance of Ikea.

Austin drove to Geneva each day, and often I went too. I had several short-term writing contracts over the years, including for a while, a regular feature for the UNHCR magazine, which both Piers and I had moved on to after Mark's work. Later I wrote occasional articles for WHO's *World Health* magazine, a glossy monthly which began from my work with Mental Heath and a feature I did on their Alcohol Programme.

The magazine's editor was John Bland, ex-features editor of the *Daily Telegraph Magazine* - so we had something in common. I'm sure John was much milder here than he would have been on the *Telegraph*, but of course the pace was so much slower: they could never have brought out a daily newspaper!

Austin and I usually met for lunch on my workdays, mostly at ILO near the WHO building, but sometimes in the summer we walked to the Botanical Gardens for a slice of pizza in their outdoor cafeteria. We often went out to dinner in favourite restaurants, maybe two or three times a week: *fillets de perch* by the lake was a favourite. Austin would enjoy a glass or two of wine, and I did occasionally, although at that time I rarely drank.

One of our greatest pleasures – for Austin more than me – was to walk most evenings into the meadows and fields behind our house. At weekends we often walked further along the pine-flanked road of the Jura, or drove up the mountain to walk in the pastures at the top.

A year or so after we moved in, Mark took a flat in a small apartment block at the bottom of the village. From then on he and we became firm friends and close companions in this faraway place we had landed in.

But London was never far away, and in 1983 I became a student at the first College of Healing course set up by *The Atlanteans* in Malvern. *The Atlanteans* were a group of people who from the 1960s had followed the teachings of a discarnate guide called HA – Helio Arcanophus, or High Priest of the Sun. According to this guidance, four core families had now taken an extraordinary leap of faith and bought a joint property just beneath the Malvern Hills – with separate living units – and set up Runnings Park, a healing and conference centre and hotel.

Although I was intuitively wary of the psychic nature of 'guidance', I didn't need much persuading to apply. To begin with, this was the first healing course I had ever heard of but, most important, its founder members were Ann and Tony Neate (it was Tony who channelled HA). It was they who had so impressed me at Bruce McManaway's first healing weekend, and I had met them subsequently at one of their own psychic development workshops. Ann and Tony were amongst the first healers to work at the new Bristol Cancer Help Centre.

I had two questions to take to the healing course. One: just because I could (feel what I assumed were healing energies) should I? The second: what level was I doing it at? In fact neither of these questions was answered until much later, but the experience was beyond anything I could have asked for. Runnings Park became my first 'spiritual home'.

The course comprised three separate weeks of study at Runnings Park, followed by extensive comprehension papers completed at home, and a final exam. The course had to be taken over not less than eighteen months. In subsequent years (and hundreds of students later) the course became far more extensive, to fit with Healing Federation rules of qualification, but it was nice to be first.

Out of the original eight participants (including Sir Victor Goddard who was over eighty and a former governor of Austin's school, Bryanston), I have had a lasting friendship with Barrie Anson, by then already a gifted homeopath. In fact it was Barrie who finally managed to cure my long-term, crazy heart palpitations that no one else could fathom, so I swear by his skills.

I felt that the College did not teach me anything I didn't already know, but it gave me a 'tool kit', a 'holdall' to deposit the myriad threads of information and experience I had gathered over the years. We did do healing practise but the received wisdom on how this should be done was not my way. I had already established a 'listening and responding to the body' way of healing, rather than opening up to spiritual energy and 'imposing' it on the body.

But the effect on me of Runnings Park was immeasurable. I began to extend my etheric energy work by asking the client to describe in words what the body was feeling. Through my journalist training, rather than any real counselling skills, I could begin to draw out the emotional causes of the body's discomfort. One woman, acting as a guinea pig, presented pain in the uterus, which we then found out was the body's reaction to the pain of her daughter's decision to live with her father.

A major lesson I learned was that being able to displace energy was not necessarily healing! Of the three younger men on our course only Barrie felt effectively 'neutral'. It did not surprise me that the wife of one of the students was agoraphobic, since his 'healing' energy was more like being wrapped up in cotton wool and giving yourself up. I could see why she couldn't go out! Another man 'healed' like Julius Caesar – shoving energy into you whether you wanted it or not.

It was not the first time I realised how careful we must be about who we allow to work on our energy fields. All sorts of personal foibles and emotional difficulties can be imposed on the client in the name of healing.

The certainty that to truly heal we must clear all the karmic shadow material and emotional blocks has stayed with me throughout my career. In the end I did not start working with clients until 1995, ten years after my completion at Runnings Park, and only when I felt I had reached a plateau of clarity. Even then I did not – and do not - call myself a healer.

What remained constant was my dislike of the psychic, though the Atlanteans were clearly a psychically-literate group. Amongst the healing arts they taught psychic development and psychic protection. On one occasion when a student complained of being attacked by entities, Ann Neate and David Furlong did a healing for her in her room. Unaware of this, her room-mate opened the door and was hit by 'a wall of energy', so strong it bounced her out again. It terrified her.

I knew I would never have the mental strength for some of this mental healing work. But I also became increasingly convinced that 'entities' could be regarded not as alien to us, but part of ourselves that had been 'lost' along the way, through some kind of emotional trauma, and was now 'bothering us' to be reintegrated. This was eventually born out when I began my client work.

There were aspects of psychic work that I had no idea about, like astral travel and 'meetings on the inner planes'. I didn't like channelling because it seemed to require the channel to leave the body to meet the guide, and therefore be in need of protection.

I felt the psychic and spiritual dimensions were literally different realities. Also, although I didn't have the language or experience then, my intuition told me that the spiritual realms were to be embodied now: we shouldn't need to 'travel' anywhere. So when Ann and Tony asked me in 1984 if I would write a book on HA's teachings, flattered though I was, I wasn't sure I wanted to do it.

I proposed to the families at Runnings Park that I write the story of their lives, rather than simply collate the teachings of HA. It appealed to me far more to chart their progress from platform mediumship – which is how Tony began in the late fifties with his first wife Murry Hope – to running a respected centre for spiritual education. I spent a cold week in January, living in Trisha and Henley Thomas's guest room, and interviewing the eight adults.

Ann, Tony, Trisha and Henley were original Atlanteans. Their children had been educated at Wynstones, the Steiner Waldorf School near Stroud, where Trisha and Henley taught and Tony was a governor. Diane and David Furlong were younger but had followed HA's teachings since they were nineteen, and Diane was just beginning to channel HA. Julie and Mick Jewell preferred to stay in the background, to concentrate on the practical side of things.

All that week Tony insisted I have a session with HA, yet it was a moment I was dreading. There were so many things in the teachings I was uneasy about, or experienced in a different way. I need not have worried. HA, through Tony, gave me a 'courtesy translation' of what he wanted to say, by couching it in suitable psychological language for me to understand. He also said that the teachings had come through in the appropriate form for the time – thirty years before. I felt appeased.

I wrote the book - to be published again by Alick through his new company *Gateway* - in four months, typing at the sitting room table in La Rippe. The only difficulty we had was choosing a title that everyone liked. In the end *Where There's Love: the story of a community and its guiding impulse* was agreed, though I'm not sure any of us were totally happy. Without my knowing they added a foreword by Sir George Trevelyan, which would not have been my choice.

The book was launched at Runnings Park, which was fun - except for the woman who told me my photograph on the back cover made me look like a shrew. I think it brought several people to Runnings Park, but otherwise for me it was a labour of love.

I graduated from the College at the end of 1985. Although the Atlanteans did most of the teaching there was input from outsiders, including two doctors. Our intake was also fortunate to have a Dutch woman, Hertha Larive, as principal and tutor. It was Hertha, as one of my final examiners, who told me in response to my nervousness and uncertainty that I was not, in fact, a healer but a spiritual teacher.

It was ten years before I had any idea what she meant, but in the meantime it was Barrie, to my eternal gratitude, who persuaded me to go to *Le Plan* in France in November 1983, where I found the real depth of experience I had been teetering around for so long.

CHAPTER ELEVEN

Le Petit Canadeau, an old convent set in a valley in Le Plan du Castellet, Var, Provence, had been the family home of Lorna St Aubyn for over twenty-five years. The beautiful pink main house sat sideways to the glorious ochre and olive valley, much of which Lorna owned and was laid to vines to produce 'the best rosé in the world'.

Lorna's daughter Minky (Alexandra) and son Teddy had their own small houses on the property, and above these on a terraced ridge was a strip of tumble-down stone cottages which, when I first went to Le Plan, was home to the vineyard worker and his family.

Eventually Lorna, the eternal builder, turned these into small living units: one for herself, one for Ruth White, and one spare. She also converted the huge ruin at the end of the terrace into a seminar room, plus accommodation for at least twelve people. The main house slept about the same number.

It was Tom Welch who had persuaded Lorna, after her divorce from Roger St Aubyn, to open up Le Plan as a spiritual education centre. Peter Dawkins and David Furlong had added their expertise by concluding that this was the 'sacral/root' chakra and an important energy centre.

As far as I was concerned I had found my true spiritual home. I could feel at once that the land resonated with my own imperative to explore this aspect of my psyche. Whereas Findhorn I perceived as the 'crown chakra', Le Plan represented the complete opposite and what to me was far more significant.

In that sense it was strange that Lorna's first 'core group' of young people, who were brimming with enthusiasm to help run the centre, were from Findhorn. In fact, Isabel Duquesne and Peter Harper did not stay long, and after a while, when several people had come and gone, it was clear that Lorna's idea of 'help' did not coincide with the idealism of those seeking to live in spiritual community. As she once said in a fit of irritation, she was 'used to servants'. She did not expect to run her centre by consensus, and it was never easy for either side.

I liked Lorna from the first. She had an extraordinary child-like quality and my first response was to want to look after her. She also had the fieriest temper I had ever encountered! If you were lucky enough to be on her side, she was the most loyal and tireless ally, but if she took against you, you certainly knew it.

In so many ways she was outrageously difficult, reacting to the hellishly lonely life of the 'spoilt little rich kid'. But she was also uniquely egalitarian and accepting, committed to using her wealth to further the cause of an alternative view of life. This was something that her son Teddy could never forgive her for and several years later maliciously chronicled in his brilliant, witty, best-selling Patrick Melrose novels. (Lorna was inordinately proud when he sold his first manuscript; but it was hard for those of us who knew her at this stage of her life to forgive this cruel depiction of his mother.)

My own strategy with Lorna was to stay small, stay loyal to Le Plan and never 'claim possession' of someone over Lorna. I played down my friendships with Alick Bartholomew and Tom Welch, for example, because instinctively I knew she had priority. On the whole Lorna gave and received far greater love and loyalty from men than women. But, barring a few (disastrous) hiccoughs, our friendship lasted as long as anyone else's at the time.

My first two-week seminar at Le Plan – and Lorna's second – was run by Peter and Elizabeth Gill on the subject of colour. Although it soon became obvious that much of the information came from Lilla's teachings anyway, and little of the work was new, the six of us (four students including Barrie Anson), had a wonderful time, chatting and enjoying each other's company in the glorious sunshine. It was enough to hook me in.

A two-week seminar always included 'excursions'. We usually went at least once to the nearest market town Le Beausset, and sometimes to the Wednesday market in Sanary.

This first time we also went to Bandol on the coast for a wine-tasting festival, where Lorna's wine was on show. But the place that left the greatest impression on me was our excursion to Le Thoronet, a Cistercian Abbey about twenty miles away.

The minute I entered the sparse, cavernous nave I felt myself inwardly screaming to get out. So I did, as soon as I could. The experience was profound and whether or not I had really known the terrors of being 'walled up' – which this felt like - it led me on to another thread of discovery.

The idea of the Cistercians began to fascinate me, and over the years Austin and I must have visited almost every Cistercian Abbey in France and Switzerland, including the original one set up by Bernard of Clairvaux as an antidote to the excesses of monastic life as he saw it. We even had a Cistercian Abbey a short distance beyond our home in La Rippe, which as part of the local golf club remained inaccessible until a decade after I left.

Exploring the true nature of the Cistercians, the Cathars and the Templars - and their relevance to the things I was experiencing - remained in the forefront of my mind during my whole time in France. And it pleased me when several years later Peter Dawkins told me that at the core of the Cistercians were Cathars. Unlike a large number of people who came to France I never felt personally in tune with the Cathars, but it made sense that there was a connection here in southeast France, as well as in the southwest.

Le Plan was always full of ghosts. Although my own relationship to past lives was fairly indifferent - even though I knew that strands from the past were echoing through this life now – other people vividly saw and heard the stories of their past lives while staying at Le Plan.

Many seminar participants were returning to re-experience scenes of terrible trauma and death from their time in the convent – which was a sister institution to the monastery at nearby Grand Canadeau that had been sacked during Disestablishment. It made sense of some of the jarring relationships found at Le Plan: too many of us had spent too many restricted monastic lives. Lorna, just like now, had been the Mother Superior.

After that first visit I returned to Le Plan for seminars twice a year, but from that moment on only those given by Ruth White. My roommate was often a wonderfully unique, funny, enthusiastic, therapist called Dinah Malloy.

Dinah reminded me of Joyce Grenfell's sketch when 'stately as a galleon....' she held court. We spent a lot of time shrieking with laughter and running around the place like a couple of demented nuns. The seriousness of her morning exercises and ablutions at 5am, were a constant source of merriment.

Although I had not read Ruth's books because at that time I did not understand her way of 'journeying', I had met her with Austin at Enson Hall in England, where she worked as a psychotherapist and counsellor. I had also had a couple of readings with her guide Gildas.

Like many of us who over several years went regularly to Le Plan, and have stayed loosely in touch as 'the French connection', I owe more to Ruth and her incredible way of working than I could ever repay. I am grateful for the friendships and sheer fun and enjoyment of those times, but also for the stark and almost unendurable difficulties of realisations that came too.

Although Ruth saw Gildas as a 'teaching guide', I admired most the way she could 'hold the space' for us for two whole weeks. Somehow, miraculously, through daily self-development work and synchronous, meaningful interactions - whether pleasant or uncomfortable - by the end of the seminar everyone had seen, touched and released what they needed most to release and moved mountains in their spiritual process.

The times with Ruth in Le Plan, however, represented an accelerated, confirming, and usually painful recognition of what I felt I was really doing. And in 1984, on a seminar excursion to the cavern in the mountains of St Baume, I had the revelation that gave me the biggest clue to what that actually was.

The cave at St Baume, carved into the mountainside, and then used as a Catholic church, was the place Mary Magdalene was reputed to have lived for the last thirty years of her life. The drive to St Baume, round nauseous hairpin bends, takes you to the foot of the mountain. From there a forty minute walk - through what feel like timeless, primal, druidic woods, alive with elemental shapes and energies - takes you winding up to the grotto. The climb was slow and magical, and entering the cavernous mountain church was simply quite wondrous.

When I sat quietly in a pew to drink in the atmosphere or lit a candle at the back of the cave, or walked slowly down to the chapel below and listened to Herve – Lorna's favourite and longest serving helper – playing the flute, I felt no particular input. Its full impact only came in when we got back to Le Plan.

As we all trooped into the house a new young core group member Siddharta, who obviously followed some Indian philosophy and whose real name I think was Derek – happened to open his arms out to hug the woman in front of me. As I went in I automatically did the same. In the microsecond of contact, I somehow experienced direct knowledge of the energy of the Magdalene through my whole body.

For better or worse, and as unlikely as it sounds, this is what I knew: The Magdalene represented the whore energy; but not in the way the Christian church depicted her and had repressed for all time, but in the sense of the most profound letting go of everything that is; to the acceptance, through the sacral chakra, of death and annihilation within matter. It is this abandonment, this supplication to 'nothingness' and to HIM, the Christ – which in some way he is simultaneously empowering her to do – that SHE 'seeds' the Christ, through the third eye.

Although this event is wholly simultaneous, it was SHE who somehow instigates it within the simultaneity. This circulation of polarised energy was the principle of integration that constituted the goal of human existence. This was the metaphor for the integration of spirit and matter in the human being and in humanity as a whole. To me it immediately answered questions about why there was so much rape and incest in the world. At the raw, material edges of this spiritual 'truth', the imperative of these energies – un-integrated and unconscious – could be expressed like that.

The moment was so powerful and all-pervading that all I could do was cry. I was overcome with this revelation for five days, during which time I was confused by the role of Siddharta. It took those electric five days to realise that he was the mediator, nothing more, and he had no idea what had taken place.

This experience became the cornerstone of my search, and although the idea of the Magdalene as metaphor for a new relationship to the feminine and to the earth became known to some extent at Le Plan (and also became *lingua franca* in the field many years later) I hugged my own experience to myself. In fact, one of my closest women friends, Tess Nind, who I met at Le Plan in 1986, felt as closely allied as I was to what eventually became clear was the 'over-lighting' energy at Le Plan.

Although this revelation was the most profound and important, other powerful experiences continued. On one occasion John Anstey at *The Telegraph* asked me to search for a property near Geneva that could be reconstructed into an ecological house and featured periodically in the magazine. I had no idea where to go because Geneva was so expensive, and decided on a whim to use the pendulum.

The indication was Lamastre, a small village in the Ardeche, in a valley near Valence. Austin immediately pointed on the map to a place nearby and told me intuitively that something significant had happened there.

The following weekend we drove to France to research the *Telegraph* house, but near 'Austin's spot' we stopped and got out, and without waiting he began charging up the thickly forested hillside. It soon became obvious that all the paths had been closed, with fallen trees placed across to block access. They clearly didn't want anyone up there.

I gave up the climb in my unsuitable shoes but Austin, undaunted, headed straight up the middle, not reappearing until some time later. What he saw had shaken him. At the top, he said, was an old stone altar – whether or not used for current practices he did not know – but what he did know was that in some era there had been sacrificial killing there!

How he picked the exact spot I will never know, but that night in our hotel in Lamastre the heavens opened to an electrical storm and howling gale that were beyond coincidence. Whatever Austin had done the elementals were released.

The only other time I have known the elementals disturbed so royally was when Isobel came to Geneva. Some time earlier, during a meditation at Runnings Park, David and Diane Furlong had recognised my difficulties and tried to help me combat the cripplingly oppressive energies of Geneva. Their explanation was that the Deva of the River Rhone – which ran fast through the middle of Lake Geneva – felt trapped by the energy bowl that enclosed the lake, located as it was between the Jura and the Alps.

But when Isobel McGilvray came to stay she 'saw' the energy metaphorically in a way I could understand. She felt it was her task to release the hitherto undiscovered and ignored primal feminine energy. That night we witnessed the most incredible howling gale that rattled the windows of the house all night. 'She' was clearly pleased to be out!

I have only ever talked about these parts of my life in a limited way and to very few people. I'm pretty sure that I have never been seen as anything but 'normal'. But I believed that, for whatever reason, I had chosen to live 'an archetypal life' and that my life experiences, or the inner affects of those experiences, mirrored the past and present evolution of humanity. Whether I liked it or not, as well as addressing personal karma I was attuned to 'the collective'. I say this only to explain why what seemed to be an exciting and adventurous life – which it was - was at the same time so painful.

An astrological reading by Darby Costello – well respected in her field - went some way to explain this. She told me that my task was to teach men to love. In order to do so the heart had to break over and over again because it was only in the breaking that another level of the heart could be reached. To her it seemed a 'harsh and rocky road', one that she would not care to tread. I would always take men to the edge of their hearts until they broke, where the partnership would reach a new level, or - as mine was about to do yet again - would end.

She also told me that I had a life that was more bizarre than I would wish for myself, and that although I knew what I was doing, I would not really understand it until I was much, much older.

It all made sense, but the problem with astrological readings is that you can also be told things you don't want to hear. Darby's skill caused me real heartache, not only once but twice. I had met her first during my endless 'waiting for Lyall' period: introduced to me by Isobel. We already had much in common. Lyall's book *Lightning Bird* was the extraordinary story of a man Adrian, who was once Darby's boyfriend. He had captured Lyall's imagination because he was a renowned shamanistic 'white witch doctor', and had tragically died during an epileptic seizure. Darby had been devastated.

Lyall had written to me three or four times since I had been in Geneva – which still caused my heart to somersault – so I knew about his 'homage to Africa'. I also knew that he had sold his Oxford house, acquired a flat as a central London base, married and divorced a journalist called Jacquey, and was now living alone in southern Ireland.

But it had been Darby's reading for Lyall that made it clear to him I would not be a permanent feature in his life. So it was like a dagger in my heart when, these years later, Darby's reading for Austin condemned me to a similar fate!

Lilla had said my relationship with Austin would last three years. In a way she was right, but it soldiered on for almost seven. Since neither of us was strong enough to sever links – we did still love each other very much – we ground inexorably on. Although for a long time I put my head in the

135

sand, I think we both had the underlying sense that at some fundamental level this was not working.

In some ways life went on as usual, but what became increasingly agonising for me was Austin's loving, yet determined and secret, detachment that allowed him to look beyond us. After a while I realised he was sparing nothing to find new lovers. I saw evidence that he had joined a dating agency in London. I also found letters to a woman he had recently met – at a New Age community he was supporting in Ireland – asking her to marry him! These *sorties* came to nothing, but unlike me he was not hoping for the best for us, or waiting.

When I realised this, something irrevocably broke inside me, and I had to face the truth. It was helpful to have a comment from Gildas that we did still love each other on a soul level, which made sense of our continuing closeness. But it didn't stop the loneliness and despair of a long, difficult and reactive separating process because, apart from an occasional hint or two, it was not openly stated. I was never sure if it was real or not.

In 1986 a marvellous opportunity arose, for me to edit the occasional *Appropriate Technology for Health* newsletter, for the Strengthening Health Services (SHS) Division of WHO. Claudine Brelet, who had the niche before me, had left Geneva to work in Paris for a while.

I loved the job, which was to produce a sixteen-page magazine on worldwide primary health care initiatives. I continued Claudine's format and added my own enthusiasm, and since I was a one-man-band I decided to include, subversively, some alternative energies to my 'appropriate' magazine. If only they knew that I chose my themes by picking Angel Cards from Findhorn's *Inner Game*.

The Angel for my first edition was 'Purpose', so I depicted on the cover a mountain summit with a flag for *'Health for All by the Year 2000* – then the current WHO slogan. For an issue on inner city miseries in developing countries, I picked the angel of 'Light', so headlined it *Light on the City*. I would also use quotes from people and ideas with an added dimension of meaning.

My job was to write articles myself by interviewing the experts in and around WHO and other UN agencies, and to put together or edit other people's words from projects around the world. Occasionally, when I was in England anyway, I would visit a relevant organisation, like the Institute of Child Health at the *School of Hygiene and Tropical Medicine,* to gather information.

I also had to design and lay out the text, which I learned on the hoof. I had met, through Sybillah's dance class, a woman called Maggie, who I was amazed to realise I had been aware of in *Petticoat* days. She had been a whiz-kid layout artist and worked on new magazine dummies for IPC, but like me had been lured to Geneva by a partner.

Maggie's main job now was as a fitness instructor, but she generously gave me a lesson in how to lay out columns and drop in pictures – in those days with a ruler and arithmetic! My illustrator for ATH was Jacqueline Bradshaw Smith, who I knew through the *World Health Magazine* was the best artist for 'multicultural' faces.

It was all hard work and good fun. I enjoyed 'going to the office' for three months a year for the next three years, and being part of the organisation. The magazines seemed to be appreciated and considered useful, and my 'Cities' issue received a short hand-written accolade of approval from the incumbent Director General, Hafdan Mahler.

At the end of those three years the magazine was taken out of my hands because desktop publishing was just coming into view and my old way of production was too expensive. I had used a local printer, chosen by Claudine, who happened to be English, and I liked him because he understood what I wanted. When ATH was handed to a competent computer person this decision looked risky to me: a computer expert is not a journalist. I had already left Geneva by then, but I believe the magazine just folded.

1986 was a busy and hair-raising year. There were many significant meetings. At one point I was exhausted through lack of sleep and more or less at the end of my tether, so I decided to ask Lorna if I could join a seminar half-way through. This is an unforgivable request in terms of group dynamics, but to my astonishment she and Ruth said yes.

The seminar was entitled *Finding the Inner Guide*, which I hadn't thought relevant to me as I was inherently distrustful of guides and guidance. It seemed to me that in these realms it was harder to distinguish the psychic from the spiritual. But I couldn't have been more wrong. A couple of the women in the group were hostile to my intrusion and wouldn't free up a bed by sharing a room. So Lorna, with extraordinary kindness, offered me the spare bed in her own personal bedroom. I remember my first night in that room when I 'begged someone to help me sleep' I suddenly 'saw' a nun at the foot of my bed. She was holding my feet, and as I felt the energy drain from my head I fell asleep!

I had missed the session where the group had found their inner guide, but Dinah, determined I shouldn't miss out, took me aside on a trip to the beach at Cassis. As Ruth's occasional co-leader, she gave me my own private meditation. I had no idea what to expect – especially as at that stage my ability to allow inner pictures was hopeless. I was better at 'insights' that imaging. But I was astonished at what came through.

Dinah, who had a guide called Keith - because he looked like actor Keith Michel!! - led me to an awareness of a monk called Hubert. He was small and round, obviously French, with a great sense of humour! For good measure, my 'inner animal' was a black panther with orange almond-shaped eyes. I was still distrustful, but I decided it did no harm to believe it.

As humour would have it, Hubert talked to me in images! If I asked him something, I could feel him slightly off to my right. I would wait until I was sure I had the image he was sending, then feel into the meaning of the picture and interpret it into words.

It was quite a long process, but it seemed to work. Someone told me later, that this was the way I could most readily accept the idea of guidance at this stage, but that Hubert was just a tiny aspect of the width of vision I would experience eventually. He stayed with me in that gentle, friendly form for six years.

The most significant bi-product of that seminar, apart from Hubert, was meeting Jay Ramsey and Carole Bruce. Although Jay was fourteen years younger than Carole – who was a divorced woman with four children – they looked good together. Jay was a poet, and the sheer force of his intensity drew me to him first. We enjoyed running rings round each other in our spiritual intellectualism.

Carole was quietly beautiful, and although she touched me hugely when I melted into the safety of her motherly energy, at that point I judged her to be 'less up to speed' than Jay. It was a gross misjudgement. In the years to come Carole and I were like two peas in a pod. We talked and shared about everything under the sun, and for a long while I valued her as a woman and a friend more highly than anyone.

At another seminar I met Tess Nind, who became the firmest of friends instantly. She, too, became a Le Plan regular and was vital to my well being for many years until her death in 2005: in some ways she eventually took the place of Vlyn. Tess was eleven years older than I was, a Gemini, and we didn't stop talking from that first day.

Tess's identity was as a vicar's wife, although we met at the most difficult period of her life when she was going through a divorce. The church was the foundation of her life and her spirituality at that time, and marriage, especially to a priest, was sacrosanct. It took many years for her to trust that there could be meaning in this most devastating event.

Tess's job was community organiser. She had lived for seven years with her husband in a parish in Jamaica, and later, in Brixton, where Rob had a real commitment to black politics, she set up a ground breaking voluntary agency *Help 21*, for local people. When we met, she was Director of *Advance*, a government funded agency for volunteer training in London, but like many of us on the path, soon after we met Tess had to go through the indignities of letting go 'old form'. I was with her when she literally collapsed with exhaustion and after a seventeen-day sleep cure had to leave her old world behind.

Tess particularly enjoyed groups and was determined to form them! As another enthusiast for the work of Alice Bailey she came storming into Le Plan, to form us into a 'tenth group'. As it happened Lorna, Ruth, Dinah and I were already forming a gentle bond, but all of us were allergic to the idea of being corralled into a 'group'.

In June that year, while Austin was in India, I went on the first of two-month long trips to America. I stayed with a friend of Austin's, psychotherapist Jane Tear. When she suggested I take her place at a summer camp conference with Robert Bly in Portland, Maine, I couldn't believe my luck. Robert Bly to my mind was the only person talking about a new kind of male, connected to the earth.

After a quick hop to San Francisco and Los Angeles to meet Linda Larson's brother Jon on campus at Berkeley, and back, I took the Greyhound bus to Maine with no idea what to expect. To my surprise I met Robert Bly almost immediately because he was picked up in the same van as me. My instant reaction was not good!

The camp itself was a bit gross and cold, and badly organised, and the whole tense experience brought insights tumbling in, in totally unexpected ways. I began to understand something new about 'maleness', but in the most negative sense. I saw Bly manipulate his audience unmercifully, moving constantly between the father and the hero archetype which caused projections to fly.

I didn't speak to Robert, except one morning, when to my shock and horror, he suddenly stood up in front of everyone (there were eighty people) and pointed at me. 'Did you write *The Wise Virgin?* Why didn't you say so?' Apparently he had discovered the book two years before and had loved the ending particularly and recommended it around! He demanded

I stand up and tell the audience what it was about. Put on the spot like that I could hardly remember my name. It was a truly embarrassing moment.

His fans loved him, but another woman I met, a novelist with a PhD, also rejected the 'groupie/guru' structure of the conference and we decided to leave a day early. She kindly offered me a lift to Connecticut, which in itself led to another weird experience.

By the time we got to her home it was late and she offered me a bed for the night. Her husband took us both out to dinner, which was charming, but over dinner she told me about her fifteen-year old son who was schizophrenic, and insisted I should meet him 'because we talked the same language'. The warning light went on.

I knew from my experience with my millionaire friend Robert, and also from Sylvia, that the nebulous energies I could reach quite sanely could act like nectar to a disturbed mind. I didn't want to go down that route again, but as I gently tried to extricate myself she suddenly freaked out and went hysterical. (Jane Tear told me, on my return to New York, that her behaviour indicated she was borderline schizophrenic too).

Whatever, it frightened me, and while she was in the ladies room I asked her husband if he would take me to a nearby hotel. Clearly he knew the signs because he assured me his wife would be well again in the morning – after they'd had sex. I said that was fine for him, but since I wasn't the one having the sex I'd rather he helped me leave now, which he did.

At the Bly conference I had also met a woman called Ann Wiseman, who told me about an international Dream Conference to be held at the Carlton University in Ottawa the following week. Since it was cheaper to go there – including the cost of the conference and travelling by Amtrak – than to stay in hotels in New York, I phoned to book a place. And for someone who doesn't dream, except at seemingly significant moments, it was a riveting experience!

Papers were presented by the top people in dream work: academics, scientists and psychotherapists. The most gruelling part, though, was breakfast, when every participant brought out his or her 'dream book' and proceeded to relate the nightly dream, blow-by-blow, to anyone who would listen. Ann Wiseman turned out to be the most interesting person there.

Ann was an artist and therapist from Cambridge, Mass. who worked using artistic materials. A video of her work was shown in which she encouraged the parent of a disturbed child to literally build a picture of the family situation, using bits and pieces of fabric and paper. She was thereby able – through the parent – to effect a healing on the child.

I was captivated, especially when over dinner she did an experiment with me, using the orange peel and strips of sweet pepper on my plate, to give me a picture of my current situation! These healing techniques are common today, but her demonstration was enough to persuade me to return to America a few months later to do some therapeutic work with her.

Back in Geneva, Austin and I were flailing badly. For a long time I had been feeling unwell. I had a lot of dizziness connected to headaches. I had done several therapeutic sessions with Ruth in Guildford, and sometimes when I was feeling especially unsteady, the prospect of seeing Ruth and the fun of staying with her overnight was all that kept me going. She even let me stay in her flat while she went away.

I can only assume that it was all due to the fear of what in my heart I knew to be impending change and separation. Austin and I had quite naturally evolved to a mutual understanding that I would soon be leaving La Rippe, although we still did not say – or even believe – we would be parting forever. Our letters were warm and sad.

I had put my London flat up for sale, and it was now a matter of deciding where on earth to live. I had been to the summer exhibition at the Royal Academy, and it was quite clear that the 'greenness' of England did not appeal to me. I preferred paintings of dry, rocky terrain.

My second visit to the States, while Austin was in Madagascar, came in November. I went to Boston to see Ann

Wiseman for therapeutic help, and then on to New York where I stayed in B & Bs. I was also determined to visit an astrologer who lived in New Haven, Connecticut, who I had consulted by tape a year earlier.

Over a cup of tea, John Ramsay told me that only two people had ever found their way to his door: I and another Leo, Sophia Milewska. A French woman living in England, Sophia's birthday was the same day as mine! What was more, he had confirmed to her that she and her husband Peter Afford would soon work as part of a core group in a spiritual community in Provence – Le Plan!

In my own reading John had turned to the importance of France for me, but now he added the idea of the 'over-lighting' of 'six sisters' by Mary Magdalene. The Magdalene, he said, made the seventh sister of the Pleides! I couldn't help doing my sums. With Tess and Sophia we were six!

In December everything fell into place. This was the moment when Ruth was already planning to give up her life in Guildford, to rent one of Lorna's small houses and live permanently in Le Plan. At Christmas Austin and I went down south for a break, and he saw to his astonishment that Le Castellet, the bijou medieval walled village near Le Plan, was where in a dream he had seen me living.

This was my future home.

PART THREE

PROVENCE

CHAPTER TWELVE

One of the most prized possessions in my life was my VW Polo, the first new car I had ever owned. I bought *Poppy* on the French side of the border in January 1987. She was my pride and joy and my passport to independence and freedom. The day after we picked her up, Austin kindly drove me to Le Plan, where Lorna offered me Minky's house to stay while I looked for somewhere to live. Austin went straight back by plane which made me sad.

I divided my time between house hunting and putting together my second ATH newsletter. After one or two false starts I really did find a house in Le Castellet and thanks to Lorna's committed support, set things in motion. I then returned to Geneva by train where, despite rolling inexorably on towards separation - by packing up and clearing away and completing lots of work for WHO - I continued to believe I would now commute between our two homes and we would remain in partnership.

So on the night before I left, 7 May 1987, despite knowing Austin had been deceiving me for years I was devastated to find out – in the most chance way – that he had been living a secret life. That evening, at the last minute, we decided to do the *I-Ching*, and Austin's card plainly indicated that he was having a relationship! There was suddenly no-where to hide, and he had to explain.

He told me that two months earlier he had met a woman, thirty years younger, who lived with her family in Marseille – only forty minutes from where I was going to live! She was a gifted psychic, he said, a student of Alice Bailey, and he was going to marry her! In that moment my world crumbled.

I began, then and there, to take down pictures and remove anything else I had planned to leave behind in the naive expectation that La Rippe would still be a home for me. I finally went to bed at 2am and after two hours sleep, took the train to my new life in a fog of unhappiness. When I arrived at Le Plan, at her new little house on the ridge, Lorna sat knitting in comfortable, kindly silence as I wept my heart out. And yet I knew in my heart it was for the best. Although I couldn't understand why I had to suffer any more gratuitous blows from life, whether I liked it or not, a new life had to begin.

With Herve's help – Lorna allowed me to hire him – I set about painting white throughout my beautiful medieval house and planning a workable kitchen corner in the salon. I also chose carpet for the upstairs sitting room, though tiles were more usual in Provence. Ruth was installed at Le Plan and together we made journeys to Toulon or Aix en Provence to buy fabric, organise utilities and generally look around us in wonder and tell ourselves 'we live here!'

My only consternation was realising the dishonesty of both the estate agent and the sellers regarding ongoing legal proceedings about a window. They had told me about the litigation, but implied that the window they had installed in the main bedroom - which the neighbours were now objecting to because it offered a view onto their balcony (if you leaned out of the window) - was only slightly larger than the original it replaced.

In fact, when the result was known I discovered there had been no window at all and the ruling was that I had to have the space walled up again! I was beside myself with worry. A house with a bedroom with no light and no air was a nightmare, and besides anything else would have no resale value.

Lorna, her builder Francis, and I tried to find a solution, but a skylight, for example, was not an option. Finally, in despair, on the day before I had to comply I took Lorna with me and we begged the neighbour to have mercy on me. Unfortunately he was merciless, but eventually agreed that I could keep the window provided I put in small squares of opaque glass.

At least I had light, and two tiny glass ventilation bricks. Then, on Lorna's suggestion, Francis made a large curved window in the wall between the two bedrooms, where I hung Laura Ashley white lace curtains, so I got attractive 'second-class' air. It served to calm me, and the system worked well, even with visitors, but until I sold the house several years later I lived with the shadow of fear that it might be difficult.

Almost immediately Austin wrote loving letters. He offered to support me financially with amazing generosity while I found my feet, and for several months gave me £1000 a month. Understandably Pascale began to complain after a while and although I was scared to lose it, I knew my needs did not justify this amount. I suggested a much lower figure and within a year I asked him to stop my 'maintenance' altogether. It was better that way.

But more than that, within weeks of our separation I began to suspect from his letters that he was seriously wondering what on earth he had done, and whether he had been taken in by psychic glamour. He was charmed by her ability to 'channel' information, including that they were meant to be together to run a healing centre.

Without any thought for how it might be for me, he asked me to meet Pascale and brought her over for tea at a cafe in Le Castellet. I screwed up all my courage to make it easy for them, and despite excruciating discomfort could not dislike her. She was very quiet and very young.

The saddest thing was that after his marriage two months later, on 18 July, (attended by friends like Mark and Celia, who loved Austin but were loyal to me too) he spent the rest of his life regretting his haste. Austin and Pascale lived in La Rippe for the next three years, but eventually moved back to France on his retirement – even though he had always dreamed of retiring to England. He bought a huge joint property with Pascale's parents and grandmother. The healing centre never materialised.

Pascale's mother Andre was a determined woman, and although in some ways when I eventually met her I liked her, she acted like a raging demon to Austin. Andre's anger made Austin's life a misery. He didn't deserve that. He knew he had made his bed and must lie in it, but Pascale never seemed able to separate from the mother and show love to Austin.

I set a pattern and spent July and August in England, letting the house in Le Castellet to Ann and Tony Neate for a week. Those two months were always too hot in France for me. I had agreed to cat-sit in Southfields for my long-time journalist friend, Jan and her husband Barrie, so I could see my friends in London. (Jan, who I met on *Petticoat*, and Sally who I knew even earlier on *Fabulous* are still in my life, and over the years we have met as often as we can.)

I then went down to Vlyn, which coincided with the 'Harmonic Convergence' on August 17th. This, apparently, was a spectacular moment in history when light and energy were poured on to the planet at an unprecedented level. It meant a great deal to many people, and while Vlyn and I did join people like Tom Welch and Lorna for a meditation at Buckfast Abbey, it meant little to me. I felt sick and was suddenly angry with Austin.

Vlyn and I decided to do an intuitive painting course on Dartmoor – more for her, I thought, than me. But when she played up, missed the whole point and disrupted things in the group, as only Vlyn could do, I got disheartened. I was fed up and angry with her, too, and thought I would never go there again (which I felt fairly often anyway!). I missed the companionship of Austin and being able to talk things through. I'd lost the plot on what life was about.

I returned to France on 1 September. A letter from Austin suggested he 'had made a mistake', and in a tearful phone call he told me 'the laughter has gone out of my life'. I wanted to make it better but I knew that these loving messages were leading me to a false sense of security. Talking to each other in the wrong way was stirring things up. I wished he'd go away.

Later that month I went back to Geneva for a long weekend to sort out some *Newsletter* material at WHO, and to act as contact point for discussions on a film SHS wanted to make on district primary health care. On my last visit to England I had found a film-maker and a scriptwriter – recommended by an *Open University* contact, Janice Dolley, and my boss John Martin had invited them both to Geneva to put some ideas together.

I was lucky to stay with Mark, but it was bizarre to be in La Rippe and not 'go home'. I met Austin for lunch in our favourite spot, the Botanical Gardens, and he was depressed enough to talk about his new life as 'an arranged marriage'. I guess from that moment on, whether it was fair or not, whether I liked it or not, I became Austin's emotional stability in a life of continuing upset and anxiety. It was often painful to hear his voice or read his letters, but as the hurt grew less over the next years he became my truest friend.

Back in my house in Le Castellet, which was beginning to look good – and it was a lifesaver to have Herve popping in and out - I had my ATH work for now, and a regular aerobics class, but it felt pretty empty. Sometimes I would leave the class, which seemed full of young mothers, feeling bereft.

The land was beautiful and I looked at it a great deal, and as Vlyn once said cuttingly 'you've got friends and freedom, what more do you want?' I know, I know, but much of my life in France was about sitting or strolling alone for days on end, wondering what on earth I was doing.

The area was yet another 'womb', and I often felt the familiar heaviness and inertia, though it was different to Geneva. At the same time, I loved the place: paradoxically, I felt a vibrancy there. It was as though my body was in a constant state of abundant expectancy, and indeed many people living there experienced it as highly creative.

Although I found 'living close to nature' a difficult idea to comprehend because I did not tune into trees or nature spirits, I did feel the nuances of the land, the spirit of the place, acutely. It was as though my body lined up with the centre of the earth, not the surface. I felt 'shifts' right now very strongly, things that were in the 'collective air', in resonance with astrological configurations, as well as my own shifts when a meditation with Ruth, for example, would affect a release.

Le Castellet was a bijou village banned to cars in the summer with chic shopping for tourists. The tourists arrived in

149

great numbers when the shops opened in mid-afternoon and then the village came alive. I often felt I was living in a hypermarket, especially on Sundays, in the summer, and on Christmas day. Winters were better, but by the time I left six years later, the popularity of the area meant it had become almost unbearable.

My passion was to wander down in the early morning sunshine when Le Castellet was empty, to the only cafe for coffee. Occasionally I would leave very early to sit in a cafe overlooking the marina in Bandol, and buy *The Times* as a treat. I became a local coffee and croissants connoisseur and when Ruth was around one of our favourites places was fourteen kilometres away in Cassis. I loved France for being open at 7am.

Le Castellet was a village for locals and I don't think they ever got over their suspicion of a single woman living alone amongst them. The only other comparable *etranger* was an English woman – who totally ignored me. I only discovered later, when she moved to the next village, that 'Elaine' was Paula Yates' mother.

Sir Anthony Deakin, Churchill's one-time Private Secretary (who I never saw) and his Rumanian wife, Pussy (who I passed the time of day with), also lived there. It was through their friendship that Lorna first came to the area. But my only real friend was Annie Maynard, a French woman my age who served in the leatherwork shop next door. We chatted a lot and it was through her that finally my French took off, because she did not speak English.

Annie was divorced from the local postman, but her love in life was politics. When I met her she was having an affair with the powerful local mayor (who Lorna hated for his influence and corruption in local affairs). In the end Annie decided to play safe and marry an older, retired politician who had once been in charge of a district in French North Africa. She moved to his house in Sanary, as a safe haven for her daughter Celine who had learning difficulties.

A few yards from my house, next to the Mairie, was the lovely church of St Mary Magdalene. I often popped in. I had first seen it on one of Lorna's excursions during an early seminar. Even then it had caught my imagination and I had sat in the church for longer than I meant to, mesmerised by the bright blue light coming through the stained glass window.

This church became a refuge for me in really miserable moments, but I would also often drive to the church on the hill above Le Beausset at Le Beausset Vieux. I would plead with the Magdalene to help me – as so many people had done before me, judging from the many votive pictures in the side chapel depicting the miracles she had brought.

I did a great deal of knitting in Le Castellet – a mountain of simple mohair jumpers! I would often take Poppy to my favourite wide sweep of beach at St Cyr Les Lecques and sit knitting with my back to the wall, as the later afternoon sun was setting.

I still never doubted that somewhere there was 'meaning' and that I had a purpose, and that by being here I was moving even further into my exploration and understanding of consciousness in matter. I continued to read copiously, but there were endless times of quiet despair, isolation and excruciating boredom.

Lorna continued to be kindness itself. She included me in trips and lunches, and on one occasion introduced me to one of her potential seminar leaders, Soozi Holbeche. I knew of Soozi's 'special relationship' and devotion to the highly regarded spiritual teacher, the late Paul Solomon – who I never quite took to from earlier days. But, although friendship wasn't feasible as she always gave the impression of being too busy doing bigger and better things, I was pleased to experience a healing session with her.

Her work was expensive, but each session took three hours. Working with crystals, she touched on many past life patterns and pains, and I had two helpful and strangely comforting insights. One was that I had never been happy on this planet, only in my 'real home', somewhere far away in the universe, which made sense.

In the second I saw myself in a cartoon character kind of way as a 'giant' who had been forced to go to earth. When I arrived I was so huge that when I bent down to pick up a tiny seedling (earth people) in my hand, I knew I was 'too big' to be here. I had so much love to give and I was totally inappropriate. In utter dejection and disappointment I fell to the ground. I did not fit on earth, and could not go back to heaven. I was destined to live in the ethers between the two, which is exactly how I had felt all my life!

Over the years the metaphor of this experience, its impact and its resolution became an important tool for explaining humanity's collective woundedness from the 'Fall from Grace'. Ultimately it led to one of the basic tenets of my understanding; that we are born with an original 'soul wound', not original sin.

In October 1987 there were hurricane winds in England, when millions of trees were flattened. The energies felt chaotic. At the end of that month I went back to Geneva for a couple of weeks' work at WHO, to put together the editorial of my final newsletter. Staying with Mark was still bizarre, especially when Austin and Pascale brought down 'my' sheets for me to borrow.

From there I flew to England. Leaving Austin always made me sad, but so it was for him. He told me often in the following years that he loved me more than anyone else in the world and his heart was constantly in pain. Yet we were both resigned to our fates. After two busy weeks with friends, Tess and I drove back together to France in her car to attend a seminar. We learned a lesson from that drive.

We had a one-night stopover at Chateau Thierry and then hurtled on towards Provence. As usual we never stopped talking, rattling on and on, hardly taking breath, not eating and noticing very little. An hour from our destination we finally stopped at a service station, but the moment we stepped out of the car (into a puddle) we both felt horribly ill. We managed to drag ourselves into the cafe, order a coffee and croissant and use the loo, and stagger back into the car again.

The next morning my hair began to fall out in frightening amounts, so much so that I asked Gildas what was happening. Apart from being practical and suggesting a daily thirty second bout of ultra violet light on my head for two weeks, he told us we had journeyed down completely unearthed, so that when we touched the ground in a puddle it was like throwing an electric fire into a bath! He suggested that in future we talk less, eat more and get out and hug a tree occasionally!

As always the seminar was intense and challenging, facing parts of ourselves we no longer needed to hang on to. I also found a 'lamp' practitioner for my hair, a kinesiologist in Le Beausset. I also phoned Barrie Anson who promised to send some homeopathic potions. In that sense the crisis was soon over, and over the years Tess and I both calmed down and managed to earth better, but those were heady electric days.

And Tess now had a home in France, too. Although she continued to live and work in London, Lorna had found her a small apartment, three floors up at the top of a typical Provencal house in the old square at Le Beausset. Her plan was to come down as often as she could, and to let the flat out at other times, although that didn't happen very often.

Although we all came and went constantly, our 'network of community' was growing. Despite being weighted down with female energy, we had a huge amount of fun. On the whole we got on very well, and were all predisposed to enjoying ourselves! This was our first Christmas together, and it established a kind of tradition.

On Christmas Eve we had supper at Le Plan, prepared by Herve. He then drove us in the minivan – all except Lorna - up the mountain road to La St Baume. Alongside crowds of other people carrying candles and lanterns, we walked up to the Grotto for midnight mass. The mass went on for an hour and a half, much too long, but it was good to have done it, and when we got to the bottom again Herve poured us all hot chocolate. We got home at 4am.

I managed to sleep until 10am, waking to glorious sunshine, and stayed in bed until one! I had tea with Tess and then we changed for dinner at Ruth's, where we played silly games and had a generally cosy time. It was established that Ruth had Christmas, I had New Year, and Tess had Epiphany. We enjoyed the routine. The only rule was that we never did the washing up in anyone else's house.

This year was slightly different. With the idea of 'a group' forming and Tess's determination to make it formal, Dinah stayed on, and we held our first official meeting. For me it was ten days of confusion and increasing fury. The more Tess warmed to her subject of 'our group' in Le Plan, the more the rest of us resisted the idea. And, as miraculous as it was that Sophia and Peter Afford were now at Le Plan, there was no way Lorna would have accepted a core group member as equal in status to us. I didn't even mention it.

Whatever the reality of it all, after endless conversations and tuning into our various forms of guidance, including Hubert who gave the group some nice pithy images, we never quite found a focus. This was a huge disappointment to Tess, who as a relative newcomer to the glamorously vibrant and psychically charged New Age energies, understandably found it all more 'important' than we sceptics did!

Tess's vision had rather changed a gentle and cosy grouping, though not our friendships. But I was also relieved. Apart from anything else, it gave me the opportunity to get to know Sophia – who is like a sister to me today – and Tess and I were able to explore the Magdalene energy in our own separate ways.

After our meeting I went to Geneva and enjoyed getting back to the *Newsletter* layouts. It was far more satisfying and much less 'head-stuff'. Meetings with Austin continued to be painful. Carrying my own heavy heart through feeling bereft was hard enough, but at times carrying his heart, too, seemed unfair.

From Geneva I flew to London, where I took part in my first meeting as a Trustee of Lorna's *Michaelmas Trust* at her other home in Parsons Green. Lorna, Nick Rose, David Furlong and John Gordon had invited me to join them as a trustee when Tom Welch retired through over–commitment. Michaelmas offered small grants and loans to individuals and projects that could not attract funding elsewhere, usually because they were considered too 'alternative'.

For example, it was a Michaelmas low-interest loan that supported Anghous Gordon in establishing Ruskin Mill near Stroud. Ruskin became a highly successful creative centre for craft and woodsman skills, and an education centre for socially disturbed children, based on the work of Rudolf Steiner. Michaelmas would also sponsor training in what were then unusual therapies, such as reflexology, and we raised money for *Visions of Hope*, a video film on near death experience.

The job of trustee begged a lot of questions for me. Sometimes I wondered how people had the confidence to ask, and whether there weren't more deserving people who would never dream of expecting someone else to pay for their dreams.

But I was honoured to take part and did my best to evaluate requests, although sometimes we were just signatories to Lorna's decisions. After a while *Friends of the Earth* became a major beneficiary. We financed a PhD student's research on Nirex's proposal to bury nuclear waste in an underground bunker at Sellafield. Her report contributed to the idea being abandoned.

Apart from anything else, a Michaelmas meeting was a great excuse for a chat with old friends and lunch at the restaurant round the corner. At this particular lunch I heard that Lyall had agreed to take part as a keynote speaker in this year's *Mystics and Scientists Conference*, held annually by the Wrekin Trust and subsequently by the Scientific and Medical Network. Apparently one of David Furlong's friends, the conference organiser, had bumped into Lyall in Watkins bookshop, and taken the opportunity to invite him.

Mention of Lyall's name could still make my heart leap after all these years, but I was surprised that he had accepted. He had lectured at the *Festival of Mind and Body* in the early days when things were vibrantly new and exciting, but not long after that I had heard him dismiss any interest in the ideas of the non-materialist science community because 'no one was saying anything new'.

I returned to Geneva by plane and immediately took the train back to France. Ruth and Tess were at Bandol to meet me, which was lovely. Ruth was now busy with another seminar – which we were not attending – and I did some editing for the Nutrition Division of WHO. When I could I helped Tess who was sorting out her apartment before returning home. On one occasion we went to Toulon to buy material and I borrowed Lorna's sewing machine to make her curtains.

There were many times when neither Tess nor Ruth were there, and although I never really knew what was happening in their lives, from time to time I felt I became the soft landing spot for various members of the core group. Herve was always loyal to Lorna, but for some of the others life was often difficult. Lorna had a propensity for thunderous, sweeping contempt for the unwary. There was a lot of pain at Le Plan, which I suppose is why we were all there, to redeem it.

Being at Le Plan needed a 'couples health warning'. The energy was so challenging for individuals, few relationships survived – certainly amongst the core group. Sophia who is a romantic mixture of French and Polish (brought up in Brazil) and speaks four languages fluently was employed as general administrator. Peter, who is English, worked in the garden. Apart from Lorna's, sometimes impossible, demands and expectations, other things were beginning to undermine them.

Claire, a young French girl with a degree in physics, was the Le Plan cook for two or three years. She originally came from Findhorn with her boyfriend Hugh, but after one season he left and Claire stayed on alone. By early 1988 something was going on between her and Peter. Sophia and I spent gentle times together, sometimes having tea, going to a movie in Toulon, and once walking on the Gros Cervaux near Le Plan. She would talk about Peter and Claire.

I continued to sort out my house, which became a tourist spot for Lorna's seminarists. I have since come across people I don't recognise who say they met me on one of these occasions. Lorna would also invite me to circle dancing evenings or an occasional supper during seminars.

We spent nice times together. She even invited me to dinner at the *Castle Restaurant* in Le Castellet with Milton Shulman and Druscilla Beyfus, the parents of her prospective daughter in law. The women remained respectfully silent while Milton put on a grand story-telling show, lubricating his Canadian tongue with extra bottles of Lorna's most expensive wine.

My equilibrium continued to go up and down like a yoyo, between a life of fun and meaning and a life of depressing banality. In March I felt a need to phone Austin (they were still living in La Rippe at this time), and was shocked to pieces to hear that Pascale was pregnant. Only now did I have the courage to tell my ever-loving mum – whose only wish was that I should be looked after – that Austin and I had properly separated.

The next few days I spent crying, as though in 'outer space'. Austin wrote to acknowledge my pain – and his – and sent me a book called *Black Butterfly* by Richard Moss, which I consumed in one day. It tackled the paradoxes that seemed to render me into inertia. Death was at the surface of the book – as the 'other side of God' and it added ammunition to my own ideas towards the 'matter' book that I was hoping eventually to write.

Linda came to stay on her Easter break and was there when Sir George Trevelyan marched into the house, followed by old-Etonian David Lorimer, on one of the Le Plan excursions to Le Castellet. David, who I didn't know, was Director of the Scientific and Medical Network, and of the Association for Near Death studies, so was connected to Lorna's near death experience video.

I had first been alerted to David, who I knew was a friend of Jonathan Porritt, when I started work at the *Newsletter* at WHO. I had found a letter on my desk written by him to Claudine Brelet about some useful link-up. He was my sort of British man: tall, dark and thin, and seemed a nice person.

As it happened David was going directly from Le Plan to Geneva to do a lecture for Mark's Association. He was staying with Austin! I was going, too, to get my proofs from the printer, and staying with Mark. Since Pascale was staying with her family for this month of her pregnancy, I had supper that first evening with Mark, David and Austin. A few years later it struck me what a karmic evening it had been, especially since I was on my way to the *Mystics and Scientists Conference* in Winchester and would meet Lyall again.

Tess met me at Gatwick and we drove together to Winchester, arriving just in time for Lyall's first lecture at 6.30. My first reaction was that he had put on weight, but I wanted to see him. When he spotted me he seemed pleased to see me but he couldn't get away, and although no bells had rung, I hardly slept at all.

The following day, after his second lecture, he suggested we 'catch-up'. When we did, at lunchtime, he told me, 'you caused me more pain than anyone else I have ever known. I hated you when we parted and I didn't think I would ever get over it, or be able to see you again. I always loved you – and still do.' I couldn't believe what he was telling me because it was he, I told him, who had caused *me* that much pain! 'What are we going to do?' he said.

In the evening Lyall came for a drink with Tess and me, but I didn't see him again until at the end of the conference. He asked me to dinner in London the following evening, and finally, eight years on and fourteen years since we first met, the bells began to ring again.

There was no opportunity to meet again for a while, so I continued my usual circuit of meeting friends and staying with Vlyn. I felt bolder and more 'up front' than I had for a long time.

Being with powerful women like Lorna, Tess and Ruth – even Dinah – was wonderful, but sometimes in my inability to express the lonely, inner, underworld explorations I was making, I felt completely unseen. Although he said he still wished I wasn't searching for meaning, for this precious moment I did feel seen – by Lyall.

CHAPTER THIRTEEN

Back in France the core group seemed to be dispersing. Peter and Sophia were leaving for the UK, in the sadness of separation. Just before Claire left, Ruth, Herve, Claire and I went on 'an exotic trip' for breakfast in Italy! We set off at 6am on the hottest of days and drove for two and a half hours along the Cote d'Azur. We had breakfast by the beach, lazed a little and left at mid-day for lunch in Menton, then tea in Monte Carlo. We arrived home exhausted!

I continued to feel anxious about everything; the likelihood of Lyall hurting me again, how I would manage on a smaller allowance from Austin, whether I would ever get in touch with what I wanted to write. But I did enjoy putting down notes, fed by the books I was reading, like *The Virgin and the Whore*, and *Sacred Virgin*.

I was wrestling with the relevance of related 'dark' concepts like Pluto power absorption and assimilation, and I pondered on where the force of gravity and 'black holes' corresponded to the continuous pull I felt of consciousness towards inertia.

Over the years we made several trips to Les Saintes Maries de la Mer. In October and May each year gypsies from all over the world congregate there to celebrate the voyage to France of the three Marys: Mary Salome, Mary Jacobi and Mary Magdalene, and their black servant Sara – the patron saint of the gypsies.

It was on one of these visits to the church that I had another profound experience to add to my continuing thesis. The only other person I knew who understood that humanity had not yet fully incarnated into matter was Ken Carey, through some channelled teachings. My theme was that Christ had incarnated spirit on to the earth, but it was the feminine descent, the feminine crucifixion that would anchor the spirit of humanity fully *into* matter.

On this occasion I was sitting in a gallery pew meditating, looking towards a statue of the Magdalene – who incidentally is the patron saint of Provence and distinguishable from the Virgin because she stands on a box. Suddenly I felt a rush of energy through my whole being, which spiralled down and down and anchored, as though into the depths of the sea. It was an energetic experience of spirit anchoring into matter.

On June 1st Lyall came to stay. After a month in Africa he looked great; the thinner Lyall I liked with longer hair. He brought me a beautiful locket, with a sliver of cloth from a third century Coptic desert fathers altar piece, showing an 'eternal flame'.

He told me that after three very low years he had reached an equilibrium, which he was afraid I would upset. I asked him to listen to a Gildas tape, which suggested that Lyall and I were part of the same soul stem, and that we each did part of 'our half' of the soul's experience which the other could not do. In some ways it seemed to confirm the strange sense I have always had that 'he was me and I was him', that we were the same thing. We even looked like each other.

As always there were no promises made, but although the projections and hurts were still there, we managed to talk. On his third evening we took Ruth to dinner at a nice, timeless restaurant in Evanos. The following morning we drove to the medieval village of St Paul de Vence where we stayed overnight.

The next day we set off early for Nice to watch *Sea Cloud*, the boat that had taken the place of *The Lindblad Explorer*, come into the harbour in full majestic rigging. Lyall had left some things on board that he wanted to collect. We then drove all the way back to Marseille airport where I left him, and picked up my mum and aunt who were coming to stay for a week. As always Lyall's ability just to leave brought a sense of loss, but for now it was not too bad.

Of all the places I have lived my mum and her sister-in-law, Auntie Trudy, loved Le Castellet the most. They were very easy to please, and if I took them to Bandol in the morning and picked them up mid-afternoon there was nothing, give or take a few excursions they enjoyed more to do in the day.

France was already too hot and a couple of weeks later I was back in London. I took a taxi directly to Lyall's studio flat in Bulstrode Street. He told me his visit to France had left him confused, and he needed to understand in the next days what I wanted from him. Our fears and questions were always the same, yet the healing of the bitterness, he said, had been worth the meeting.

We shopped in Portobello Road for suitable gifts for his Japanese connections. His work to stop the Japanese whaling had impressed them so much that he was now in the middle of negotiations for the honour of bringing Sumo wrestling to Britain. We went to the movies, ate out at restaurants, or watched *Eastenders* – to my astonishment – over the kind of delicious luxuries only he could prepare.

When Lyall left for Japan (from where he sent me one of his beautifully crafted letters gently wondering 'can we make it?') I, too, set off – eventually to meet up with Tess, Dinah and Ruth for a long-awaited excursion to the Cistercian Abbeys of Rivaux and Fountains in Yorkshire. Sadly Lorna had had a very minor stroke and was not well enough to travel. On my way I stayed a couple of days with Lilla who was living in Chester at that point. It was good to see her.

But most of that summer I spent working for WHO in Geneva. I had a two-month contract with the publicity department, working under its director Ann Kern on a brochure to mark the organisation's 50th anniversary, including writing an introduction for the incoming Japanese Director General Nakajima. Austin had arranged for me to live in his daughter and son-in-law's flat while they were away, and it was good to be up and out at 7.30am with somewhere to go again, and something to do.

It was oppressively hot and I hardly slept for two whole months. The work was gruelling because it was never right, the brief unclear, and I lived in a permanently hyper state. The concept of the booklet changed again and again until I wasn't sure who was more muddled about what was required: me or Ann Kern. It came together in the end, but considering how much they paid me it seemed a horribly expensive enterprise for such a small booklet.

Didier's ex-girlfriend Andrea (Tosca) was getting married, and I was invited to their wedding party. She and her new husband, Oumar from West Guinea, went for their honeymoon to Le Castellet. I kept up the copious correspondence with friends, which was a vital part of my living abroad (no emails in those days!) and saw friends in Geneva.

Linda was down for the summer and Austin and I could still talk abundantly. Back from Japan, Lyall called me two or three times, which made me want to see him even more. We arranged to meet in Paris for a weekend.

Paris was the hottest and most uncomfortable I had ever known it, and there was so little time to re-enter our relationship because of the consuming difficulties of the work in Geneva. We went to the Eiffel Tower, to the movies (as always) and restaurants, but were quickly back to the old hurtful patterns, both parrying pre-emptive strikes when we sensed another attack coming. At moments we did not even like each other.

By the time I left on the Sunday we had just about managed to salvage our friendship, but a letter from Lyall expressed for us both, yet again, the confusion and hurt. 'There are ways in which we are so much alike that we cannot help but wound each other', he said. 'I don't know how to proceed.' He left open a meeting we had planned in November.

A note of congratulation from Ann Kern as the final approved text of the booklet came down from the D-G's office, made the long haul seem fine in the end, but I arrived in England with my brain addled and exhausted. Three weeks later, which included a visit to Vlyn – but not to Lyall as he was in Africa – I was back in France.

The Sexuality/Spirituality seminar began early October, and a title like that was guaranteed to stir things up. For once there were several younger participants, including not Tess but her daughter Fran. Watching the group process (and muddles) was a drama in itself, and for the second time at a workshop the 'Raymond factor' came sharply into focus.

Raymond was a young Dutch healer, married with children. Like several of us he had become a regular participant, and from the beginning he had a magnetic attraction that drew people to him. After several workshops it became clear there was a purposeful positioning of where he sat in the group, to create a dynamic power base with Lorna and Ruth. They certainly favoured him in an uncomfortable way.

After one particular meditation Raymond and I were partners for the sharing. To my astonishment and confusion, it felt quite simply that he knew me more completely than anyone had ever known me before, as though we just had to be together, because he was like a twin soul. Yet even as we talked I tried to weigh up what was happening. How could I feel like this for someone I didn't know, when I was in love more than ever with Lyall? It didn't make sense.

The spell was soon broken, so I could watch once again the webs being woven. At one point a young woman came to me in great distress. She had been making friends with a girl she liked a lot, but somehow Raymond had come between them and lured this girl into the haze of a 'special relationship', which had caused hurt and misunderstanding between them. Whether coincidentally or not, the marriage of this woman also broke up.

During the seminar I drew a picture, which I called the *yellow octopus*, to register what Raymond's influence felt like. It was as though an aspect of feminine energy in the male was sucking unwary people into a black hole through use of the sacral or sexual energy. It may sound over-dramatic, but it felt important to hold the angels of 'trust and balance' for the group as well as myself. Whether Raymond was ever conscious of what he was doing I still have no idea –and suspect not - but his 'wizardry' eventually spoiled the legacy of Le Plan.

I went back home exhausted, and gave myself a few days to weather the storms that always kicked in after a seminar until the effects were assimilated. I often thought it must be unbearably difficult for those who had to return immediately to 'normal life', especially to partners who had no idea what these life-changing seminars involved.

At the end of October Austin and Pascale's baby, Gael, was born. It was discovered shortly afterwards that she had a hole in the heart, but fortunately after several weeks of anxiety and concern an operation was able successfully to correct the fault.

In November I went to London via a brief stopover in Geneva, which at that time was the cheapest route. At the end of the month I went with Lyall to visit his exquisitely appointed and typically non-inclusive home in Ireland.

I have never taken to Ireland but my first impression, in the wonderful autumnal sunlight, was of the beauty of the coastal landscape. But by the time the sun had begun to set, I was feeling depressed and alone. As always, being with Lyall highlighted this feeling of isolation, and talking about my inner world of meaning only unnerved him.

The next morning I asked Lyall if his pain was as present as mine. He told me that whenever he was with me I seemed to offer a promise of bliss, which simultaneously came with the pain of knowing that it would never be fulfilled.

In our despair it was a tender morning for us both, but by the time I left, a few days later, the sense of loss was as powerful as ever. He assumed I wanted 'all or nothing', which wasn't true. I did not want 'all', but I did want 'something'. I could not just 'wait' as I had always done before.

I came back to France to a long period of sleepless weariness. There was a degree of edginess between Lorna and Ruth on the one side, and Tess and I on the other. Tess had been attending another Ruth seminar while I was away, and she, too, was unhappy about Raymond's influence.

Linda came for Christmas and New Year, and on Christmas Day I was touched by many phone calls, including from Austin, Lyall, Herve and Sophia. Christmas dinner with Ruth was fun with games, carols and presents and candles, but

165

a straight talk from Lorna the following day made it clear that Raymond was a fixture of the new healing school being established, whatever Tess and I felt.

It was to Lorna's credit that five years later when the healing school had disbanded and Ruth and Lorna had irreconcilably fallen out, that she admitted we had been right. But this talk finally brought an end to anything like 'a group'.

I asked Hubert for a resume of our situation. For Dinah there was an insect pollinating eagerly; Ruth was deadheading roses; Tess was trying to get out of the web she was busily building; Lorna was endeavouring to extricate her wings which were caught, while I was struggling out of my chrysalis to get my wings free. The images spoke for themselves.

Early in January 1989 I asked Ruth for a counselling session because I felt I had lost all structure to my life. Pluto in Scorpio had done what it threatened to do. Everything had to be let go, to die, but I didn't recognise at all what was emerging.

In the session I saw myself going over a chasm on a pulley. When I looked down I saw a black hole of black liquid. I could choose to drop into the chasm, but it was hard to let go, and it felt as though I could be suspended forever. Then I saw that I could climb down the other side with other people, and it seemed less dark. In fact, 1989 was the worst year of my life, when indeed it did feel as though I had dropped into a hole of black liquid.

Although I did a couple of short-term jobs for WHO that year my connection with Geneva was virtually over and I was anxious to find alternative work. I felt I should chase up some contacts from my old way of life, so I drove back to London with Tess. I stayed with Jan and Barrie, but since I planned to stay a couple of months I wanted to find somewhere independent to live (my mother was away for three months in Australia with my aunt and uncle). Eventually, after a couple of days together, it was Lyall who came to my rescue. He offered me his London home while he was in Japan.

Jan, who has never failed to carry the brightest energy and enthusiasm, had passed on to me a 'famous person in glasses' article for an optical magazine. In the end I interviewed Cynthia Lennon, who gave a nice quote about Beatle wives: on one occasion when they met in a restaurant they all pulled out their reading glasses and decided they were getting old!

I made myself phone Unity and she invited me, with Sandy, to meet at *Joe Allens*. She looked exactly the same after nine years and Sandy was now doing very well writing features. I came away from lunch on a high, excited to have glimpsed the old world and to feel so energised by it after years of feeling so 'underpowered'.

Lyall came back after a week and my confidence stayed stable. It was strange how timeless our time together always was, as though we lived three years in a day. With Austin the time had fled by.

I continued to meet friends, like Mary who was going to live in Australia following a new love. In February I was able to stay at her flat. Claire Buloc, too, was back in London. She and Peter had not stayed together and Claire was teaching French privately, obviously enjoying meeting 'ordinary' people and earning money.

Sophia had met and was now living with a new partner, Jeremy Smith, a marketing executive for UNISON, and Dinah was at last to marry CJ, just after her fiftieth birthday. But living between the two worlds was also odd. I didn't quite know where I was.

I had begun to be more engrossed in astrology, doing several weekend workshops with Darby Costello and Howard Sasportas, and eventually an evening class in Queen Square near Mary's flat. On Tuesday evenings I stayed with Tess in Stockwell and we practised our calculations and interpretations. On one particular occasion we decided instead to attend a Ben Creme meeting at the Friends Meeting House, Euston Road.

For many years Ben Creme had been telling Britain that Christ was about to appear again, this time in Brick Lane in the East End. For some reason this prediction had captured the collective imagination, and was even reported in some serious newspapers. There was no appearance yet, but apparently it was still on the cards. Tess, who was open to the Alice Bailey idea of The Second Coming in physical form, was interested to see what Ben Creme sounded like.

There were quite a number of people, seated in large semicircles in front of him in the room. He began by sweeping his eyes over every individual, which immediately made me 'close down' instinctively and not look at him back. After the talk, which was fairly standard stuff, he closed by sweeping his eyes over the room again, and this time I decided I'd open every chakra to feel the measure of him.

Immediately he looked my way I felt a 'zap' on my third eye, and the headache I already had increased. That night I couldn't sleep a wink, and although I felt fine in the morning, I knew that whatever Ben Creme thought he was channelling, it wasn't the Christ. He was using power on the third eye.

A couple of days later, when I went to Sophia's biodynamic therapist, Miriam, I registered the full impact of the Ben Creme event. She massaged my head, forehead and face, and suddenly I dipped into what felt like a past life. I experienced a really angry 'how dare they', and a sense of Nazi domination and manipulation on the third eye.

I had known for several years, through an experience with Austin, that it was the male, not the female who ultimately had the deeper connection to the earth. I felt that this understanding would lead to an awareness of a different kind of non-patriarchal male leadership. I did not know that this expected outcome of the current descent by the feminine into matter, would take many more years to materialise, or at what cost. But it seemed relevant to understand these negative male archetypes.

I had an article to write for the *Guardian* Saturday magazine's New Age column, about prisoners who had taken up yoga. This was based on another Michaelmas sponsored project, *The Prison Phoenix Trust*, which aimed to get a book on meditation called *We're All Doing Time* into every prison.

In March I went again to Ireland and vowed I would never fly again. The landing in Cork in a blustery gale was horrendous. Lyall was caring and attentive, but it felt as it always did, as though it would never be different between us.

The flight home was equally terrifying. As we took off in 55mph winds, the pilot told us we were going up very straight and very fast! Back at Mary's I was full of anxiety. I had no idea what was going to happen if I couldn't continue as a journalist. When Lyall called and suggested ours was a crazy way of carrying on (though he changed his mind later), I felt dizzy and ill. I wanted love, I wanted meaning, and to act with effect. I wanted Life – now.

For once I did not go down to see Vlyn. Instead she came with me to Le Castellet for Easter. We took the sleeper to Marseille and Tess met us at Bandol and invited us to supper. As we sat at dinner I suddenly flipped into a sense of Vlyn as my mother, Tess as my father, and I as a boy child.

I had the sense of the child having power to allow the mother and father the freedom to be together again, and that would leave the child to be free. I knew it had something personal to say. But I also felt it offered a wider sense of allegory.

The child, the earth, must detach from the mother, the moon, to do its own parenting. This would allow the moon to return to its full relationship to the sun. Was this connected to HA's idea of Lucifer the Deva of the Moon, which had usurped Michael as the rightful Deva of Earth?

Whatever, it was difficult to have Vlyn and Tess together as they tended to end up in combat! It was a relief when Vlyn was gone and Tess and I went on to do Ruth's *Black Madonna* seminar. I decided to do an *I-Ching* beforehand and 'darkening of the light' sounded about right.

For some reason the seminar was deeply unsatisfying. It should have been the most relevant to the journey I was taking, but somehow it did not touch the depths I needed most to go. Most of the time I couldn't concentrate and felt angry about everything that went on. Towards the end I caught a cold, and after several sleepless nights I felt physically as well as emotionally dreadful. Usually the process of a seminar ended in resolution. This time I just wanted to get back to London.

When I got to Mary's, via a stopover in Paris to see Herve, I was still down in the dumps. What was the point of all this inner agonising, when 'the world out there' couldn't care less? There was no movement on the work front.

My classes and weekends in astrology kept me going. Pouring over transits and aspects meant there was still a possibility that life was on course. Jupiter transiting Uranus and Venus surely meant something nice! Confirmatory conversations with friends like Isobel and Tess about the effects of collective energies we were all experiencing held me together. I had lots of coffees out with my ever-accepting mum, although I was never able to tell her how much pain I was in.

I was hardly sleeping at all, maybe a couple of hours each night. I was now seeing Miriam regularly and also doing singing lessons as a therapeutic tool, with opera trained Kate Tierney in Ravenscourt Park. Despite the awful noise I made the effect was grounding and deepening, and usually provided a temporary respite from anxiety.

It continued to be a year of headaches and sleeplessness. Lorna held a sixtieth birthday party at her home in Parsons Green, for which I bought a pair of royal blue silk trousers. I went to the one-day astrology lectures given by Liz Greene at Regents College. I was also writing up articles that for one reason or another never got published. *The Guardian,* for example, took on a new magazine editor who cancelled the New Age column.

Telephone calls with Lyall, who was completing a book in Ireland, were no help at all, and usually ended in mutual desolation. After one agonising exchange I got an unhappy letter saying he felt gutted every time the strains appeared. We had a closeness that was maybe called love, but too often it felt like hate. 'All in all I don't understand you very well: or at all. Sometimes I don't even like you'.

The letter ended by saying he didn't know if it was worth going on, but he had bought the enclosed (a ticket to Cork) as a peace offering. I went at the end of May, and through the usual frustration of non-relating, took precisely seventy-two hours to de-stabilise things again.

We came back to London together, but I was crying in the dark. I felt disintegrated and angry. I went to stay with Jan and then with Mary. Yet for the first time ever, and nervous though I was, Lyall came with me to a friend's party – for Tess's birthday. It was clear, however, that he was enjoying his space and the threads were weakening. I felt overwhelmingly lonely and longed to speak to someone who loved me.

Austin and I continued to write regularly, especially during the time of Gael's heart operation, and the fears during her recuperation. Towards the end of June he came to London. We met for supper at Tess's and again for breakfast a day or so later before he went back to Geneva. It was warm and nice to see him, and he told me he was far from being detached from me and sad not to be sharing my life. He said I deserved to be happy.

By comparison my lunch with Lyall straight afterwards was hell. When we met the pain of loss and the human condition was so dreadful I felt like vomiting. I wondered if I'd ever been happy. I felt dead. The last straw was when Lyall took me out for my birthday and stayed overnight at Mary's and it felt like a one-night stand. He rang afterwards to thank me!

This was more than about relationship. Life had lost its meaning, and right now I could not think of anyone who could help me. Even my many friends suddenly seemed sparse and far away. Suicide? I wouldn't know how. I felt I had been promised a 'transition' at the beginning of the year but since that was not true, what was?

At the April seminar several participants had given rave reviews of a psychic called Dave Cousins. In desperation I sent off for a tape, which now arrived, two months later, in July. In a perverse way it fitted my mood for a while because it acknowledged my negativity! I was only using four percent of my energy, he said, and suggested some long and complicated breathing exercises to ground me, which I religiously started to do. He also told me to sound the OM for twenty minutes twice a day, which was a bit alarming considering the thinness of Mary's walls.

He said that I had extremely 'virulent' energies, which meant that relationships would always be difficult. I had also, he informed me, been the 'full stop' in many men's lives and that in this life I would have to account for them all! It explained a lot! As depressing as it was, it helped.

Over the last few weeks I had been helping Tess clear up her house in Stockwell, and on 1st August she moved to Abingdon. It was still her dream to be part of a group, and it was hoped that St Ethelwold's, the home of an elderly spinster Dorothea Pickering who wished it to be conducted on Benedictine principles, would become a community- run house for retreat and healing. *The One Work* was the vision of Catherine Tetlow, a psychotherapist colleague, and Tess had been invited to be co-worker and housekeeper.

I continued to see Miriam and Kate, and on one particular occasion when I had tossed and turned all night I dreamed about 'my star'. I was born with my sun in Leo, but on a full moon. I had only ever had reflected light; my men would never let me shine. As Lorna's little booklet said, I needed to 'find my song and sing it'. I needed to shine.

It was a huge relief to leave London to visit Vlyn in her new flat in Totnes. Her criticisms were still biting and irritating, but it was part of the nurturing package. I should have made time to see Linda, who was completing her time at the Waldorf School, and about to spend a year in Geneva to earn some decent money, but I needed Vlyn more urgently, to combat the panic.

On the eve of Vlyn's sixtieth birthday, we sailed with numerous guests down the River Dart on a hired boat. She and her daughter Gail did the magnificent catering and the champagne flowed. It was a beautiful evening. On her actual birthday we had a fish and chip supper for ten.

Back in London, though my nights were disturbed, I was now just grateful if I woke up without a headache. I felt I wanted to hide because my inner world and my outer world were collapsing on me. I wanted to leave them both behind. I also wanted to leave behind Austin and Lyall who still both phoned occasionally. Although I would not be victim, and could see 'the greater meaning', on a bad day they had simply both betrayed me.

August had been a terrifying month, with the loss of all motivation and light. In September I made up my mind; it was now or never. I would commit myself to three therapy sessions a week (adding art therapy with a girl called Kathleen Wood). I would work on all the blocks that stopped me from moving on, giving myself an ultimatum to be clear by the Alchemy seminar in December.

As Dave Cousins had said, I must get rid of all limitations and everything that had been a hindrance. I decided that this had to mark the completion of my work at Le Plan, and then I would write my book.

In preparation I began gathering up all my notes, trying to fit the pieces together, but I had too much time to think, and my mind went back to despair and panic. Perhaps looking at my childhood pain with the therapists was doing me more harm than good. Was the spiritual path dangerous for me? Was I living in a world of illusion? I was afraid to ask for more guidance in case I was fooled again, and in any case could not show anyone how vulnerable I was.

There were days when I couldn't sleep at all, when the fears and terrors overcame me, and on one occasion Kathleen suggested I look at the fears. I drew a dot in a circle, and suddenly the dot became the eye of a primeval lizard. I felt myself at the centre of the earth. What did it mean?

On particularly bad days I cancelled meetings with friends, although this was the one aspect of my life that made it right to be in England. Sometimes I just lay on the sofa, and at

173

one point my mother, who thought I had flu, took pity on me and brought down some sleeping pills she had begged from a friend!

The last straw came after a weekend of astrology at Regents College. I was so low I could hardly function. On my way back to Mary's I walked through the rose garden in Regents Park and out on to the Euston Road opposite the Marylebone Church. When I saw the large notice inviting anyone in for healing, I knew at that moment that no one on earth could help me.

I felt there was not even an 'elder stateswoman' like Barbara Somers who would know what I was going through. I begged God for mercy, and promised Him that if ever I survived, I would give my life to bringing others out of these depths of death.

On November 10 the Berlin Wall came down after twenty-eight years. It was amazingly beautiful and moving to watch the extraordinary scenes, and it somehow held significance to everything that was going on for me. By the end of November I had completed all my therapy sessions. On my last meeting with Kathleen, I drew a large foot, which was almost over the line! And at last I went home to France.

The *Alchemy* seminar began on 4 December. On it I had put all my hopes for survival, and for the first two or three days I felt fragile and silent. With her usual extraordinary creativity, Ruth had devised an 'alchemical game'. The idea was to build up a picture day by day towards our own personal understanding of the final '*conjunctio*'.

Throughout the fortnight we meditated at each stage of the alchemical process, using the symbols of the planets and their resonant colours. It became clear to me that this was to be a review of the whole of this phase - of a ten-year journey.

During one particular exercise we had to tune into colours 'energetically' without seeing them. When my turn came I sensed the group was holding up the colour orange, and I had the most violently angry reaction. Later in the day when we went to the chapel to 'sound' these colours, my group kindly offered to 'do orange'.

As everyone tentatively began to sound a note for orange, I heard only Gill Pichler sounding 'my note'. When I picked it up from her, which made everyone else follow, I had an overwhelming feeling that I was 'singing my own note'. The release that came from this recognition was immense.

As we did the Moon journey, I saw the moon as me. I saw there was a 'Second Fall' and a 'feminine crucifixion'. I saw again that the child, the earth, had to separate from the moon, the mother, so that the moon could see herself, and then unite with the sun. Only then could the darkness go.

The following day I did a session with Nadia O'Connor, where I saw 'the mother' as an overprotective power, a witch who clamped my power. I did not know what to do with my sense of wonder: unless I could tell someone about it I could not see. I was blind. By the end of the session I felt wracked and could not move.

The next day Ruth had planned a healing ceremony and I asked a Dutch member of the core group, Jan, to be my healing partner. He told me afterwards that he had touched my essence, which was fragile yet authentic, and that we were surrounded by bubbles of joy.

In the Gold journey of the Sun I became a swan that was 'ready', swimming with purpose down the river to a crystal city. It had three cygnets (which needed light) behind it.

The next evening was the 'mystic marriage' or Coronation finale. The 'pre-marriage' tension during the day was intense, but in the event I felt blessed. I saw the black Queen of Sheba coming down the steps to give a necklace to the King. The King was crowned.

Although there was more personal unhappiness to come, I knew I had completed in some way my contribution to a universal journey. I had somehow reached a plateau, beneath which I would not need to descend. Nothing could be so existentially painful again.

CHAPTER FOURTEEN

'Life is not just a 'product' of matter, as heat is a product of fire. It is an organising principle beyond matter. Once chance and the laws of nature had formed the basic building blocks – the amino acids – life intervened to organise into more complex forms, ie. vitalism. The process of evolution can be described as the insertion of more and more freedom into matter. Amoeba is a small 'leak' of freedom, while man is a large leak. Life – or freedom – stands above matter and mechanism. Life (or mind) can overrule the laws of nature, i.e. magic." Philosopher T.E. Hulme.

The beginning of 1990 felt like my third incarnation in this one life. The first time I had felt 'reborn' to a new dimension was in 1975. Now I just wanted to get on, to serve, to create. No more Self, looking at my own navel. In my humanness I contained 'the gods', or access to them. It had no glamour or inflation, it just was!

I could now plan my book on *freedom within containment,* understanding how spirit could be free within the confines of matter. The working of humanity through the spirit of Love rather than the Will of matter, and the fine dividing line between taking power and finding one's note.

I had made up my mind to write the book as a metaphor, in novel form, and began wading happily amongst the symbols I would use, and sensing how the Greek Gods could be depicted in my story. It surprised me to read back on the prescience of what I had written in my diaries when Austin and I first got together, about opening up to earth energies, preparing for the descent.

I asked Hubert for some images to help with the story. I saw action under water amongst Greek caves and rocks. I saw underworld laboratories and the final days of Atlantis, where there was experimentation on others, physically, mentally and emotionally. It crossed my mind that it was going to be a dark book, which worried me.

It was around that time I learned that silica, or sand, was at its purest around the Le Plan terrain, through the particular folding of the land. Research by Don Robbins for his book

Silence of the Stones, about accessing information through stones, had said that the clearest messages came through pure silica!

I knew, however, that I did not want to set my book in France, despite the fact that everything I had experienced stemmed from there. Landscape would have to be the prime player in the story, and a descent book needed black earth. The only place I could think of with black volcanic sand was Santorini.

Robert Graves said: *'The Black Goddess is so far hardly more than a hope whispered among the few who have served their apprenticeship to the White Goddess. She promises a new pacific bond between men and women in which the patriarchal marriage bond will fade away. The Black Goddess has experienced good and evil, love and hate, truth and falsehood in the person of her sisters. She will lead men back to that sure instinct of love which he long ago forfeited by intellectual pride.'*

In February I went to London to continue my research. As usual I stayed with Jan and Barrie, and they decided they would like to go to Santorini with me for Easter. We arranged I would fly from Marseille and they would join me from London. But before I went something happened totally out of the blue.

At the beginning of April, David Lorimer came to Le Plan to run a seminar. As usual my house was on the excursion list, so it never occurred to me to question when David invited himself to tea one afternoon. By the third occasion it began to dawn on me... and when he suddenly put his arm round me on the beach in Bandol, I realised he was asking a little more from me!

Although I had met him in Geneva, I knew very little about David, except he had gone to Eton. I had the impression that he had not had many girlfriends, but I learned afterwards that this touchingly tentative approach had come at the suggestion of his long-term friend Monica.

I had just met Monica for the first time a short while earlier, although I had been aware of her for several years. In the mid-eighties I read an article by her, introducing the work of German microbiologist Prof. Dr. G. Enderlein. The article had rung bells for me because I had always sensed this journey into matter held a resonance with microbiology – in a similar way the 'cosmic' journey was mirrored in quantum physics.

What amazed me when Monica and I met was that she was such a young woman, still only thirty-one. She had already achieved so much in the field of nutrition and had pioneered an ecological approach to health and the concept of probiotics. At the time we met her awareness of the 'descent' was as great as mine. Despite the difference in our ages, we became firm friends, and continue to be so.

Age was also an issue with David. In his gentle wooing of me, he did baulk a bit when he learned he was seven years younger than I was, but he gamely carried on. A relationship between us was mooted the day before I left for Santorini, and he went back to the home he rented on the property of Serge Beddington Behrens in Gloucestershire.

As it happened, Jan and Barrie could not get a flight until four days after I'd arrived on Santorini, which turned out to be fortuitous. I made my way from Fera to Oia, and found myself accommodation overlooking the Caldera. *Lauda's* was a family run hotel, set on sloping white terraces, with rooms that tunnelled into the cliffs. Much of the time there were elemental winds, and thunderstorms over the volcano, but it was also sunny.

My purpose was simply to write myself a location for my story, and I spent the days walking up and down recording in words as accurately as possible everything I saw. I took local names from the sides of vans, walked down to the harbour counting the steps, and asked the tourist office obscure questions about flora and fauna and weather.

In the evening I would sit on the terrace with a glass of wine, look across the sea to the volcano and imagine a life for my notes. On the following day I noticed that another girl was doing something similar at the next table beside me. It was inevitable that eventually we would speak. Myrna Denis was typically gorgeously French, and spoke perfect English.

Myrna was here preparing to write a novel! This was her sixth visit to Santorini, and she was somehow recapturing memories and experiences that would eventually constitute the book. It became clear that while I was using Santorini as a backdrop for my novel about my process in France, Myrna was 'processing' – somehow in a less conscious way – through her relationship to the island itself.

Neither of us shared exactly what we were doing, but we knew this was a significant meeting and we had to stay in touch. In the following years I stayed with her in Paris two or three times, and she brought her new partner to dinner in Le Castellet and Le Beausset (where unbelievably, his parents lived). But it was five years before we talked about the exact nature of our respective plots and discovered we had touched into the same book!

Although in the end Myrna did not begin her book until nine years later, I discovered, through my own guidance, that hers was the real story of the Santorini earthquake, and mine was not. But we had both set up double time scenarios about failed earth initiations (involving a brother and sister), and lives that were redeemed in the current incarnation. Myrna's book was an exquisite literary creation while my book was a more mundane attempt to explain an evolutionary process. But by anyone's book it was an astonishing meeting, and until her untimely death, we were as close as sisters, particularly in the early years.

When Jan and Barrie eventually arrived we spent a day or two together, and I then took a ferry to Naxos, to follow the thread of earthy Dionysus and his relationship to Ariadne and Theseus.

When I got back to Le Castellet I set up my typewriter in my upstairs sitting room and began putting down words as if they came from nowhere. I forced them out thousand by thousand, often like pulling teeth. In two weeks I had fourteen thousand words.

Ruth, Lorna and Tess were all in France. The healing school was underway, which really had set a wedge between us and the atmosphere remained fairly tense. I think Lorna would have distrusted me even further if she knew one of my main characters had suddenly become modelled on her builder Francis. In his early sixties Francis had obviously been the prize catch of Le Beausset at one time. He had once been Lorna's lover for thirty years (she'd apparently 'seen off' Pussy Deakin) – and had been the reason for her divorce.

He had even backed me up against the wall a couple of times in my house, but when I made it clear I was not available, he begged me not to tell Lorna. He had never married and still lived with his ageing mother, and was ideal for my sinister, charismatic character Georgio Vassilou. From the moment he entered the plot, I would see Francis almost every day driving around in his van in Le Beausset!

There was no doubt that events were being attracted for the book, which made it vibrant and joyous. On a short visit to Le Plan, David arranged to visit me again. We walked in a meadow nearby and on the way back he told me he had 'seen' us together on this exact same path, as two black and white monks (Cistercians?)

Later, when I went to my favourite contemplation spot, the breakwater at St Cyr les Lecques, I saw two extraordinary birds perched together on a yacht mast; one was black, the other black and white. Another sign? David's existence in my life, though tenuous at this point, lessened the tension between Lorna and I. If Lorna wanted to continue her friendship with David, she now had to have me!

During my writing the image of the swan, on a postcard on my table, was my constant companion, and I turned to Hubert a great deal for images. I was dividing the book into sections encapsulating the descent into the 'velvet beauty' of matter by journeying through one Greek god or goddess after another, to show the cyclical mythical nature of evolving life. I had left Demeter and was now in Persephone.

At the same time I was reading Jung's ideas about myth, fantasy and symbolic thinking, when suddenly I felt as though I was being overwhelmed, as though a huge force was trying to speak. It was too big for the small vehicle in front of me, too big to handle. I knew it wasn't Hubert, who always came from my right hand side. This was coming from behind me.

By June, with everyone gone, I was exhausted. On June 15th I went to England, because by sheer coincidence David and I had both been asked independently by David Furlong to be on the editorial board of a new alternative magazine he was producing. David and I agreed to meet at Runnings Park for an editorial meeting and worked on some text together, but we both concluded it was not for us.

David invited me back to Hampnett and we began to get to know each other. After a moment's hesitancy and gentleness David's fear left him and we embarked on a full relationship, marked by a lot of laughter. He was clearly pleased with his newfound pleasures and bought a big blue double bed. Much to Serge's amusement.

Thanks to Serge's generosity, David was currently sharing his cottage with a uniquely wonderful woman, Naiad Ellis who, divorced with two children, had recently jumped the ship of her life and ended up temporarily with nowhere to go. To me she was like a thoroughbred colt, wild and beautiful but funny and kind. She skittered away from intimacy, but surprisingly, since we were so unalike, we got on famously and still do. Later that year she met Peter Hewitt, another writer friend of David's, who owned a house in nearby Cheltenham, and we became a regular foursome.

My most immediate and obvious problem was David's mother! On this first visit to Hampnett he spent an hour and a half on the phone to his mother in Scotland, defending my honour against accusations of being a 'slut' (as I had been married before).

Although I did not meet Mrs Lorimer for quite a while, over the course of our relationship the issue of David's mother proved almost insuperable, not least because she had a lot of psychic power. She also continued a campaign of emotional blackmail and to me was the Plutonic personification of the dark mother.

At an earlier time, when David was keen to join the Ivanoff *White Brotherhood,* she had threatened to 'destroy them both', and persuaded his father to cut him out of his will. Once she had had her way the will was reinstated, but throughout his relationship with me she he was cut off again.

When I did finally meet her, I was surprised to see she was actually a young woman – only ten or so years older than me! She was incapacitated by a weak heart, and sat in her sitting room surrounded by piles of old newspapers. She showed me round the house pointing up the family heirlooms, proof of their elevated heritage.

We sat round the table and I could feel the manipulation, as though she were daring me to reveal my own background. I was angry with David for not coming to my rescue or challenging her unforgivable behaviour. I began to feel a psychic darkness and called on everything I could for help.

Suddenly a huge wave of calming energy came over me, and the song 'you are a child of the universe' came into my head, and I knew I was safe. David knew I had held the ground between light and dark, and it felt like a timely release of the dark mother. I just hope it did him some good that someone held out against her.

Nonetheless, despite his seeming gentleness and sensitivity, and choosing the spiritual path, David did have the air of 'ruling by right'. After Eton, St Andrews University, and teaching at Fettes and Winchester College, he was now Director of the Scientific and Medical Network. But it was also known that Sir George Trevelyan considered David to be his successor as the 'leader of the new age'.

Sir John Whitmore had said to me in 1975, 'isn't it interesting how the leaders of the new age are all from the aristocracy?' That had not gone down at all well with me then, and certainly would not do so now. David's book: *Whole in One: the near death experience and the ethic of interconnectedness,* was published that year by *Arkana.*

It was also frustrating that the Network only acknowledged external qualifications and achievements - only people with degrees were allowed to be members. In my view the Network paid lip service to 'beyond the brain' but by virtue of its set up those operating 'beyond the brain', were not regarded. I know it is different now – and David disputes that it ever was! But on several counts, then, David belonged to a club I could never join.

Some of David's friends were scary. Bright sparks of extreme intellect, out on the vanguard, while I had for many years, though reluctantly, been forced to ride the waves behind. Yet I had come far enough and was sufficiently creatively occupied right now to hold my own. David was so much in the public domain and while I had wanted to keep this year quite isolated and independent, life had clearly conspired otherwise. At least there was not the continual 'loss and crisis' of my other relationships.

David was tender and caring and there was beauty in the relationship, but he needed his space. The deep spiritual mirror we provided for each other was intensely sexual, yet sensitive not sensual. I felt my own 'spiritual beauty' in close contact with him. A Venus kind of 'by seeing you, I see myself. By giving to you I give to myself'. It was as though the instrument were being played at a high vibration. And because we had many separations that year, new layers and dimensions could be added, and a closeness was possible for longer. He said he felt loved.

For part of that summer I rented, through a contact of Austin's in Geneva, a small flat near the British Museum. (Though still travelling a great deal, Austin was now winding down his life in Geneva for imminent retirement with his family to the house in France)

The Bloomsbury flat was rather primitive but the location was wonderful and I enjoyed adding to my research at the British Museum library. To my astonishment and pleasure it was Jan who came up trumps in a big way, and we spent hours together working out the finer details of my plot. She was sympathetic to my idea of metaphor but led the way in

183

imaging scenes and situations. I went back to France at the end of August to continue writing.

My routine was to write from about nine to twelve; three hours was always enough. The afternoons I spent 'lounging', as though the well needed time to fill up. I would read and reflect. I missed David and thought of his intense attachment to his family and his history. I saw I did not exist in relation to my own birth. It felt as though I floated within my whole history.

The plot ground on and three weeks later David came to Le Castellet. It was fun to invite Nadia, Lorna and Jonathan Powell, who were attending another Ruth seminar to tea with us. The afternoon before, we had been to watch the sunset and moonrise at St Cyr, which left us feeling a unique peace and contentment, as though together and independently we were in a state of grace and innocence. We were experiencing extraordinary intensities within a framework of freedom.

It wasn't all roses however! There were moments when I felt a deep rising anger and irritation, for what seemed like no reason at all. It was as though I was rejecting the excessive passivity in David, and I realised the anger I felt was a projection of David's anger on me. It made sense of his otherwise imperceptible Mars in Scorpio, and passive aggression in itself holds enormous power and control.

We talked about it, and he went back to his earliest memories of passivity, through his mother's determination to break his will (at three), and his lack of passion, which has turned into negative projected aggression (hence his being bullied at school).

When he left three weeks later I had lost my equilibrium of earlier in the year, and fear was beginning to take hold of me. As I worked with the plot, the intensity of the fear kept growing. Without realising it I was writing in a character guaranteed to frighten me to death and bring me face to face with my worst nightmares – psychic terror and madness.

At the age of seven I had had a bad accident. My brother and I were racing on the back of David and Brian Taylor's bikes when my ankle twisted and my heel got caught in the spokes of Brian's back wheel. My screams finally stopped the race, and a saviour in the form of a postman dismantled the spokes and set my foot free. An ambulance was called but I was too shocked to be left in hospital. My mother wheeled me back and forth to the hospital in a pushchair to have my wound dressed, twice a day for two months, eight miles a day.

As a result of the accident my nervous system was shot, and for almost seven years I lived with mind-bending terrors. I was afraid of everything: Sundays, shapes on the wall, that my parents were damned because they didn't go to Church. I lived in dread in a way that I felt no one could ever understand. I was endlessly afraid of everything. Eventually when I was twelve, I was so desperate I made a decision and with gigantic determination and will power, I cut off my imagination. My creative faculties were stopped.

It was only when I met Lilla that I understood what had really happened. She told me that the accident had knocked my 'third eye' off-centre, which meant that I began to experience my own fears as external 'entities'. This in turn touched into old past life fears of psychic abuse and misuse of power.

That this was 'meant' to happen I have no doubt. It instigated the chain of events that went on to inform the rest of my life. But at the time, it was my mother who sat with me night after night reassuring me over and over again that it was 'just my imagination', and quite simply kept me sane.

Now, however, my character Professor Marinatos, who was experimenting on mind control, was creating a re-run of that time and bringing back the same recognisable fears that threatened my sanity. Despite everything I had invested in this project there was no option but to stop the book. I was too terrified to go on.

A few days later I got a call from an American woman Helene Shik, who had been given my name by John Ramsay 'because we were both preoccupied by the same things'. She was on a research trip for a pilgrimage she was planning on the Black Madonna, and because she was nearer to Rennes le Chateau than me, I suggested she go to see Celia. It was her enjoyment of Celia that brought her back to me, and the following weekend she came to stay, with her English companion and driver, Alison.

Despite the number of times these things happened I was staggered at the miracle of the process. Our conversation, the sharing, the acknowledgement of the journey was magical. We soared and sorted and tested ideas. Her major interest was the significance of the blood – which also fascinated me.

We got closer and closer to the terror of the psychic, of being controlled and giving up power. Suddenly I saw a life in Atlantis; the action of priests who 'programmed' people on the third eye to enslave them. It made sense of my terror of madness.

I knew then that Helene could do the healing, and what she did was like deep powerful surgery, a psychic operation. The imagery was very precise. SHE (the Wise Virgin?) was there above me, and it was she who pulled me out of the dark, primal death. At Les Saintes Maries de la Mer I had seen the 'plumb line' go down into matter, but I saw now how close I had been to not making it out.

It was over now, and thanks to Helene I knew now I could continue writing the book. I also knew I was nearly ready to leave Le Castellet, and began to think of selling my house. By December 22nd I had the semblance of a finished product. Although there was still much to do, I had the sense it was now possible. Despite parental pressure David came for Christmas and New Year, and on December 31, another Harmonic Convergence, we meditated together.

On New Year's Day we opened the book *Mystérieuse Provence* at random and took a trip to St Victoire, the glorious red mountain near Aix, captured so intensely by Cezanne. Against an astonishingly deep blue sky and a strong Mistral, we climbed to the ridge beyond the Refuge de Cezanne and talked to 'him' – the huge mountain being, over-lighted by a vast angelic presence.

When David left I went back to my book. I felt what I now called 'the externals' somehow closer and available, bringing gifts and synchronicities. I continued to check in regularly with Hubert, to keep faith with what I was doing. I also kept in regular touch with Geoffrey Arnold, whose guide Darius had from the beginning been helpful and encouraging.

It was Darius who had told me that Hubert was the acceptable face of guidance for me, and that he would eventually show himself to be just a small part of a far greater system of guidance. It was also he who told me that the story of my life was the story of the history of the universe.

At the end of January I spent ten vibrant days with David in Hampnett. He was blossoming, and had just been invited to an educational meeting at High Grove. Naiad lent me a large piece of rose tourmaline, which I put beside the bed. Suddenly one night, I saw a huge energy bursting, rocketing from the inside out of the crystal. And I knew that whether crystal or cauliflower, the power of growth, the power of life was LOVE; that all nature is love by its nature.

When Paul Solomon had talked of a new energy, to me the new energy was love, and was in some unfathomable way mirrored by scientists' continuing search for a new, cleaner energy through nuclear fission.

Back home in France I wanted to finish the book by the time Saturn conjuncted my moon in Capricorn. David, in the meantime, had gone to see his family and was experiencing more dissention, presumably because he had spent Christmas with us in France. He was having a hard time, but so far was holding firm. His mother, he told me, was ranting yet again about age and babies, and family and what I did and did not do for mine; she continued to hit at my weakest spots.

Hubert had given me an indication that I was facilitating a rough ride on the waves for David, but that I would not go into despair or be the scapegoat. And Dave Cousins had said I would work more consciously and constructively with the negative. But still the attacks felt pretty poisonous. I had no ammunition, but could only hold true.

I walked in the sun and wind to clear away the debris, and to breathe in the air to clear myself. I read Donna

Cunningham's book *Pluto*, and remembered my isolation, the Plutonian heritage: to pull back, withdraw. I was angry again with David for his emotional passivity in not protecting me. I got the image of burning and him letting me down. How dare he. I had taken on my own family stuff as a child; I would not take on his.

Then Lorna told me of her Cathar visions, and it touched me greatly, her sense of classlessness. A Cathar trait, she told me. She later sent me a letter expressing the 'now' of our friendship. She said we were all expecting a breakthrough on the trip to Cathar country, which would be part of David's up-coming seminar on the Templars and Cathars: a movement from persecution to empowerment.

CHAPTER FIFTEEN

Although I was not part of David's Templar seminar, I was invited, approved, and accompanied by Lorna, to go on the five-day trip to Cathar country. There were several heavyweights like Sir George and his companion Rhoda. Tom Welch and Alick Bartholomew shared a room, and apparently talked about their individual relationships with me – a gossip point now I was with David. I'm glad there were no tales to tell!

Gill Pichler and I sat together on the coach on the way and talked non-stop, touching into helpful insights for each other. She saw the 'ugly' truth that as a Templar guarding the Cathars at Mont Segur, she had let them down to save herself. Although I did not resonate with the Cathars (and did not recapture the feeling on this trip), it did fit with my vision of David's betrayal and 'letting me burn'. It touched Gill's issue of not being depended on.

We got to my previous insight of being the giant who wanted to nurture and the huge 'disappointment' at being too big for the tiny earth, because too much love overwhelmed them. Gill helped me to see I felt 'how dare they' – for being let down by 'my planet' for not realising I was inappropriate.

Thanks to David's negotiations we were allowed to go into a Cathar cave not normally open to the public. Suddenly, Lorna, who was helping another participant who couldn't walk well from the bus to the pathway, told us felt she was replaying a scene when the Inquisitors tortured the feet of the Cathars. This gave Gill a clue as to why her son John had been born with a foot distortion, and had had trouble with his feet all his life.

For some reason all candles were extinguished to meditate in the cave, and immediately I went into total terrified panic. I coped by saying 'I'm safe, I'm safe' over and over again, but it was all I could do not to beg someone to put a light on. The fear subsided when we said the Lord's Prayer (the Cathar prayer), and I wept, I was so moved.

Later I put the events together: my feeling of abandonment by the gods, and disappointment at not being welcomed on earth, and as a result living eons of lives in 'no-man's land'. In this life, fearful of belonging nowhere, my life had been a fight to be safe. And I allowed myself to be a victim, instead of assuming 'mea culpa' which I always did because I knew had chosen this life. For once I could say to the gods 'how dare they', and forgive them, rather than asking them to forgive me, and move on.

All the next day I cried because I then knew that 'they' were from my planet and would not let me down this time - it was 'they' who had pulled me out with Helene. The rest of the trip was fun but did not affect me as much as others, who clearly saw themselves as former Cathars.

At the end of March Naiad came to stay. She was an independent soul and because we planned to return to London together I could get on and finish the novel while she amused herself. Except the ending of the book was stuck! But on the day before we were due to leave we were talking at breakfast as usual - about La St Baume and Mary Magdalene. Suddenly I felt a huge surrender. It was 'that surrender'; the surrender I had experienced in the St Baume cave five years before. 'She' was so beautiful. She 'came in' and pulled me down to a deep, full place of resolution.

I ran upstairs to my desk and completed the book, at least in essence, in forty-five minutes. But the plot had completely turned round. I had seen the book in modern time, resonating back to a distant past life. Suddenly I was in the ancient time, looking forward to a potential life in the future. It was magic!

David's elderly father died two days after we returned from a visit to his mother in Scotland. We decided to find a flat together, choosing Bath as our milieu. In the end we took a modern flat at the 'back end' of town off the London Road. It wasn't ideal and to neither of our tastes but there was little to choose from. For me it was just another temporary location, but for him it was scary, leaving security for the unknown for the first time. I did not realise quite how hard that was for him.

David set up an office for the Network in one bedroom and we had a sufficiently spacious dining and sitting room - though I felt oppressed by the family furniture and books. (Lyall, Austin and David were all men with thousands of books and the energy of the old had always depressed me). Austin and Pascale had moved to France and Austin and I continued to write copiously. He had begun an *Open University* degree in history. David gave me two days work a week doing Network admin, filling in for the assistant in Hampnett.

In June my book was delivered to Tessa Sayle, the literary agent I had always had, but who had no relationship to the 'alternative' view. At the end of June it was rejected, and quite simply I was embarrassed and devastated. That night I had a dream: the Fool is looking frantically for his place in the play. He can't find his lines anywhere and he isn't sure whether he has missed his entrance. It looks doubtful he will find the script as the play goes relentlessly on.

My self-esteem once again went to zero. If I was not a writer, I had no identity left to relate through – especially in the face of a powerful and successful man. Once again I was struggling to keep my validity intact.

There was always a nagging feeling of 'wrongness' about the 'brightness' of David's path for us to be together, and then came another 'last straw'. Obviously to combat how unsettled he was feeling, David told me he wanted to go back to Winchester to teach. I fought to not react, but just be, and finally I did find a place of stillness, and could see myself, with him in Winchester, without drowning or dying.

The Network AGM was also a trial. I held my own, but still felt threatened by the busy women who surrounded David and obviously adored him: Gill Wright, Hertha Larive, Teresa Hale. He was a social man with many friends and that kind of socialising scared me.

David was learning Bulgarian and each morning at breakfast he would work on his books at the kitchen table. This was to further his work on Peter Deunov whose teachings did not draw me at all. At the AGM he offered a session on Paneurythmy – the accompanying movement – but this also felt too 'high' energy – when everything in me was about bringing down spirit into matter. I did enjoy the Qi Gong, however, and learned it was the Tao, the movement out of receptivity, that worked for me.

As always it was my female friends who were there to confer and confirm. Carole Bruce became my closest ally, and along with Naiad was my closest friend at this time. She and I did a meditation together and I saw the image of menacing sharks roaming in the water. Then I saw the oyster with a golden pearl inside and the sharks could not reach me: I was too small for them to see me and I would stay safe. Suddenly the pain in my back intensified until I felt myself trying to give birth but couldn't make it.

In the night I woke in panic. I had not given birth in the physical - the book - but I saw that it was the journey to give birth to myself that was not complete. My back felt jammed solid, the 'key' a long pointed one – was the key to a chastity belt. I felt shame; shame down the female line: my mother's shame, my shame and above all shame of my creative issue; my work and my books.

Strangely, I was not ashamed of this dear child, this book, even though it had been rejected. I knew then that I must stay in ordinariness. No more addiction to intensity because it led me to 'flying out'. My addiction to movement and escape had been an escape from shame. I had to learn to 'stay in', act out of receptivity and not die. To sit in the place of the feminine where action follows non-action: the Tao.

I decided to take Carole's advice and visit a favourite friend of her and Jay's: Bronwen Astor. After the Clivedon debacle Bronwen became an ardent Catholic and practitioner of Rebirthing. I visited her twice at her beautiful Manor home near Guildford.

The colours, the flowers, the butterflies were gorgeous and Bronwen was charming as we talked of the 'shame' event.

If it was a man who had locked me in, she suggested (as I had seen David the Crusader do in the name of God, and killed me as a witch) a man must let me out: an Inner Male.

Astonishingly, during the work I saw an 'Inner Crusader! His rapier was the long, odd shaped key I had seen. My body went into contortions; my mouth puckered, jaw clenched. I loved my mother, why didn't she love me? I needed to be fed and was denied it. Finally a woman came to comfort me: not my mother but The Mother.

Then it subsided; my thighs began to ache and were locked. I saw myself as a Crusader in the Temple Church in London, entombed in stone. And then 'he' came alive, and 'with words' I saw God. I needed to have *seen* God before.... what? More and more it was difficult to grasp things with my mind. There were so many questions with so many layers and these came round and round for the next many years.

Bronwen, too, talked of the feminine crucifixion and the approaching resurrection. She, too, felt unseen, wondering when and how to present her story – the spiritual dimension around the Profumo affair. I did a ritual to release myself from my mother's shame. I burned it and buried it under an apple tree, and by the time I got home the pain had gone.

Towards the end of the year David and I went to France and brought my car, Poppy, back to England. We stopped overnight at *Chartres* and went early into the Cathedral. To me – and to many others – *Chartres*, built on the lines of sacred geometry, holds 'it all'.

I looked again at the luminous Blue Virgin window, in which the head of the Christ is in the heart of the Virgin. I said a prayer in the chapel of the Black Virgin, and was now gazing at the glorious north rose window. And then I knew: it was no longer either Virgin or Whore, but the integrated feminine - and the counterpart of Christ - the Sophia. I knew, now, I could leave France.

David continued to be attentive. He needed to feel loved and didn't seem to need me to be 'wise', and I felt loved back, though I still felt I needed to protect myself from the Network. In September Helene Shik came to London.

Over the years our meetings were always manic, exciting and vital. Our minds and intuitions would leap all over the place in recognition. Helene, however, was always the authority. I realised over time that our collective experiences led to the same understanding, but hers were always dramatic events to suit her supremely energised and dramatic persona. Helene was German by birth but had lived in the States since her marriage – and subsequent divorce – to a Hungarian. She was nine years older than me and had three adult children.

David's circle of friends was often intimidating. Darby once told me that my Capricorn moon in the first house meant that I 'appeared and disappeared' to myself, and at my most insecure I looked in control; so I guess I got by. With his Edinburgh friends he would hold Haiku evenings, where everyone had to speak in this Japanese form of verse! His brother Willie worked at Christies, and together they lay down wine, and loved to drink special half bottles – at a time I no longer drank wine.

His sister Katy worked as assistant to the head of Glaxo, and was closest friends with Kevin and Pandora Maxwell - we went to dinner at their home in Chelsea when Katy was babysitting their children. We also spent time with Peter and Sarah Dawkins.

My greatest difficulty, however, was with the woman I had held in such high esteem at Runnings Park: Hertha Larive. Hertha was attached like a limpet to David. She had become a member of The Network herself, and seemed to take personal responsibility for boosting David's status. She began phoning him regularly at 10.30pm at night.

I was passionate about David and every night was spoiled because I literally couldn't keep awake any longer. Quite simply, it spoiled our sex life. Though charming enough to me, after a while I suspected that, psychically or otherwise, she felt I was not right for David. On one occasion she invited us to a party and introduced us both to a lovely young woman

Catriona, who was just opening up to ideas of the new. I spent most of the evening talking to her, but a little while later I realised Hertha had other ideas.

David was a trustee of Sir George Trevelyan's Wrekin Trust, which was now based at Runnings Park. A celebration, organised by Lorna, was to be held in London for George's retirement as head of the Trust. He was in his late eighties then, and for many people it was an occasion to honour the work of a great pioneer and I went because David was involved.

As we entered the hall, although Hertha beckoned us down to the front, I stopped to talk to Lorna. When I looked up again David and Hertha had been joined by Catriona, and it sent out warning bells. To save myself from fear I stayed with Lorna, irritated by the whole event, and incandescent with rage at David's defection.

I felt George's retirement marked the end of the perpetuation of the light and bright of spiritual life, which completely ignored the darkness within the psyche. And it was shortly afterwards that I came home one afternoon to listen to the answering machine. It was a message from Catriona for David, saying she would be delighted to meet him.

I loved David more than I had loved anyone. I had even, for a moment, wondered if we could have a child together: I had wanted to marry him. But true to my style, our separation did not take long. He told me he could not see his future with me. He had tried to go with some of our plans: like moving to Oxford with Peter and Naiad, but he said he had to go to Winchester. And I knew, of course, that despite my love for him I could never do that. Devastated I phoned Tess and Isobel and they both immediately said 'just come'. I packed my things, put them in my beloved Poppy and left.

For three days with Tess I was catatonic, unable to speak or believe it had happened again. I then spent ten disbelieving days with Isobel, who simply let me be what I needed to be in my distress. Once again I had loved a man into being able to love, and he had left me to love someone else.

Many years before, Isobel had devised a way of working through the psychological process by creating a pack of 'monsters', as she called them, using various cards with art images as a divination tool: she now had five packs. By picking cards and using the symbols or feeling into the energies portrayed, it prompted the inner processes. We worked with this system tirelessly.

I went back to Bath to pick up my things, and in my sadness I tried to comfort myself by knowing that David could never have married an older woman. I met Naiad who found it unbearable to be with my pain because she couldn't assuage it.

I went to France in December when Tess was there. Austin visited too, but for a while I felt more alone, more bereft and more 'not me' than I had ever been before – and yet, the opposite suddenly felt true. I was becoming more me than ever before, more full, more secure. So small, so subtle, it reached so far down, to the place of beauty: the Grail Cup at the base of my body, to the Who I am.

Suddenly I saw it was at that place that David and I met. The Crusader and the feminine meet and merge. It was here that David met me and I came home. He was the one I was to marry. I did marry him, and through him I came home. All those questions about how to bring the two polarities together. The two energies merged and the gap was bridged.

I was ready to release the men I had 'had to account for'. I wanted to thank them and be forgiven and released. I wished to take up my birthright as a woman who had integrated her masculine and feminine as nearly as she could and to emerge from that to be and act in a way that my soul, fully operative and conscious, desired to act.

Relationship was my tool for growth and understanding. But it seemed it was written; it was inevitable. I dreamed I was wearing totally broken shoes and needed new ones. I sensed that the new Earth Father was Saturn. I thought of France over the last years - of 'gathering in' time, from the past.

Peter Russell saw the speeding up of time to a moment of collapse. To me it felt like a 'switch point' of consciousness, which would include the future in the now, as well as the past: a place of timelessness. It felt like a huge space of becoming, full not empty, but not known or seen. The next moment I felt dreadful again. I felt abandoned, despite the visions and expectations. I felt more publically vulnerable, recognising how armoured I had been to survive my life.

I went to Le Beausset Vieux church as usual and begged Mary Magdalene to intercede. I asked Hubert why all this, and for David I saw a puppy dog let off a chain. For me a hermit crab coming out of the shell.

The New Year dawned and I felt calmer and began my life again. I picked a tarot card for the year: the Knight of Cups. We laughed: a knight of romantic love who fights for women. I also had a healing session with Tess, who was now working with pendulum and stones, which suited her as a former geologist.

Myrna and Edward came to dinner with Tess and I at Le Castellet. I was still trying to send my manuscript to individual publishers, and giving up hope. Myrna told me a little about her plot and we saw how similar our efforts were. As early as 1986 she had 'seen' a divination game while on Santorini. Later she had seen the actual game in the museum in Heraklion, Crete - though the museum could not identify what it was. Her plot revolved around this game. (Myrna never did publish her book and mine was finally self-published in 2016 under the title *Shadowplay*.)

I woke one morning with an *I-Ching* number in my head: 43 Resoluteness.

'The issue of the time is to decide to come into being. Fill empty vessels with precious fluids and your time will come: a point of great determination to accomplish the new. Seek a balanced attitude, organise your resources and your aim can be achieved: time towards clear, creative manifestation'.

Back in England I was terrified of confronting the future, dependent and unprotected. I stayed with Jan, and felt on another planet - I stood on the platform at Southfields and had a panic attack. I called Ted Partridge, a marvellous man Carole had discovered, who did absent healing by phone.

Ted gave me a deep translucent mauve at the solar plexus; a tranquilising blue and lavender; and a cone marking the acupuncture meridian for sleep. He also gave me an emerald green disc with a silver circle in the middle and said I should visualise the disc and throw at it all the negativity and fear. Before sleeping I threw rocks of anger.

I learned that David was not with Catriona: it hadn't worked out. By the end of January 1992 I had panicked enough and went to the States: I thought if I got to Boston I would be okay, and Ted with his magic healing to reduce my fear of flying had got me there.

I stayed with Carl and Aida and despite being a zombie from lack of sleep had a good two-day intensive with Aida. Together we saw how the British class system held the Grail myth energy and why David was the most symbolic of that type of man. Aida's word for the non-hierarchal way of being was 'mutuality'. I saw more clearly why the 'new king' must arise from the UK, on the ashes of the old.

I went on to Vermont to visit Helene and we had a marvellous healing time together. Helene's particular interest and insights about the blood were evolving. She had already told me she wanted to write a book about the blood: the story of consciousness, and I decided to let go of every piece of the precious information I would have used, if I had written my novel as a 'fact' book. We spent three weeks talking non-stop, Helene taking and comparing notes.

Holy Blood, Holy Grail, about the holy bloodline was significant. At one time genetic engineering kept the spiritual bloodline, but now the spirit no longer needed to be passed through 'holy blood ' or 'blue blood'. It could be seeded from within. The blood must change, and I saw that polluting influences might even be playing their part. Acid rain, for example, which changes the PH balance in the earth, could in fact affect the PH balance in the blood, and have an evolutionary purpose. I felt that global warming might have positive meaning as well as negative impact.

One of the most profound insights came during my time with Helene, and explained the intrinsic karmic impossibility of the relationship between men and women. I saw an Egyptian life as a priestess. Helene saw a circle of priests ready to consummate union, and then their unbearable pain because they did not get what was promised.

By going out of body, the priestesses began to withhold the consciousness or intelligence they received from spiritual sources, using it as a way of keeping the priests from misusing the power of the vision they would be given – as happened in Atlantis. She controlled them.

This picture, of putting locks on the throat and the sacral, leaving the men who saw so much promise but were left unfulfilled and disappointed made sense of my relationships. In that way the priestess keeps the information to herself and becomes powerful. Several years later I saw a re-play – of allowing men to receive information but not now through sexuality.

We are the Grail, to seed the Christ, and serve God. We are needed to connect the higher to the lower. Only by incarnating, anchoring fully into matter and becoming wholly human are we released from this oath of allegiance to God.

I saw the Grail courtly love, the knight and the maiden clean and washed through: the innocence of the maiden, not the whore, starting again. The nun throws off her habit with abandon. What is my work in the world? To expand with joy.

Naiad had told me about Catherine Bean Weser, who channelled Dwal Khul, one of Alice Bailey's *Masters of Wisdom*. While I was with Helene I called her in Santa Fe. Catherine told me that *in relation to David I was letting go a particular image that I had projected on to my own masculine counterpart.*

I was moving into a femininity that emerges from innocence, which was the primary foundation for the way I had explored this lifetime so far. And yet that innocence had almost been lost in my perception of what

femininity could be, rather than expectation of what it was. I had to carry
a deeper respect for myself, in order to come to know who and what I was.

I had created crises and experienced life as shattering, not so much
that my life needed to be felt as shattering, but I needed to perceive it as my
way to create something new. It was my way of creating a better image of
Self over and over again as the new image failed.

I had not been returning to an essential state of being, an essential
innocence, but creating more and more protection so it would not happen. I
was now moving into a deeper respect for Self. I was as clear as any
subjective feminine being can be on this planet. I must recognise my
innocent feminine and the divine marriage even more.

When I left Vermont I knew I had to go to Egypt to
complete the journey Austin and I had made twelve years
before, and Helene was taking a party on a sacred pilgrimage in
March. I felt the last three months had been a gigantic healing
of this life blocks. I had asked Hubert a year go what needed to
happen before I could do 'the work', and he said 'let the damn
burst'; a washout of the emotional body.

Although I missed David and the hurt was terrible, the
process since 'the completion', at the Alchemy workshop in
1989, had not been as bad again. I returned to England and
back to Jan's, still feeling in a precarious position. But I realised
if I stayed in London the panic attacks would continue.
Carole's relationship to Jay had ended painfully, and she had
moved to a lovely redbrick house in Painswick near Stroud.
Despite a very new partner, Jonathan Nunn, she welcomed me
warmly to take refuge there.

The day I arrived she was planning a house warming
party and although through my level of confusion and
uncertainly I was inclined to stay in my room, I ventured out.
One of her guests was Hugh, the BBC television producer I
had met in 1980. He had moved locally with his family so his
children could go to a Steiner school. It was a vibrant re-
meeting and he said he would call me. I suppose at the back of
my mind was a fantastical wish for a job. I put an ad in the
local post office for somewhere to live.

In March I took a plane to Cairo where I was to meet Helene and her group from the States. I arrived at my room in the hotel late at night, and my roommate let me in, although she had been asleep for several hours. In the morning they left me sleeping while they went on their trip.

Helene's energy was insatiable and indomitable. I kept up with the pace for a day or two, but was soon exhausted. Most of the fortnight I dragged myself alongside a group of enthusiastic Americans as we got up at unearthly hours to visit temples and sites before anyone else was up. Helene had a knack of getting people to do what she wanted, including entering places where no one else was allowed.

Her programme was to progress from the most southerly part, Abu Simbel, up through the chakras, ending at Giza, the crown chakra. Process washed through me at every port of call. We took an overnight train to Luxor, and after the Temple of Isis I woke with horrendous sickness and realised once again I was tuning into a life when I had been buried alive and suffocated! My body was wracked, I was sick, and totally wiped out for the morning.

As we progressed up the Nile: Dendera, Abydos, Kom Ombo, the effects subsided, and by the time we got to the magical cream coloured light and vast expanses at Mount Sinai, the throat chakra, I felt so huge and expanded I wondered how we would ever squeeze back into 'real life'.

At 2.30am we made a magical climb up Mount Sinai to watch the sunset (where Moses took the Ten Commandments). My blood pressure suddenly sank alarmingly in the cold and my hands and arms went numb. A stallholder made me put my hands into his precious hot water - hauled up the mountain in order to sell tea - and our guide wrapped my head in his scarf, to make the blood run again.

We completed in Giza, the Great Pyramid and again we were there before anyone else. I sat on the floor of the Queen's Chamber and found myself swaying: clockwise, anti-clockwise, backwards and forwards. 'She' gave me the sun from her headdress to take to the King's Chamber. It was a joy there and

201

I had this swaying rhythm a short time later and recognised it as a way of freeing the sacral and connecting most fully with earth.

In the King's Chamber I sensed that the last 'darkness' from the third eye was removed. I was told that the light would not go out. I was given a black book now closed. In the granite sarcophagus where the initiates lay for three days as their souls went out, I felt myself being pulled upwards and my head being 'repositioned' – drawn up and back, affecting the jaw: and a sense of 'serpent' at the brow.

I was pulled back and back and changed posture and heard 'hold your head up'. I felt I could sit in a position of dignity far more easily. It was a profound experience of love and light. I asked my question, 'how does the king come out of the tunnel?' 'By becoming a crystal' I felt fire, a burning away, a cleansing and purification, and light inside. Again, I did not realise that all these threads have many turns and only in later years did the threads weave into a fuller pattern.

When we returned to the hotel my roommate Lucy felt something was not complete. I did some healing with her, joining her sacral to the earth. She felt a deep sense of release of something that had always held her back.

Egypt had brought a sense of selfhood and a wish to share my journey with other people. I went back to France; my time marked by the books I read, as I had no car and couldn't go out. I was reading Teddy St Aubyn's dark, brooding autobiographical novel *Never Mind* with a sense of how our compassion for Lorna's humiliation, and anger at her compliance had touched our lives. All our lives were like fiction and we were all players and pawns in each other's stories.

On Good Friday I took a plethora of new beginning cards from a Tarot pack. 'Where am I?' *The Fool*: a quantum leap; trust the voice in your heart; dare – even if fear holds you back.

'What does a courageous leap look like? *Princess of Wands*: release from fear; increased perception.

'What is the next step?' *Queen of Cups:* find it fearlessly; learn to transform fear. 'What do I need to stop brooding?' Universe. Completion.

Every day I was getting better and better.

PART FOUR

BACK HOME

CHAPTER SIXTEEN

In response to my card in the post office, Richard Savage and his American wife Lydia had offered me The Old Meeting House, a virtually self-contained flat attached to their lovely old stone home, Well Farm in Wick Street, in the Gloucestershire countryside between Painswick and Stroud. It was a perfect place to be, and near to Carole and Naiad.

One of the saddest occasions that year, 1992, was hearing that Unity Hall had died. She had had a stroke and for many months was paralysed all but her eyelids, movingly described by her husband Phil in *The News of the World*. I wrote to Phil my enormous gratitude for her example of fearless determination. Several of 'her girls' went to her memorial in St Brides, Fleet Street.

I was invited by Nick Rose, who was a Michaelmas trustee like me, to join his *Gloucestershire Initiative*, a small group of old age New Agers, including Carole briefly, Serge Beddington Behrens and Naiad's Peter, to find a loose way of embracing the local New Age people. While we hung out, nervous of 'coralling and organising', enthusiastic newcomer Michael Ratcliffe, a Cheltenham businessman, chivvied us along to 'do something'.

Michael offered to pay me £60 a week from his charity funds to do a PR job gathering potential people, and was eventually responsible for writing a public statement. The initiative got a wide response, including the Gloucestershire Health Authority, one of the foremost acceptors of complementary therapy. Peter Hewitt set up a regular newsletter, a notice board of practitioners and events that went on for many years. We had an introductory tea party at Michael Ratcliff's house.

I had let my house in France, but I was grateful for a job to pay my rent and to trust that I could keep body and soul together. I got £500 in royalties for *What Colour Are You?* and felt miraculously cared for.

John Mills the wonderfully sardonic owner of the health food cafe in Stroud once added. "It depends what your expectations are". Right now I had no expectations, of myself or anyone else. I no longer had any questions because I did not know what questions to ask. But something strange was happening. When I listened to my being I heard more space around my molecules, as though I was being 'worked on', and the space was filling up.

And yet, when I heard that David had met Jane McWhirter - who he eventually married and they had two children - it hurt all over again. I wanted someone to be there for me. Tess and Isobel were happy to stay single, while Carole, Naiad and I felt we were meant for partnership. When Alice, another Stroud friend and married, yearned for our kind of 'space' from men, we felt she had no idea what 'alone' meant.

I continued to be Austin's confidante at a time that was extremely difficult for him, and we wrote to each other two or three times a month. He and Pascale had now left Geneva and were living in France in the joint property with Pascale's parents. While their part, virtually derelict, would take a long time to complete, they all lived together in the parents' part.

Pascale's grandmother had recently died, and now her father was seriously ill. When he eventually died, Austin – who had himself had a serious intestinal operation – was more than ever at the mercy of Pascale's mother and her relentless rage against him. His life was soon to become virtually unbearable.

Hugh called me as promised and invited me to lunch. He told me that all those years ago, in 1980 when we had first met, it had shattered him to be attracted to someone just as he was about to get married. He clearly wanted to get close now, but I was not about to have an affair with a married man. (I had vowed a long time ago that as mad as my relationship life had turned out to be, I needed my men to be free.)

I was meeting many charming people. One of the nicest encounters early on was being taken under the wing – as several of us had been – of an elderly couple, artist Sir Oliver Heywood and his wife Denise (Ollo and Sneeze). In early July they invited me to go badger watching with them and to supper afterwards. Their home offered such a depth of stability and security.

On the following Sunday I invited them to supper, and felt so loved, as though it mattered that I existed. Very soon afterwards Ollo died, of a heart attack while circle dancing with another new friend Dr Judy de la Hoyde. We all went to see him – I had never seen a dead body before - and he looked beautiful. The atmosphere, and Sneeze in a 'state of grace' – although her life fell apart after the funeral – was a celebration of his life (on his birthday) and we all felt his amazing presence.

A few days later I went to Bronwen Astor in Guildford, a year since my first rebirthing session, which had brought up the 'male issue' and had taken a year to clear. At this session Ollo – his love - was there all the time. Although I knew at my actual birth I had not wanted to be born and 'left immediately', in my session Ollo became the perfect father and Mother Meera of all people became my mother.

In reality Mother Meera, who was beginning to draw many people to her ashram in Germany did not seem the right energy for me, but here these two people were, creating a sacred space, and suddenly I was 'born'. Ollo took the baby and comforted me; I was shouting 'I choose, I choose'. By choosing I felt I would finally be in control of my life – at forty-seven!

I felt very fragile and a short time later went to Judy for a massage. Talking to Judy she said she felt Ollo had been there for all of us who needed it: the father who did not abandon us, the father we could rely on.

Monica became a regular telephone correspondent (able to give me updates on David and Jane), and Isobel was present too. There was so much change going, but the overriding influence on my return to life in the UK, apart from my enjoyment of the women's friendship and solidarity around me, was Hugh. The electricity between us was unmistakeable, and despite my horror at his being married, and was not surrendering to the inevitable, it was nonetheless inevitable. He was persistent; he told me he loved me and was happy when he was with me. On July 10 I looked at a picture of Mother Meera and heard her say 'have fun, have fun'.

Later in July he offered me a research job so we could work together on a TV series on spiritual journeys, for HTV transmission in the autumn. Then Lyall called – three years on – and I realised Austin had called that afternoon. These three were there as profoundly as in 1980! They were all now an integral part of my being: the rocks, the stones, the structure of who I was, whatever that was.

Hugh was away filming for two weeks. He called from Islamabad. The only people who ever knew about us were Carole and Naiad. But I still felt guilty. I drove to Birmingham especially to ask Geoffrey's guide Darius what on earth I was doing. 'Let the juice run down your chin!' he said. *This man would lead me up the mountain path; the steps had already been forged, and I could climb with the sun on my back. His task was to hand me on to the person who would take me to the top.* I have had to trust guidance for a large part of my life. I had to believe I was not sinning.

On August 14 I saw Lyall in London. And for the first time in eighteen years I did not feel the magic. I had changed. He said he was still there for me; I could still 'wrap him round my little finger'. He told me I could have had anything in those days (when I thought he was giving me nothing). He asked me if I would like to go on his new paddle steamer boat in the Mississippi, and I suddenly knew I did not. I liked my new Gloucestershire life. The link was finally broken. It was sad.

And yet, as ever, it was not easy. I was learning to love unconditionally, a man who was very Saturnian, anchored to his life, his marriage and his emotions. I was learning to be strong; I could not fall into expectations and outcomes. We met virtually once a month, romantic idyllic suppers in local pubs. We talked of spiritual matters – his own path was not mine - but we got to know each other most through our sexuality.

But in between times I was alone. He never once stayed the night and one attempt at a few days away left us both in high anxiety of guilt, and we went home early. I could not speak about the relationship, or explore it, because it was going nowhere. Hugh would take no responsibility for what was happening so there was endless talk with Carole, my day-to-day companion.

I wrote to Austin, who was clearly unwell despite his operation, telling him there was the beginning of a new twelve year Jupiter cycle: it had returned to the place where it was when he and I met. I asked Hubert where would the next Jupiter cycle go; what did I need to 're-hydrate? *The happy child.* What does she need in soul terms? *Radar.* The idea of me becoming a 'radar dish' had been around for a long time.

Carole had become adept at tuning in and writing down messages. We spent so much time together and often asked about the moment-by-moment dilemmas we were in. Her guidance assured me that the relationship was having a profound effect on Hugh because I was 'watering parts of him that had never been touched'.

The year was intense and sometimes the collective Uranus-Neptune conjunction was almost physically agonising. (This was the Queen's *annus horribilis*). The talking and comparing and 'pushing through' with Carole and Naiad were a lifeline. Naiad's relationship with Peter was often dark and distressful and at one point of retreat she came to stay with me. We would 'workshop' for hours, using astrological symbolism as a means of looking at, and responding to shifts.

One night I woke up dead! I wondered if I had died. I became aware that in that deadness I was inside myself, inside my womb, and at peace. I could invite things in, but did not have to go out to anything external. I saw that what made us human was 'I', the eternal 'I'. And 'I' was the mind that makes things conscious. I could invite the 'I' of the mind into my womb, penetrate it with 'I', that is, with Light, the eternal self. Therefore 'Light is the Mind', and the mature place of safety (not infantile bliss) was the womb.

I asked Hubert, 'what is the essence of my soul journey at this time?' *Communication. Playful dealings with all possible forms of communication: expression of creative potential.*

Catherine Bean had said the DNA itself was changing. Carole had talked about restructuring at the primal level. It was almost surreal at times. It was almost a surrender to annihilation at a fundamental particle level: a sense of real change in time and space. It was as though this time shift meant that everything had to be gathered from the past into this moment, an implosion into matter, and to clear the emotional body, to see the reality of who and what we are. I could not go forward to reach a goal any more, could only allow things to unfold. No forward motion. And external realities were mirroring our internal process.

In October I went back to France and completed business on the sale of my house. Tess was keeping her flat and with the money she gave me for my television I bought an Afghan rug, as a symbol of change.

My instinct in the tense times was to withdraw my boring process from the eyes of the world: to retreat into isolation. Hugh was abroad filming for six weeks, which meant I didn't have to deal with that. When we met he was full of love and packed a sensual punch, but left me bereft every time it stopped. He told me he was so happy and felt so much joy; that I soared him out to the stars. But he would never be a partner on the end of the phone.

One person I met during my search for people for the series was Kirsten Bolwig. (Whose father by some extraordinary quirk of fate was Lyall's tutor in zoology at the Witwatersrand University in South Africa). I had met her briefly before in Bath, and although she was not quite right for the programme, we became and remain good friends. Kirsten was an aromatherapist and healer, and in the next year or so it was through her that I felt most healed and helped. In one session I saw the joy I have in communicating with parts of myself in the 'other dimensional world'.

Kirsten told me I was active and dynamic in that fourth dimensional place, in touch with my own light; source light. It is who I am. I am safe and cared for. I am creating my own security.

Her work on the body brought up yet again the pain of not wanting to incarnate. I breathed life into my body as though I had never breathed before. Later that night, linked with 'source' and joy as the other dimensions descended into me, I saw the negative I had imprinted into everything. I was self-contained: there was freedom within the containment of the human body.

I held the integration for two days – until Hugh showed me his wonderful new home in a nearby village. It was he, not I, who had the security: the money, the wife, children, the lifestyle, a future, and a proper hold on reality.

Early January 1993 I wrote to Austin, who was now having chemotherapy. I told him that the last year had totally changed who and what I was, or had ever perceived myself to be. There were no longer any goalposts, or reference points about past or future, no maps or pathways to explain things. There was only trust in being in touch with the creative present moment. The more I tried to explain it the more looney it sounded! But, as always, for me the reality was so vital and huge.

I had an eighteen-week contract in total with Hugh's production company. Twelve weeks were spent searching the area for the suitable lives to hold a forty-minute 'talking head' programme on spiritual journeys.

I felt I had found the 'right' people - those who were really in touch with themselves, not just in the head. Hugh, of course, had his own ideas, and all were thoroughly researched. It was fun to meet so many good people, and although I worked from home, I occasionally went into the office, which made me feel I was doing a 'real job'.

When I had completed my list of possibilities, Hugh, as producer/director and presenter – which is how he always made his films – returned to see them for his overall opinion.

We finally came up with a list of ten people of varying faiths, experiences and interests. During filming I was assigned as PA, looking after the practical stuff and logging films, which much to Mary's horror as a real PA, I was taught to do in one afternoon session!

But working together made us unsettled. Back home I would go to bed at 7pm and 'sit inside myself' for comfort. There I found an amazing state of joy and peace. I recognised the 'ecstasy' and knew that, for whatever reason, I had reached a level of surrender I had never managed before. I had begun to understand what sexuality/spirituality could be; I knew what it was to be full and spacious and whole.

It seemed that when we are so alive and in touch with ourselves, we are paradoxically in touch with the rest of the universe. Once the 'inner marriage' is real, the universe begins to impinge on us and everything becomes available, as though the 'inner marriage' is surrounded by 'the waters of life' where all information is held.

In the gap between shooting I went for a few days to Geneva, a half-way point to meet Linda who was now back in the States, but attending a conference in Dornach. Austin's daughter France who was now pregnant had organised a B & B with a friend for me, but after two days I went to the home where Linda was staying.

During the filming coolness had set in between Hugh and I and when my work was finally finished at the end of April, it was clear the relationship should be over. Unexpectedly I found myself a new house, though in fact it was artist Naomi Brandel, one of our women friends, who found it first, but had decided she needed a bigger garden.

In July I moved into Daisy Bank in Stroud. It was a tiny Cotswold cottage on three levels, up a narrow alley and opposite the park; delightfully quiet. It wasn't exactly my dream for the rest of my life, but with everyone else's enthusiasm and the sunshine, I began to love it too.

With the help of the local young handymen I made the alterations, most importantly lopping off the ice cream *artex* that was everywhere, and painting it white throughout. We enlarged the basement kitchen by knocking out the original fireplace. A new carpet was laid, and I moved in.

Once I was settled in I wrote Hugh a letter. I wanted to set out as truthfully as I could what I was thinking. I wanted him to know before my birthday, so I could break the cold 'impeccable behaviour', and at least find a warmth between us. I also went to Alice Friend for a birthday reading. Her guide Golden Flame spoke of 'channelling at a higher frequency'. But it was Kirsten who, towards the end of 1993, during a healing session, suddenly came through with the message: 'go home and start channelling'. So I did!

Carole once said, 'the trouble with you is that you believe your own process'. It was true: I did believe that if I had an experience, a shift to move on, it was real! It was only later, when I worked with clients myself that I saw just how possible it is to choose not to move on!

Something strange was happening to Carole. She had begun to suffer with ME, and was more and more confined to bed. From time to time I offered healing, and it was only on reflection that I realised that on these two or three occasions, she professed to feeling worse the following day. She had even admitted herself to the Priory in London on one occasion, and Park Atwood on another.

Over these last months, a feeling of 'betrayal', prompted by current events with Carole, had surfaced now and again, and it was during a session with a local cranial osteopath, that it suddenly made sense. I saw my last life as a Jewish writer in exile in France, and that it was a friend in this life, a member of the Resistance, who had betrayed me. (I already knew I had died in a concentration camp.)

A little later when I was able to glean something more profound from my own channelling, I literally saw Carole unconsciously stamp her foot on the ground, and say 'shan't'. She had somehow, for her own reasons, chosen to be ill. I knew from then on that despite Jay calling in the whole community to rally round, and the hundreds of pounds she

213

spent on an unimaginable number of healing methods, she was not going to let anyone heal her – until she was ready. For the last twenty-five years Carole has virtually been confined to bed. Many of the community withdrew, but Jay and Jonathan Nunn remained loyal.

But that was way ahead, and now that I was beginning to channel, too, Carole and I had a lot of fun swapping advice for each other. I spent hours and hours practising what can only be called 'automatic writing', filling endless notebooks with channelled information. The writing was distinguishable as my 'channelling writing', and a bit more curly than my own sharper style.

The first guidance described itself as 'the Hierarchy', which had the task of realigning the earth to the planetary logos - the driving motor in the planet's etheric body. They told me I was being given a higher dose of energy, and as I was feeling a bit physically disorientated, I would soon be comfortable with these levels of 'universal mind'.

The second level to make itself known was 'Morning Star', which was responsible for the relationship between the planetary logos and the light body of the planet. I would be working from the realm of light, which would become familiar again. These dimensions were the dimensions of wisdom connected with the Sophia, the feminine that encompasses all: the soul of God. She was the Mother of the World, and it was her work that I would be asked to do. She is as the Child, the wisdom of the child and the Mother of the Divine Child.

Hugh, I was told, would hold the space for the earth plane. My new partner would hold the space of the Sophia plane. *You will be a communicator of several systems, as you always have been.*

You are being allowed to realise your true nature as a God being of Light, to come forward to take your place amongst the light workers. The planet is undergoing the most significant changes that it has ever done. You with others are being trained to hold the band of light around the earth in order that the eclipse may be experienced in the gentlest way possible. As earth passes through its shadow to the light, you will stay the incredible fear that will result. Like Lilla you will be able to run the gauntlet of dimensions.

'Your task is to relay information through the planetary light body. You deal with the electromagnetic structure and the planetary vibrations that are connected to the solar system and beyond. The vibration you resonate on is the Resonance of the Mind, the power of the Universal Third. This is the vibration that holds the hemispheres in balance, the vibration that sings throughout the solar system and carries the energy back and forth from the star beings in the ultra dimension of space.

'This is why travel has been important to you. You are a time traveller and this is the stream that permeates your being. Time is the key to Light, and time will soon be very different to you. You are experiencing the marriage of spirit and matter, the true integration of parts of yourself. A time of trust.'

The third level was 'Alpha Omega', which 'relates planet earth to the dimension in which the universal mind is at its finest before the incoming Christ Consciousness'. Unlike the other two levels it did not consist of previously incarnated souls and had to be 'sipped not swigged'. The first time it came through I had to rest for a couple of hours afterwards! As someone who hated the idea of 'hierarchy', they reassured me 'we do not want the dimensional aspect to feel like 'more or less'. It is according to disposition'.

In October I went to Santa Fe for a gloriously warm month with Linda. One of the most important things we did was to visit the Light Centre made famous by Shirley MacLaine, whose spiritual journeying had been so well recorded in her best-selling books. We attended a lecture about the significance of the land there, and hence their ability to work with the light body.

Afterwards I spent the night 'hovering' above my body. I knew that for all the talk of the light body, many people were calling it down but not incorporating it within them. They had not worked for the privilege of soul consciousness and the information would be distorted.

On my return to Daisy Bank I was assured by the guides that the physical discomfort I had been feeling all year was simply the changing of energies from the old to the new. But Carole, Naiad and I decided we were fed up with the static nature of our lives and drove together to Wales to see a woman psychic someone had recommended, Jan Angelo.

We each went in separately but she gave us all the riot act! We had to listen to our souls now, not our personalities. To me she said I would have no options, and that next March I would meet a man, a writer, who would take me to China, where I would live for a year; and that this was more my country than England!

I wanted my soul to lead; it was what I assumed I was moving towards. On the winter solstice the guides suggested I do a 'ritual of intention', which I took very seriously. I prepared the idea and was ready on Christmas Eve. I bought a 'red rose of intention' (which Carole later dried for me), and sitting on Austin's Afghan rug, and with their guidance, I spent two hours releasing everything that might be holding me back from emerging as my full self, and taking responsibility for who I was, and no longer a cast-off from other people's expectations or picture.

They could not promise it would be easy, but this was the beginning of a great adventure.

CHAPTER SEVENTEEN

Virtually the whole of 1994 was about guidance, despite my scepticism and anxiety, filling notebooks and files on every conceivable question that came up for me or Tess or Naiad.

The guides had suggested I bring prayer into my life, and one afternoon when I was trying to explain to Carole and Jay the knife-edge of being in a state of 'nothing', it was Carole who told me about the 'Jesus Prayer'. It was one of the most profound things to happen that year. 'Lord Jesus Christ have mercy upon me'. In fact the prayer concludes, 'upon me, a sinner', but I couldn't say that.

That night in bed I said the prayer over and over, and the effect was instantaneous and extraordinary. It induced in me a level of surrender that I had not experienced before. I felt the humility of giving over to another, very loving source, which was an acknowledgement that I simply could not do it myself.

I woke up in a lifted state; more joyous and relaxed, hardly describable because it was as ordinary as any other day, but more optimistic and peaceful. I was enthusiastic to read the tiny pocket book *The Way of the Pilgrim*, the autobiography of a pilgrim whose only wish was to live in interior prayer. It was he who was given the Jesus prayer, the prayer of the heart.

The next morning I walked into town saying the prayer over and over again, levelling it into my heart, and just for a second I caught a glimpse; a glimpse full of fear. I suddenly felt a level of love unknown to me, and my fear was that if I were to love that much, who would I be, what would I do? I believed, like the pilgrim, that those words resonate with Christ energy, and it could somehow resonate Christ into the heart.

The guides at no time indicated I would be with Hugh, only that I was creating a better life for him and his wife, and the gaps between our conjugal visits were widening unacceptably. Waiting for Hugh was not what I wanted for my life.

In February 1994 Austin who was very ill and still undergoing chemotherapy, began writing a book for me. It came to him in a dream that he should write a book commenting on world events, and as he said on its front page, 'it was modified by you tuning into your wider self, who proposed that instead I write on the changing consciousness of Britain'. In the end it turned out to be the most unbearably heart-rending account of the last painful year of his life, a wonderful document to have, but one I cannot bear to read again.

In February, too, I went to see Isobel in Sheffield for the weekend. As usual it was a powerful experience. The theme was confronting some gruelling shadow aspects we would never have known; also that the kaleidoscope of life was somehow being shaken up completely, waiting to settle into a completely new pattern.

Our tool this time was a new exploration of Isobel's 'shapes' idea: that we hold a basic shape, an archetypal shape. Of those she had devised, I was a rose, she a triangle. On the train home I realised my intention was to somehow bring the archetypal down to the personal. I knew I had contributed to Isobel's perceptions and process in a visible way, and the weekend served to reinforce for me that my connection to those dimensions were real, valid and true.

An important part of the weekend was seeing the film *Age of Reason*, with Daniel Day Lewis and Michelle Pfeiffer. The characters are caught in who they are by the circumstances and culture they find themselves in. Above all, it was a film about sexuality and fidelity, which reminded me of Hugh and me.

I woke next morning with a heaviness that wouldn't leave me. I felt compelled to wash my hair, have a shower. The guides then said I had held the affect of the film – connecting to Hugh – in my crown chakra. They said my relationship was complete; I no longer needed to be his mistress. He had given me back to myself – and I had 'washed that man right out of my hair'.

A few weeks later Hugh invited me to a London screening of one of his films. I was in a sufficiently strong mood to decline an overnight, and was rather amused to be chatted up by his brother John, who phoned me a few days later to invite me to the theatre. This was less amusing, since it was more than Hugh had ever done, and I did not accept.

There was a sense of 'no-where to go' in the air. I was hugely frustrated that nothing at all was happening, a blank wall: no job or occupation. I could not make things happen yet with the help of David Hubbard, the chiropractor and 'process chats' with Tess and Naiad, there was a growing inner strength and integration.

In April, Celia Wyndham organised a series of showings of our series at the Quaker Meeting House. The first evening was a milestone for me. I was able to share with Hugh the questions asked, confidently and happily. It felt so good. No one could have known how impossible it had been for me to speak in public, and with the strength of Hugh's acknowledgement of me as part of the team, I spoke spontaneously.

At the end of a lovely evening – with thirty-four people – I felt present to myself in a way I had never done before. It made more possible the idea of a workshop that Tess and I had talked of for July.

As always the changes in me had a profound influence on Hugh's relationship to me. The evening had been magical. Again I saw how the feelings he inspired in me could be pulled back into my own being and experienced fully by me, through me. I could create my own self-sustaining wholeness, and live in the present moment.

Stroud energy was beginning to feel impossible, though I valued the protection it had given me for so long. The guides confirmed what Anghous Gordon had once said, that Stroud forms the interface between two ancient cultures that represent the paradoxical principles of masculine and feminine. Out of the tension between them comes the third, the child: the new creative child.

Alice's guide Golden Flame had also told me that there was a 'winged disc' over Stroud, which enabled people to 'find their blueprint' – which indicated to me that when you found it, you should leave.

I worked with my guidance, mostly with Tess. Although in the last years she had been completely taken up with Katherine Tetlow's way of healing and considered Katherine her psychotherapist, Tess was insatiably curious. It was she who took the idea of guidance from the 'Hierarchy' and 'Morning Star' seriously, and always wanted more information. It was she who kept me from total scepticism. On one occasion in France the guides had said that if I doubted myself, I doubted 'them', and I saw how disrespectful that was.

The nature of my guidance was at base therapeutic, which made sense. I had always said I did not wish to 'save the world', but preferred to save 'you and me'. It was clear that the aim of my guides – as indeed my whole life had been – was to 'clear the instrument' to embody true soul consciousness, or, realise our full creative potential; the magnificence of what it is to be human.

The guides described the gift as 'embodying more and more of the universal mind'. And although at one level 'they' looked more separate from any way in which I had accessed information before, I also knew that what I was now able to do was incorporate more of 'me', more of 'all that is'. As I read in Barbara Marciniak's books *Bringers of the Dawn* and *Earth*, channelled from the Pleiadians - not all of which I took as gospel truth - the human being on earth was the 'Key to the Library'.

Although at first the guides brought information, laboriously written down word for word, eventually the client was asked to take part in a dialogue during a kind of guided meditation. They would take the meditation into the most apposite – and difficult – realms, which the client was able to recognise. And by shifting those mental, emotional or physical symptoms held in the body - connected to the search for spiritual understanding - they would effect change.

To my surprise, one of the most widely used techniques by the guides then (and for several years afterwards), was taking people into past lives, to show how the patterns were being repeated in the present life. Although this was to become quite a recognised way of getting at emotional blocks, since my training at Runnings Park I had regarded it as a dangerous practice, and been extremely wary. I had a general idea of collective issues from past lives, but - except recently with Helene - I had never centred on them, and had gleaned my experience in other ways.

It was past March and I had still not met 'the writer who would take me to China'. I asked Jan Angelo about the 'waiting without waiting' she had predicted, that would end in March. It was a comforting conversation. She said things were in place, except for 'something in the cupboard' that needed weeding out. 'Are you ready to go?' she asked.

I realised that the thought of my 'real partner' coming into my life made me unbelievably sad! It meant I would have to leave Hugh and all I had received in Stroud. Although I found 'community' difficult in this close-knit town with so many acquaintances in the alternative field, I would miss my closest 'mirrors', the one-to-one friends. When in my third yearly reading from Alice, she told me I would meet a 'simple gardener', someone very different from anyone I had been in partnership with before, I was a bit disappointed. As someone who was a hopeless and disinterested gardener, I didn't like the sound of that!

In April Austin returned all my letters and cards and 'other expressions of love' that I had sent him over the fourteen years I had known him – exactly to the day, he told me, that I had written my first letter to him from Waterloo. He said the synchronicity of the sevens was irresistible, including that when I wrote I was thirty-five, and he was forty-nine.

He felt he could not destroy the letters, but it was right to move on. Our love was still there on a stronger, purer level: unconditional love. He told me too, he had had a dream in which his masculine, feminine and child were all fused together. His masculine was emerging and he was grateful for

221

my insights. He would write it all in the journal for me, and felt I was living through this time with him.

I went to visit Isobel in Sheffield again. Originally from New Zealand, she was about to return towards home and settle in Australia. I immediately noticed the effect of the blue of her earrings, which she told me were bluejohn stones, given to her that morning by her group.

Bluejohn was only found in a particular cave in Derbyshire, and she had had a powerful experience when she visited the Speedwell cave when she first arrived. She was sure she had been alive when the Romans had first discovered the caves, and she was somehow meant to 'protect their sanctity'.

When I tuned into the small piece she gave me I 'knew' the bluejohn was her. It was the energy of a star system to do with cats! (Isobel always had several cats.) What was even more strange, was when Tess arrived on her way back from visiting her father in Derbyshire, the guides told her that the necklace of blue stone that she had dreamed about many years ago – and had set her on her path of spiritual exploration – was a necklace of bluejohn!

In May, urged by Isobel, I took an eight-hour journey by bus to Norfolk to visit her friend Gill Birley (who later adopted the name Hannah, which felt very natural). She had suggested to us both that our meeting was important. As expected, we talked through our journeying, and one of Gill's fears was of the impossibility of coming through to her true being.

But it was quite a surprise when, during a blissful walk along the stony beach on the Sunday morning, an unexpected theme tumbled out; one that I recognised. We stopped to rest and Gill's throat suddenly went strange. Automatically I began to work on the etheric.

In her own way she repeated my own experience of the first time coming to earth. In my own image I had seen a giant who was shocked by his inappropriateness for earth, which gave me the opportunity to be a 'victim'. When Gill started to rail at God, that 'they should have known better', we were able to talk through it.

In Isobel's terms, both of us were roses trying to be roses. We had to trust that we would not be let down so badly again. The rose has to receive, to trust. There is nothing else for the rose to be. Gill had been afraid that if she were angry with God, the wrath of God would be down on her.

We began to unfold what was holding her and I together. We had left behind our stillness; both were unable to make the final commitment to 'stop', in order for action to happen. We saw a life when we had been witches together (healers and wise woman), like two peas in a pod, in stillness.

I had been reading Steiner's *Atlantis and Lemuria* on the way to Norfolk, and it seemed relevant that in Lemuria women were in complete relationship to the will of the nature forces. Gill's unfolding of this past life story suggested she had realised this way was no longer appropriate and needed to withdraw to find 'the life force'; an appropriate masculine energy that moved from the feminine into a new mode of action. But until now she had mucked it.

By getting involved with the masculine through sexual magic, it seems that those working on the 'dark side' had whipped themselves into a frenzy to destroy the white witches – including us. This was ingrained in Gill's memory: no wonder she had pushed down the masculine beyond redemption.

Gill works with the Alexander Technique and is particularly interested in exploring Voice. She has worked not only with opera singers in Paris but also with others who wish to discover the truth of their own voices. She has a spectacularly beautiful and affecting voice herself. She and I have remained friends since then and are still a 'first line of call' when either of us needs support

I was exhausted when I got off the bus at Cheltenham, which was a pity because it was the final evening of the film showings at the Meeting House. Although he had only attended the first evening, Hugh was there now to take the lead.

We met in the pub and the evening went well, the response still magical for me, and I had prepared dinner for him after the showing. Whether from the weekend, or what was happening naturally, our relating had become really deep. I could no longer understand why. All the guides continued to tell me was that Hugh was not my partner: my partner would meet me in a more whole way. I woke after four hours sleep refreshed.

A week or so later Hugh took me to the pub where we had had our first meeting exactly two years before. But all we did was talk intellectually: detached and hard about spiritual guidance. I tried to explain what was happening, and it was depressingly clear we were not speaking the same language. Hugh stated how different our lives were and said he kept his life and me in separate compartments; which is exactly how it felt when he left me after each encounter. Two people in separate compartments.

At the end of May I told Hugh over the phone that I had come to the end of the line with our relationship. I told him I had decided to go forward, to come out into the world with the skills I seemed to be acquiring, and I needed to take the whole of me, including my honesty and integrity. Deep down I knew it was time, and he knew and understood. He said we should have lunch in a couple of weeks and we could still be friends, which made me sad.

Carole did a reading and said that my relationship with Hugh had marked the end of a long journey of individuation for me, and the weaning off from a deep relating mode that was no longer appropriate. He had been 'all things rolled into one' for me: a large reference point in my life. Without a radical severance it would go on forever. I should step back now and really value myself; be bolder, pushing in 'where angels fear to tread'. My own angel was raring to go.

Carole's illness continued to bother me. I couldn't understand why she had chosen what she had, and was sad that she could no longer talk about anything but her symptoms. I wanted to wave a magic wand and get her up once and for all.

I was exhausted with my channelling, and remembered Dave Cousins saying this energy should be 'sipped like a cocktail, not swigged'. Alpha Omega was now coming through, and in early June I had my first two paying clients. One a friend of Isobel's asked for a postal reading. From now on I had to work with people's lives in complete confidence.

Answering the first client's questions required an act of trust. It was guidance, not 'law': suggesting a course of action; offering ways of looking at current aspects of the life; implying certain things needed to be looked at in a different way. I trusted that it would ring a bell of reality. The reading took exactly an hour, written down in the curly writing. Here, right then, was the reality of bringing spirit into matter. It did not seem to contain anything like the numinous, nor does it now.

I remember Dave Cousins suggesting in 1989 that I looked soft and feminine but really I was *'an esoteric heavy'! and that was what people needed from me. Some people needed a cuddle, some a push. I was the one to give the push!* The other client was a one-to-one with one of our acquaintances. Quite soon after that I did a tape for the partner of a friend, who phoned a week later to say he was delighted with the reading which was 'spot on'.

I wrote to Austin telling him that this work was an experience of detachment. It was ordinary, mundane and grounded. It 'just was'. I felt my guidance was as clear as it could be, and clients could choose to believe it or not. But it could never be predictive, because at any given moment we can choose. Our choices can shift us onto a different railway track at any moment.

In June 1994 Cathy Bean sent a channelled reading suggesting *that angels were appearing in order to assist the dramatic reorganisation of galactic energies, within the fields of all individuals who are open to receiving that quality of reorganisation. The timing was associated to the Mayan calendar. Angels have always been messengers and were being used at that time to send messages that will link, via the global mind, the consciousness of many individuals together simultaneously.*

In July Tess suggested she assist me to hold my first workshop: *Dedication to the Real Self brings Joy and Freedom.* We ran it in St Ethelwolds, and despite my terror of groups and speaking out, it was a success - especially a kind of 'chat show' at the end. But it began to cause a rift between Tess and Katherine – who did not approve of my involvement – and over the next years this was to have difficult fallout.

I still did casual sessions with Naiad, who had been doing a basic art course at Stroud Art College. Her relationship with Peter had been over for a long time, and just as I had moved into Daisy Bank she had rented a cottage two houses along from Well Farm where I had lived in Wick Street. We talked most days on the phone.

By the end of August Austin and I both acknowledged the possibility of his death. Alice, in my birthday reading, had told me that should he decide to 'go over', we would maintain the link. Indeed his death would be a huge and beautiful experience for me because we would work together, and he would contribute to my work on health.

Tess and I planned to go to France, which made me nervous. I was afraid to see Austin in his dying, but this visit was clearly about Austin. Tess always left her car parked on their property and collected it on her return, and somehow he managed to meet us from the local train station.

The relief to me was immense. I don't know if it was 'grace', given only to me, but immediately I felt something beautiful about him. Although his hair was much greyer, his skin whiter and he was terribly thin he seemed to be 'shining'. To me he did not look as bad as he had a couple of years before, when after the intestinal operation he had come to see me after attending an Open University Summer School.

I now recognise that in some people the soul becomes embodied towards death. He was tired, his gut distended, but he was managing his own pain; determined foolishly to follow some alternative healing path that was assuring him he would get well. Unwisely it stopped him taking morphine.

I just wanted to be with him, to bathe in that energy, and I was very moved. We went to see him three times, but I didn't see him like that again. He was calm and tranquil about the prospect of 'passing over' - his phrase. He had tidied up his life, organised his funeral, and the scattering of his ashes in the hills behind his home. He didn't want any drama.

Carole, Naiad and I had often discussed how we, and so many others, had become addicted to drama, to make us feel alive. That evening I reflected that it was as though, twenty years before, I had climbed into an alchemical flask and somehow a drama – the universal drama - had been unfolding; out of my control, almost against my will, and against my better judgement. Now it felt I had climbed out of that flask, and the drama was over. I was progressively experiencing calmness, stillness and peace. For a moment I think I understood silence.

Back home I felt I could no longer continue to minutely 'contemplate my navel', to analyse and evaluate my daily life as a symbol of psychological and spiritual reality. The things that had fascinated me before no longer interested me: my mind would not work in its old complexities. Cathy Bean had said I would not remember how I got here, which was true.

Someone suggested I phone Irena Morley, who for many years had been the membership secretary at the College of Psychic Studies in London. Irena was happy to suggest that I telephone the new Principal to ask if I was suitable to be taken on as a part-time medium.

The Principal called me up to Queensbury Street and asked for a reading. He told me his aim was to take the College away from the psychic, mediumistic, 'proof of the afterlife' kind of work, and bring in the 'higher' notion of Light. My work would help him do this, he thought. I was hugely relieved to hear this and we arranged that in January I would commute to London one day a week.

Austin wrote as best he could in his last days, and he even sent a tape, which was so painful I could not bear to keep it. He died on December 17th 1994, and I cried for him more than I have cried for anyone else before or since. I was distraught to lose my most loyal friend. He had given me the task of notifying his friends, and in trying to so I could hardly speak the words without weeping.

My guides told me I did not need to go to the funeral, but his sisters Sal and Charlotte insisted I should go. They both knew I had been important to Austin, particularly in the last years when his life had been so painful. The plane fares at Christmas and at short notice were beyond my budget, but Charlotte showed incredible kindness by offering to pay for me from the family trust.

I took my tied bunch of yellow roses on the plane with me, picked up Tess's car from Pascale and drove to stay overnight with a friend Cliff Swann, who now rented a property in the countryside near Le Plan.

The funeral in the church at Roquevaire was beautiful. Austin's university friend Patrick took the service, and somehow managed to make all three of us, Austin's partners, feel included. I was touched beyond words when my flowers went on the coffin alongside those of Pascale and Malou. Malou and I made peace, and it was a joy to see France, Blaise and Didier again, even under such circumstances. It completed an era.

In January 1995 I started work at the College. I left home at 7.15 on Friday mornings, took my car to Cirencester and caught the bus to Victoria. I would arrive for work around 10am. It was a strange environment for someone who disliked the psychic, and did not consider herself a medium. One or two people did want me to contact relatives who had passed over – particularly the loyal, older patrons of the College – but I had to point out that this was not my speciality.

Eventually, as they got to know me, the girls on Reception would give me the right kind of people who would appreciate that I was not a fortune-teller. I only had one client who was obviously not satisfied, which gave me a swift lesson in learning not to panic. I simply asked the front desk to return her money.

I still wrote everything down by hand, but I was also given a tape recorder for backup. The number of clients varied between two and six, and on the whole it was usually financially viable. (Eventually I was able to speak directly without writing it down – though even now I hold the pencil and 'scribble' as a point of concentration!) I was grateful for the work and the practise, and even when the Principal asked me to speak about my work at one of the welcome evenings, I managed to get through it, frightened though I was.

I was even more grateful that my own guides were now saying they felt 'the companionship you seek will be here soon'. They predicted my partner was waiting as impatiently as I was to enter my life.

I met Martin (William) Davison through Lorna in early April. He had written to her as an independent television producer because he liked her book *Rituals for Everyday Living* very much. They had arranged to meet in Bath, and after she and I had watched together his BBC 2 documentary film *Circling the Dragon* made in China - about the disabled son of Deng Shao Ping - I asked her to ask him if he needed a researcher.

Martin contacted me soon after and suggested he come to Stroud to meet me. I did not immediately understand that here was the partner so long promised to me, but he told me later that he knew I was the one the minute he knew I existed. Thank goodness he persisted.

The guides told me that when I made the commitment to Martin in full measure, I would cross a bridge that was almost intolerable to me. They suggested they were saying this in great love, because the pain I had suffered for my commitment to God had been almost insupportable. He was the man, it seemed, who would 'take me to the top of the mountain'.

EPILOGUE

Martin (now called by his second name, William) and I married in June 1996. He was, as Jan Angelo predicted, a writer - of television scripts. And we did go to China, where William produced and directed a series for Shanghai television on *Cool Britannia*.

He also volunteered to work for several months for *Handicap International* in Beijing, ostensibly to train the national staff in film making, but also to produce several films, including one on disability in Tibet – in Tibetan! We were in Tibet for seven weeks. He also made a film for Sheila Purves of the WHO Collaboration Centre for Rehabilitation in Hong Kong, where we had an amazing time exploring.

I learned Mandarin Chinese for seven years, both in the UK and Beijing, and spent a year in total living in China. During these years we have also moved eight times, including a seven-year stint in Normandy.

Was he a 'simple gardener'? In a way, yes. What William has done, which none of my former partners were able to do, is give attention, credence, value and support to my work. He was and is sensitive, creative and far less dominantly male than I have known before.

Quite simply, he believes in what I do, and above all he has been prepared to trust completely and live by the guidance. He has accepted without question that for us, there have been 'three' in the marriage. He also has a fabulous sense of humour!

I have now been Channelling for over twenty years, offering individual client work and many workshops and courses on myriad subjects, both in the UK and in France. There is always the 'process work' of the moment, tackling the next block and barrier that clients present. But the point has always been to help each individual open up to their full creativity and spiritual potential, and to share in the evolving wisdom and vastness of what it is to be fully human.

This has brought an amazing 'constituency' of loyal clients, many of whom have become my greatest friends. (It is truly a huge privilege to know people at such profound depth, and to know, too, that they know you).

Although I had three books published earlier in my career - and William and I put out two books ourselves around 2006 - at the end of 2011 O-Books published what I consider to be my second 'magnum opus': *Time to Change: a guide to life after greed.* It is a wholly channelled book, and despite my dislike over the years of naming the guidance (since those first 'heady days'), this I believe was the work of the *Lords of Time.* These beings, as I understand it, are now leaving the planetary sphere of influence as our own experience of time itself is changing. They leave way for direct access to the *Masters of Wisdom.*

The guides say that the light of spirit is now, at last, docking fully into place, through the skeletal structure of mankind. The earth, it suggests, is lighting up with the recognition and pleasure of finally understanding why man is here – as the mediator between spirit and matter, which was exactly the implication of the work, which for me felt completed in 1989. It seems there are levels and levels, and levels within levels. As the guides say, when all human beings understand this conundrum, the earth itself will know it is changed.

All I know is that I continue to feel the changes, to feel the differences, to hope to ride the zeitgeist, and, despite evidence to the contrary and inevitable scary moments, along with so many other people I feel certain of an optimistic and spiritually creative future.

So, did William take me to the top of the mountain? I guess it depends what you mean by 'the top'. But, all these years on, I feel that maybe I do now have *A Spot to Stand.*

The Jurassic Coast 2017
www.guidelines.uk.com

Printed in Great Britain
by Amazon